THE SECRET OF THE BARDS
OF THE ISLE OF BRITAIN

Iolo Morganwg.

THE SECRET
OF THE BARDS
OF THE
ISLE OF BRITAIN

Dillwyn Miles
The Herald Bard

Gwasg Dinefwr Press

Published and printed in Wales by
Gwasg Dinefwr Press
Rawlings Road, Llandybie
Dyfed, SA18 3YD

ISBN 0-9519926-0-0

ACKNOWLEDGEMENTS

We should like to express our warmest thanks to the following for so kindly
giving us permission to reproduce the following illustrations:

National Museum of Wales, Welsh Folk Museum
pages 70, 131, 133, 149, 209, 218

Gwynedd Archives Service Publications
pages 132, 138, 139, 178

National Library of Wales
page 121

Western Mail
page 135

CONTENTS

LIST OF ILLUSTRATIONS

FOREWORD

THE WELSH have never boasted of pageantry. They have no Trooping of the Colour, no Highland Games, and any flaunt of splendour, like Sir Rhys ap Thomas's magnificent tournament at Carew Castle in 1507, was removed by the grey hand of Puritanism, but it is unique in having a spectacular event that is held to celebrate the literary achievement of its people. In a colourful display, of green, blue, white and gold, the Gorsedd of Bards, with its attendants in scarlet and crimson, and little dancing girls with flowers in their hair, gather to honour those who deserve merit for the written word. Nowhere else is a poet or author so acclaimed, with a flourish of trumpets and a robe of purple, and crowned or chaired with ceremony, exalted in song, and raised to the standing of a national hero.

The Gorsedd of Bards, and Bards in this connection means not only poets but others who find succour in a pursuit of the arts, is, of course, not only a piece of pageantry. It is a bulwark of the bardic tradition, a bastion of the Welsh language, a rural academy of the arts, a fount of honour and a fellowship in which its members are all equal.

It was born of the imagination of a humble, but scholarly, country stonemason, Iolo Morganwg, who came under the influence of the antiquarian revival that turned men's minds towards Stonehenge and 'druidical altars', and of the radical romanticism that was stimulated by the French Revolution. He had a dream in which he saw the land of his fathers as a haven of culture as it was, according to Caesar, in the time of the Druids, and in which its people enjoyed the freedom that Tom Paine envisaged in his *Rights of Man*. He linked the Welsh bardic tradition with ancient beliefs and created 'an arcana of neo-Druidism', and set out to 're-establish' the Gorsedd of Bards of the Isle of Britain.

In an effort to establish an understanding of that bardic tradition, I have endeavoured to explain the alleged connection with the Druids, to present the position of the bard in society and among his fellows, and to portray that 'most gifted forger in the history of the world', Iolo, before proceeding to give a history of the Gorsedd.

For a century and a half, Iolo succeeded in deluding our men of letters, and the discovery of his pious fraud, when it was made, only went to reveal him as one of the great scholars of his time.

The Gorsedd, which he created, has been the object of banter and derision in certain quarters, and there are still some squeamish pedants who would endeavour to hold it to ridicule, but it is now an integral part of our history and, if need be, able to laugh at itself. In celebrating its bicentenary, it can hold its head high and be content in the knowledge that its contribution to Welsh life and culture has already been a significant one.

This book has been written at the request of the Governing Board of the Gorsedd of Bards, and I am grateful to its members for entrusting me with the task.

My gratitude is also due to the Council of the Royal National Eisteddfod of Wales, and its Director, Emyr Jenkins; to the Recorder of the Gorsedd, the former Archdruid James Nicholas; to Bertrand Borne, Recorder and Herald Bard of the Breton Gorsedd; to Peter Laws, Secretary of the Cornish Gorsedd; to the Librarian and Legal Adviser of the Diocese of Canterbury, and the Librarian, Lambeth Palace Library, to Mrs Mair Rees and to *The Illustrated London News* Picture Library. I am particularly indebted to Geraint and Zonia Bowen in whose authoritative work, *Hanes Gorsedd y Beirdd* (1991), I was able to glean bits of information that had evaded me and which I was able to add to my original draft with their kind permission, and to W. J. Rees, sometime Senior Lecturer in Philosophy, University of Leeds, for reading the final proof.

Sir Alun Talfan Davies was good enough to arrange for the book to be published and I am grateful to Donald Martin and his staff at Gwasg Dinefwr Press for their courtesy and efficiency. My thanks are due to them, as they are to May Evans who, with her customary competence and care, typed the manuscript. Last, but not least, I wish to thank Judith for her forbearance and encouragement.

Haverfordwest, 1992   DILLWYN MILES

DRUIDS, AND DRUIDS

NO ONE now believes in a druidic ancestry for the Gorsedd of Bards, but up to the end of the last century, and even into the present, such a belief was widely held. The bardic tradition upon which such credulity was founded is traceable, however, to Druidic times, and the concept itself originated from a revival of interest in ancient bardic and Druidic lore that is difficult to explain. One might well ask, with Professor Stuart Piggott, 'Why has a priesthood within the barbarian pre-Roman Celtic religion, attested by a handful of some thirty scrappy references in Greek and Roman authors, many little known and some downright obscure, come even to be remembered at all except by scholars nearly two thousand years after its official suppression by Roman authority?'

The main classical writer on the Druids, Posidonius, in his *Histories*, written at the end of the second century BC, gave a contemporary account that provided source material for other historians, such as Strabo and Diodoros Siculus and, in particular, Julius Caesar. In his account of the Gallic campaign of 52-51 BC, Caesar stated that 'the Druidic religion is thought to have been found in existence in Britain and taken from there to Gaul. Nowadays, those who want to study it deeply still go to Britain.'

The Posidonian sources noted that the Druids were held in a position of honour in the Celtic social order as philosophers and theologians, and were associated with two other classes of learned and holy men: the *bardoi* who, as poets and singers, celebrated 'the brave deeds of their famous men in epic verse', and the *vates* who interpreted sacrifices and natural phenomena. Caesar observed that the Druids of Gaul were 'concerned with divine worship, the due performance of sacrifices and the interpretation of ritual questions'. Young men gathered around them 'for the sake of instruction and held them in high regard' and, 'in the schools of the Druids, they learned by heart a great number of verses and therefore some remain twenty years under training'.

Our only glimpse of British Druids is that given by Tacitus, in his *Annales*, of their massacre by Suetonius Paulinus in 61 AD on the Anglesey side of the Menai Straits:

> The enemy was arrayed along the shore in a massive, dense and heavily-armed line of battle, but it was a strangely mixed one. Women, dressed in black like the Furies, were thrusting their way about in it, their hair let down and streaming, and they were brandishing flaming torches. Around the enemy host were Druids, uttering prayers and curses, flinging their arms towards the sky. The Roman troops stopped short in their tracks as if their limbs were paralysed. Wounds were received while they stood frozen to the spot by this extraordinary and novel sight. However, in the end, exhortations from their commander and an exchange among themselves of encouragement not to be scared of a womanish and fanatical army broke the spell. They overran those who resisted them and cast them into their own flames. Subsequently a garrison was imposed on the defeated enemy and the groves sacred to savage superstitions destroyed (these people regard it as right to sprinkle their altars with the blood of prisoners and to consult the wishes of the gods by examining the entrails of humans).

The fact that the Roman troops were awestruck 'by this extraordinary and novel sight' indicates that Druids were not common in Britain and were certainly not a major element in the resistance to Rome, as they were in Gaul. Throughout the meagre record of Druidism in Britain, the emphasis is on Druidic lore and ritual rather than on politics or warfare, with the exception of the Anglesey incident. They were, nevertheless, suppressed by the Romans. Suetonius reported that Claudius had 'completely abolished the barbarous and inhuman religion of the Druids in Gaul' in 54 BC, and he himself set out to achieve the same object in so far as Wales was concerned.

Pliny, in his *Natural History*, gave the only detailed account of a Druidic ceremony. He stated that it took place in a grove where, as rarely happens, mistletoe grew on an oak tree. The mistletoe was gathered 'devoutly and with many ceremonies' on the sixth day of the moon: 'after they have well and truly prepared their sacrifices and festival cheer under the said tree, they bring thither two young bullocks milk white, such as never drew in yoke at plough or wain and whose heads were then and not before bound, by the horn: which done, the priest, arrayed in a surplice or white vesture, climbeth up into the tree, and with a golden hook or bill cutteth it off, and they beneath receive it in a white soldier's cassock or coat of arms: then fall they to kill the beasts aforesaid for sacrifice, mumbling many orisons and praying devoutly.'

He maintained that the word 'druid' is related, in its first part, to the Greek *drus* (an oak tree), but its second part derives from the Indo-European root **wid-*(to know). The Welsh form *derwydd* originally meant 'a prophet' or 'a wise man', deriving from the Celtic **derv* (oak trees) and was first used to signify 'a druid' in Dr John Davies of Mallwyd's *Dictionarium Duplex* (1632), the Welsh-Latin section of which being his own work while the Latin-Welsh part is an abridgement of Sir Thomas Wiliems's unpublished *Thesaurus Linguae Latinae et Cambrobrytannicae*.

With the rise of Christianity, the Druids were soon forgotten, and remained so for many centuries. They were discovered again, however, when the texts of classical writers became available to scholars during the Renaissance, beginning with the printing of the works of Caesar, in Venice in 1511. Tacitus, translated into English in 1598, and Caesar's *Commentaries* in 1604, came within the reach of the ordinary educated person in this country and created a revival of interest in the Ancient Britons and the Druids. They had to be fitted into a past, however, that was based on the Old Testament narrative, and provided with a descent from Noah, whose son Japhet had a son named Gomer, from whom, it was surmised, were descended the 'Gomeri', or 'Cymry'. This concept, together with the twelfth century fabrications of Geoffrey of Monmouth, remained to bedevil the study of Welsh history well into the nineteenth century.

The Druids were hailed by the English poets like Michael Drayton who, in his *Poly-Olbion* (1622), called them 'sacred Bards' and philosophers the 'like whom great Nature's depth no man yet ever knew', and Milton, mourning his friend drowned off the north Wales coast, in his *Lycidas*, referred to the 'steep where the old bards, the famous Druids lie' in Anglesey. They even appeared on stage in 1618, as dignified bards in John Fletcher's play about Boadicea.

The association of the Druids with Stonehenge began with the antiquary, John Aubrey. In his *Monumenta Britannica*, Aubrey stated that there had been 'several books writt by learned men concerning Stone-heng, much differing from one another, some offering one thing, some another'. The earliest of these was Henry of Huntingdon who, in his *Historia Anglorum*, written in about the year 1130, described Stonehenge, as one of the four marvels of Britain, the others being natural phenomena such as the Cheddar Caves. About the same time Geoffrey of Monmouth gave his account of its origin in his *Historia Regum Britanniae*, the definitive source of all Arthurian legends. Geoffrey claimed that he had found the story in 'an ancient book written in the British language', which stated how Aurelius Ambrosius, the British king, had sought the opinion of Merlin as to a suitable memorial for the four hundred and sixty noble warriors treacherously massacred by Hengist. Merlin advised him to 'send for the Giants' Round which is on Mount Killaraus in Ireland', and the king thereupon dispatched an expeditionary force of fifteen thousand men, under his brother, Uthr Pendragon, to counter any Irish opposition and to dismantle the stones, which they found they could only do with the help of Merlin, who then carried them to the waiting ships and brought them back to England. At the king's orders, Merlin 'put them up in a circle round the sepulchre, in exactly the same way as they had been arranged on Mount Killaraus in Ireland.'

This interpretation was repeated by Giraldus Cambrensis and other chroniclers and was widely accepted, except when John Rastell, in his *Pastyme of People* (1530), expressed the view that the stones of Stonehenge were too large to have been moved and that they must have been made of artificial cement manufactured 'from some large Congeries of Sand, and other unctuous matter mixt together.'

In 1620, while staying with the Earl of Pembroke at Wilton Park, King James I visited Stonehenge and commanded his Surveyor-General of the King's Works, Inigo Jones, to conduct an expert study of the monument. At his death, thirty years later, the 'judicious architect' had left only 'some few indigested notes', which his son-in-law and assistant, John Webb, amplified and published as a volume, in 1655, under the title, *The Most Notable Antiquity of Great Britain, Vulgarly Called Stone-Heng on Salisbury Plain, Restored*. It was the first book entirely about Stonehenge and it dismissed all Arthurian claims and stated that the monument was a Roman temple of the Tuscan order of architecture. A little later, Dr Walter Charleton wrote his *Chorea Gigantum: or, The Most Famous Antiquity of Great Britain, Vulgarly Called Stone-Heng, Standing on Salisbury Plain, Restored to the Danes*, claiming that Stonehenge was the place where the ancient Danish kings were crowned. Aylett Sammes, in his *Britannia Antiqua Illustrata* (1676) , wondered whether it could have been built by the Phoenicians, and other writers put forward other conjectures, from Boadicea's tomb to a Saxon monument. Samuel Pepys found the stones 'as prodigious as any tales I ever heard of them' and could do no more than utter: 'God knows what their use was!'

In an account of his native Wiltshire in 1640, Aubrey tried to 'imagine what kind of countrie this was in the time of the ancient Britons'. 'Their priests,' he wrote, 'were Druids. Some of their temples I pretend [i.e. claim] to have restored, as Avebury, Stonehenge, &c.' He developed the theme in his *Monumenta Britannica* in which he referred to stone circles as *Templa Druidum*, and conjectured that the inscription on a tablet that no one else could read 'might be made by the Druides'. He revealed his Welsh origin when he stated that the 'stares', or starlings, that made their nests in the gaps between the sarsen uprights and lintels at Stonehenge 'did put me in mind that in Wales they do call stares Adar y Drudwy, sc. Avis Druidum. The Druids might make these holes purposely for their birds to nest in.' Edward Lhuyd, with whom Aubrey discussed his ideas, expressed the view that stone circles 'were Places of Sacrifice and other religious Rites in the Times of Paganism, seeing the *Druids* were our ancient heathen Priests.'

In 1717, Dr William Stukeley saw a transcript of *Monumenta Britannica* and was inspired to carry on the field-work begun by Aubrey at Stonehenge. He popularised the notion of a Druidic connection with the publication, in 1740, of his *Stonehenge, a Temple restor'd to the British Druids*. He believed that Stonehenge and Avebury were serpent temples of 'Dracontia', a belief that arose from a mythical story of Pliny which stated that the Druids of Gaul used a serpent's egg as a magic charm, from which it was assumed that they were serpent worshippers. He laid out, in the garden of his house at Grantham, a Druidic grove and temple in which he buried a still-born child. He invited his antiquarian friends to form a 'Society of Roman Knights' dedicated to the saving of Roman remains from destruction 'by time, Goths and barbarians'. Each member was given the name of a Roman or Celtic notable, but for himself he chose the name of a Druid and, unable to find the name of a British Druid, he called himself Chyndonax, the French '*prince des Druides*'.

Stukeley made an excellent survey of Stonehenge and put forward the theory that its Druid builders had employed a unit of measurement, which he called a 'druid cubit', measuring 20.8 inches (53cm.), and that they had made use of a magnetic compass in setting the principal line of the whole work to point to 'the northeast, where abouts the sun rises when the days are longest.' This astronomical conclusion was pursued by Dr John Smith, 'the Inoculator of the Small Pox', who published a pamphlet entitled *Coir Gaur, the Great Orrery of the Ancient Druids*, in 1777. He divided the Stonehenge circle into 360 parts, which were 'the number of days in the ancient solar year', and set a line through the Friar's Heel to form an axis aligned to the summer solstice so that 'the Arch Druid standing on his stall, and looking down the right line of the Temple' would see the sun rise. *Coir Gaur* was his interpretation of *Chorea Gigantum*, the Giants' Round or Dance, that survives in the Welsh name for Stonehenge, *Côr y Cewri*.

Henry Rowlands, the Anglesey vicar and antiquary and a disciple of Edward Lhuyd, in his *Mona Antiqua Restaurata* (1723), presumed that the Druids, 'being so near a descent to the Fountains of true Religion and Worship as to have had one of Noah's Sons for Grandsire or Great-grandsire, may well be imagin'd to have carried and conveyed here some of the Rites and Usages of the true Religion, pure and untainted.' He believed that they had worshipped in the oak groves on the Plain of Mamre, where Abraham had settled and, more important, he associated them with the *cromlechau* of his own county and thus gave rise to the notion that these chambered tombs were Druidical Altars.

The descent from Noah, whose language was held to be Hebrew, led to the belief that there was a connection between Hebrew and the Welsh language. Even as late as the last century, a correspondent in the *Salopian and West Midland Monthly Journal* expressed the opinion that the name Stonehenge was derived from 'pure Hebrew-Welsh' and quoted, as source words, the '(Hebrew) *Shiovang*, (Welsh) *Sionge*, the stone seat of Honour or Reverence.'

The revived interest in Druidism was such that new societies, or movements, came into being bearing the name of, and even claiming derivation from, the Druids.

Junius Janus (John) Toland, the Irish deistical writer whose works had been burnt by the hangman in Ireland, had met Aubrey when he took refuge in this country, and had accepted his views on Druidism and stone circles. On 21 September 1717, the autumnal equinox, he held a meeting of Druidic followers on Primrose Hill in London, as a result of which the Ancient Druid Order was established. The Order subsequently had, as its Archdruid, successively, Dr William Stukeley, the Earl of Winchilsea with whom Stukeley had walked along the

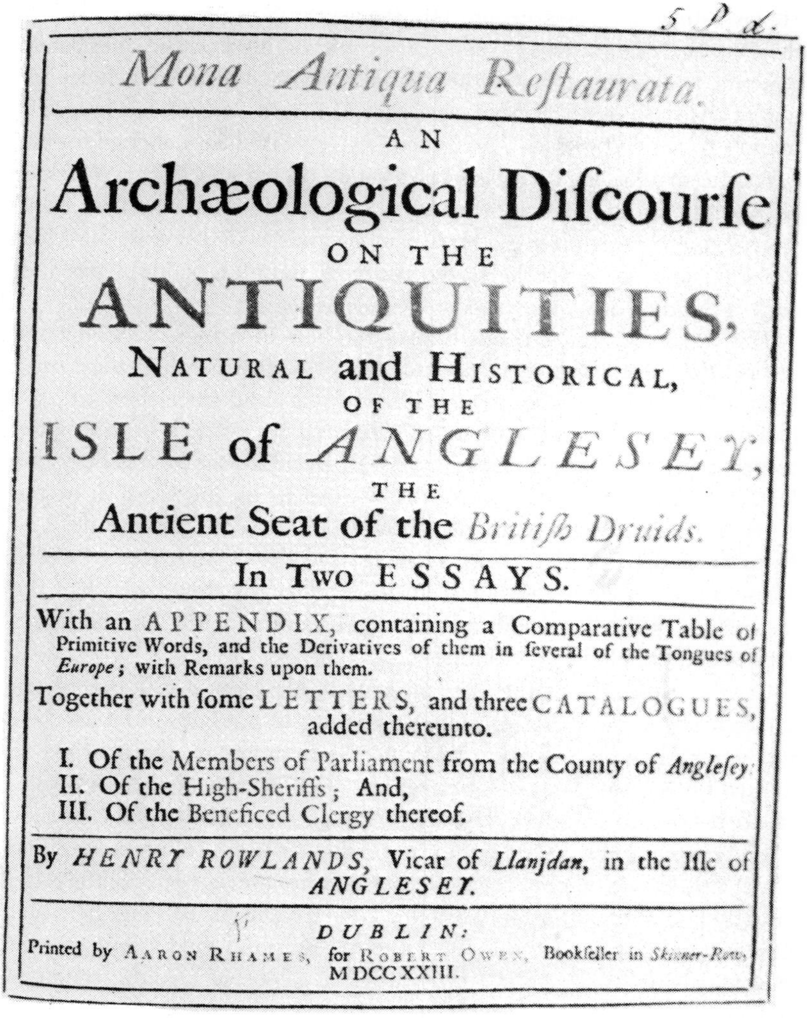

5 P d.

Mona Antiqua Restaurata.

A N
Archæological Difcourfe
ON THE
ANTIQUITIES,
NATURAL and HISTORICAL,
OF THE
ISLE of ANGLESEY,
THE
Antient Seat of the *Britifh Druids.*

In Two ESSAYS.

With an APPENDIX, containing a Comparative Table of Primitive Words, and the Derivatives of them in feveral of the Tongues of *Europe;* with Remarks upon them.

Together with fome LETTERS, and three CATALOGUES, added thereunto.

I. Of the Members of Parliament from the County of *Anglefey.*
II. Of the High-Sheriffs; And,
III. Of the Beneficed Clergy thereof.

By *HENRY ROWLANDS,* Vicar of *Llanjdan,* in the Ifle of *ANGLESEY.*

DUBLIN:
Printed by AARON RHAMES, for ROBERT OWEN, Bookfeller in *Skinner-Row,* M DCC XXIII.

Title page of Henry Rowlands's Mona Antiqua Restaurata *(1723).*

lintels of the trilithons of Stonhenge, and the poet William Blake who, as Professor Stuart Piggott has commented, had made 'the revolutionary discovery that Britain was the Holy Land, and Jerusalem not so far from Primrose Hill.'

The Order is not to be confused with the Ancient Order of Druids formed in 1781 as a secret society, on the lines of Freemasonary, by

Henry Hurle, a carpenter and builder, at the King's Arms Tavern in the City of London. In 1833 this Order was divided on the question of benefits, and the majority of the members seceded to form a charitable body called The United Ancient Order of Druids, which has lodges in many parts of the world. The Grand Lodge visited Stonehenge for the first time in 1905, its members robed and cowled and carrying sickles at the end of long poles with which to gather imaginary mistletoe, and a large number of initiates were brought blindfolded before the Most Noble Grand Arch Brother, who received them and administered an oath 'as binding as sealing wax and twice as lasting'.

There were several Druidic bodies that held meetings at Stonehenge during the latter part of the last century. A group called the Druid Hermetists met there before the 1914–18 war, and since then, at least half a dozen different groups of Druids have performed, or attempted to perform, their ceremonies, there but, by 1955, there was only one left. This was *An Druidk Uileach Braithreachas*, or the Church of the Universal Bond, which claims, without any evidence, to be derived from Toland's Ancient Druid Order. Its Chief Druid, from 1909 to 1946, was the formidable Dr George MacGregor Reid, who had the distinction of having stood, unsuccessfully, both for the United States Senate and the House of Commons.

On the last night of the last century, a gale blew down one of the sarsen uprights, and a lintel came down with it. Sir Edmund Antrobus, its owner, then placed a fence around the monument, and charged an admission fee towards its upkeep, but the Church of the Universal Bond refused to pay and demanded free entry to *Cathoir Galt*, as they called Stonehenge, which they regarded as their inheritance. The Chief Druid was ejected by the Police and he, thereupon, publicly and ritually laid a curse on Sir Edmund. Later, when his son and heir was killed in action, in October 1914, and Sir Edmund died a few months afterwards, their deaths were regarded as proof of Druidic religious power.

Stonehenge was then purchased by Cecil Chubb, a local landowner and, in 1918, he presented it to the nation. During his brief period of ownership, he had given the Druids free access, but the Office of Works would make no exception and the custodian, Mr Smith, was ordered to charge the Druids the customary fee. In June 1920 the Church of Universal Bond wanted to perform their ceremonies on two additional days, but the Office of Works refused consent, stating that 'some limit must be set to this absurd and degrading nonsense.'

The Chief Druid took offence and allowed the solstice to pass un-celebrated, for the first time, it was claimed, since 1643, which is three quarters of a century before the Ancient Druid Order was founded. In 1926 the Druids tore down the fences, but then left to celebrate the solstice on nearby Normanton Down, where they proposed to build a replica Stonehenge. When Smith, the custodian, died shortly after-wards, he was regarded as a victim of the Druidic curse, and MacGregor Reid and his followers returned to Stonehenge, and peacefully paid the admission charge.

The Church of the Universal Bond suffered a secession in 1963 when some of its members formed The Order of Bards, Ovates and Druids, who have forsaken Stonehenge and meet at Hunsbury Hill, in North-amptonshire, and on Tower Hill in London.

Druidic meetings continue to take place at Stonehenge despite the fact that it has been amply demonstrated, as Professor R. J. C. Atkin-son has stated in his authoritative book, *Stonehenge*, that 'there is *no* evidence for connecting the Druids with Stonehenge in any way what-soever ... Even if the monument was still venerated, there is no reason for the Druids to have taken any interest in it, since their places of worship and observance were "groves", that is, clearings in the forest.'

The Gorsedd of Bards has no connection with Stonehenge but the fact that some of its ceremonies are held within a stone circle indicates that the postulations of William Stukeley influenced its founder when he was seeking a place for Welsh literature and culture in the Romantic movement in which he found himself.

EARLY GATHERINGS

NO ACCOUNT of the Gorsedd of Bards can be understood without some investigation into the past of Welsh bardism. From time beyond recall, the bards have gathered together in friendly rivalry, sometimes over a pot of ale, sometimes in stern competition for a chair in the king's court. A rubric in the *Book of Aneirin* stated that 'any more than a man should go to battle without arms, so a bard ought not to go to a bardic contest without his song.'

The earliest Welsh poets of whom there is account were bards at the court of the kings and princes of northern Britain in the sixth century. Taliesin, who may have been a native of Powys, travelled to the court of Urien ap Cynfarch, ruler of Rheged, a kingdom that bestrode the Solway Firth, and sang the praise of his host, generous in his hospitality and brave in battle against Ida, King of Northumbria, and composed a lament for his son, Owain ab Urien, who was to become a hero in the mediaeval romances of the Arthurian cycle.

Aneirin was at the court of Mynyddog Mwynfawr, whose realm was Gododdin, stretching from Stirling to the Tyne, with its capital at Din Eidyn, now Edinburgh. Mynyddog gathered around him a band of three hundred warriors whom he trained and feasted for a year before setting off, in about the year 600, to attack the Angles of Deira and Bernicia at the battle of Catraeth, the present day Catterick. Despite their courage and bravery in the face of the overwhelmingly superior numbers of the enemy, they were annihilated, and Aneirin commemorated their valiant deeds in a long poem, called *Y Gododdin*.

The poet's place as a privileged member of society was defined in the tenth century Law of Hywel Dda, which recognised the grades of *pencerdd* (chief poet) and *bardd teulu* (bard of the household). 'This is a pencerdd,' the Law stated, 'the bard when he wins a chair.' He was an officer of the king's domain, rather than of the court, and he was one of the fourteen royal officers who had his own chair in the king's hall, where he sat beside the court justice, His lodging was with the heir apparent, and he was entitled to his land free. He had authority over other poets, and was entitled to receive twenty-four pence from a poet to whom he gave instruction.

The *bardd teulu* was one of the twenty-four officers of the court. The *teulu* was the royal household, rather than a family, in the modern sense, and it included the royal guard, that was under the command of the *penteulu* (captain of the guard) and ready at all times to protect the king. Sir J. E. Lloyd has suggested that when Henry VII inaugurated the Yeomen of the Guard he was, perhaps unwittingly, re-establishing a form of *teulu* that was familiar to his Welsh forebears.

The *bardd teulu* was entitled by law to receive his woollen clothing from the king, and his linen clothes from the queen, three times a year, at Christmas, Easter and Whitsun, and he had his land free and a horse in attendance. He sat next to the captain of the guard in hall 'so as to have his harp put in his hand' by him, and his lodging was with him, in 'the largest house in the townland, and the most central.' He received a harp from the king on his appointment, and a gold ring from the queen. In the traditional passing on of garments of lenten penance, he received the steward's clothes, and gave his own to the doorkeeper. He was entitled to a steer from the booty when he accompanied the household on a raid and, like the court justice, he received a 'whale-bone throwboard', which was probably a board game with its pieces, like chessmen, made of bone. When a song was required to be sung, the *pencerdd* sang two songs in the hall, one of God and one of the king and, after him, the *bardd teulu* sang three songs below the precinct. If the queen wanted a song, he sang to her 'without stint' and that quietly, so that the hall was not disturbed by him. On the day of battle he was required to sing *Unbeniaeth Prydain* (The Monarchy of Britain), which referred to the Welsh claim for sovereignty over the whole of the island.

Bardism was a craft and, like any other, it was necessary that it's practitioner should excel at his work. He learned his craft by becoming a disciple of an older or superior poet who taught not only the arts of poetry, but also the use of words, history, folk lore, legends, genealogy and heraldry, for the poet was expected to entertain his patron and praise his virtues, to be his 'memory' and to record his lineage. He would recite the works of earlier bards and, in this way, poems and stories, were handed on from generation to generation. A young poet would have to serve his apprenticeship before he could qualify as a bard, and become a member of the bardic order. Cynddelw Brydydd Mawr, in his elegy to Hywel ab Owain Gwynedd, who died in 1170, stated that he had 'taught splendid poets' and, in a lament after the death of Cadwgan ap Madog he was confident that 'our disciples know their teaching'. The disciples of Gruffudd Hiraethog, four centuries later, became the foremost bards of the sixteenth century and included William Llŷn, Simwnt Fychan, Wiliam Cynwal and Sion Tudur. Gruffudd himself had received his bardic degrees from his bardic teacher, Lewys Morgannwg and had his licence signed by him and two noblemen. He was, thus, qualified to teach the rules of prosody and the history of Wales and of Britain, and he was sufficiently knowledgeable in family history to be appointed Deputy-Herald of Wales by the College of Arms.

Not infrequently a poet would perpetuate the tradition of prophetic verse in which *Mab Darogan* (the Son of Destiny) would lead the Welsh again to victory and place a king, once more, on the throne of Bendigeidfran son of Llŷr who had ruled over the Isle of Britain. One of the earliest examples of such verse is *Armes Prydein* (The Prophecy of Britain), a tenth century call to arms in which the Irish and the Norse of Dublin, the Cornish and the men of Clyde are invited to help to drive the Anglo-Saxons from these shores and to regain the territory of the Celts 'from Manaw Gododdin to Brittany, from Dyfed to the Isle of Thanet.' The Welsh would be led by Cynan and Cadwaladr who, under the banner of St David, would chase the enemy into the sea at Aber Santwig (Sandwich). With the advance of the Normans into Wales, Geoffrey of Monmouth revived Merlin's prophecy that the Red Dragon of Cadwaladr would be ultimately victorious, and it was felt that this prediction had been fulfilled when Henry Tudor ascended the throne, having carried the banner of Cadwaladr, from whom he claimed descent, at the Battle of Bosworth.

Some of the court poets of the twelfth century were themselves of noble birth, and versed in the arts of war. Owain Cyfeiliog, prince of Powys is famous for the only poem that can be ascribed to him, *Hirlas Owain,* which has echoes of *Y Gododdin* except that the mead horn circles the hall at a feast after, and not before, a battle.

A dynasty of lordly poets flourished in north Pembrokeshire in the early part of the eleventh century. A poem of praise preserved in *The Black Book of Carmarthen,* is addressed to Cuhelyn Fardd, the son of Gwynfardd Dyfed (Privileged Bard of Dyfed), who was lord of the cantref of Cemais, with his stronghold at Nevern. Gwynfardd is given, in one version of his pedigree, as the son of Cynan Gerdd Gynnil

(Cynan of the Precise Poetic Art), and Cuhelyn's son was named Gwr-wared Gerdd Gynnil, which goes to indicate that this was a family of poets and of patrons of poets, of which Dafydd ap Gwilym was a direct descendant. Cuhelyn, according to his anonymous adulator, was 'worthy of a chair.'

Cynddelw Brydydd Mawr (fl. 1155-1200), the most prolific poet of his time, was able to claim that he had sung in the courts of the three provinces: he laments the breaking up of the princedom of Powys, where he had been court poet; he wrote an elegy to Owain Gwynedd, and a poem of praise to his son, Hywel ab Owain Gwynedd, and he composed a series of *awdlau* to the Lord Rhys, prince of Deheubarth, in which he pleaded for the restoration of the traditional relationship between poet and patron. Cynddelw had been in contest with Seisyll Bryffwrch for the office of *pencerdd* at the court of Madog ap Maredudd, prince of Powys, when Seisyll claimed descent from a long line of poets and taunted Cynddelw for the lack of bardic tradition in his family, but Cynddelw was chosen.

Stories and legends of early assemblies of bards abound, most of them born of the imagination of nineteenth century historians. Prydain ab Aedd Mawr was claimed to have 'established the Gorsedd as an institution to perpetuate the works of the poets and musicians' in about 1000 BC and Caesar was said to have written that 'the Druids held a Gorsedd at the appropriate times of the year in a sacred place that was held to be centre of Gaul.' Owain, son of the Emperor Magnus Maximus, was held to have brought order and discipline to the eisteddfod in 375 AD, and there were tales of festivals held to compete for a chair at Caerleon in the time of King Arthur, and at the court of Urien Rheged in 517, and at Bangor Teifi, under the patronage of Cedig ap Ceredig ap Cunedda Wledig. Maelgwn Gwynedd, who favoured bards rather than minstrels, was patron of an eisteddfod held at Conway in 540 and, according to the fourteenth century poet, Iorwerth Beli, he mischievously commanded all the competitors to swim the river before competing, which caused the harps of the minstrels to warp and gave the bards a clear field.

Rhys ap Tewdwr, king of Deheubarth, was believed to have held an eisteddfod at Carmarthen in 1170 at which he imparted to the bards the new rules of poetry that he had learned while an exile in Brittany. Bleddyn ap Cynfyn, Prince of Powys, and Cadwgan ap Bleddyn, his son, were said to have given their patronage to the festivals they held triennially at their courts, and the Earls of Gloucester were claimed to have endowed eisteddfodau at Tir Iarll in Glamorgan.

Edward Jones (Bardd y Brenin) who was harpist to King George IV reminded us that 'the eisteddfod was a triennial assembly of the Bards (held usually at Aberffraw, the royal seat of the Prince of Wales formerly, situated in Anglesey; likewise Dynevawr, the royal castle of the Prince of South Wales, in Carmarthenshire; and Mathravael, the royal palace of the Princes of Powys, in Montgomeryshire) for the regulation of Poetry and Music, for the purpose of conferring degrees and advancing to the Chair of the Eisteddfod, by the decision of a Poetical and Musical contest, some of the rival candidates; or establishing in that honourable seat the Chief Bard, who already occupied it.'

Gruffudd ap Cynan (c. 1055-1137), king of Gwynedd, was said to have held eisteddfodau triennially at his court at Aberffraw, and also at Caerwys and at Achlach Vale in Ireland. He had been brought up in Dublin, where his father lived in exile and had married the daughter of the Viking ruler, and tradition states that he returned to Wales bringing Irish bards and musicians with him, and that he introduced certain changes in the bardic organisation and issued regulations governing the craft of poetry under a statute known as the Statute of Gruffudd ap Cynan. It was believed that the eisteddfod held at Caerwys, 'before the prince Gruffudd ap Cynan in person,' was held there because his wife, Angharad, was the daughter of the ruler of that area. The Statute was invented, however, in preparation for a later eisteddfod held at Caerwys.

The first eisteddfod of which there is reliable account was held under the patronage of his grandson, Rhys ap Gruffydd. Rhys was the younger son of Gruffydd ap Rhys ap Tewdwr, prince of Deheubarth, and his wife Gwenllian, daughter of Gruffudd ap Cynan. He was only an infant when his mother was killed defending Kidwelly, and his father died a year later leaving his sons to lead the revolt against the Normans in south Wales. On the death of his last surviving brother, Maredudd, in 1155, Rhys became the ruler of Deheubarth but, on the accession of Henry II he was obliged, in 1158, to acknowledge the overlordship of the Crown and he is henceforth known as 'the Lord Rhys'. He regained his territories in 1165 and, in 1171, he was appointed Justiciar of South Wales. Although he accepted English ways in dress and domestic manners, he remained a patron of Welsh life and letters, and his court at Dinefwr was the resort of bards, like Cynddelw Brydydd Mawr, Seisyll Bryffwrch and Gwynfardd Brycheiniog.

In 1171 he removed his court from Dinefwr to Cardigan and,

according to *Brut y Tywysogion* (the Chronicle of the Princes), at Christmastide in the year 1176, he held a *gwledd arbennig* (a special feast) in that castle, during which he 'set two contests, one between the bards and poets, and the other between harpists, *crwth* players and pipers and other string instrument players. And he offered two chairs to the winners of the contests, and these he enriched with generous gifts. And then a young servant of his own court was awarded the prize in the music contest, and a man from Gwynedd was victorious in poetry. And all the other competitors received from Lord Rhys all they asked for, and none was refused. And that feast was proclaimed a year before it happened, throughout Wales and England and Britain and Ireland, and in many other countries.' This assembly of poets and musicians is regarded as the earliest recorded *eisteddfod*, and to it 'there repaired all the musicians of Wales and some also from England and Scotland.' While the event was considered sufficiently important to be recorded in the *Brut*, it is strange that the percipient contemporary Giraldus Cambrensis, who observed of the Welsh that 'in their musical concerts they do not sing in unison like the inhabitants of other countries, but in many different parts,' and dwelt on many other of their qualities and shortcomings, and who knew about every movement of his kinsman, the Lord Rhys, should make no mention in his *Itinerarium Cambriae* either of the 'special feast' or of any other form of poetic rivalry.

Standards deteriorated among the bards as the number of *y glêr*, the wandering minstrels, increased. The term *clêr*, borrowed from the Irish *cleir*, meaning itinerant bards, was downgraded to refer to inferior rhymesters, and corresponded roughly to the continental *clerici vagantes*, or the goliards, who were noted for their riotous behaviour. Phylip Brydydd (fl. 1220), chief poet at the court of Rhys Gryg, son of the Lord Rhys, complained that the licensed poets had to compete against these poetasters in the courts of south Wales. The 'Statute of Gruffudd ap Cynan' denounced the *clerwyr*, and the eisteddfod that was said to have been held at Caerwys in Gruffudd's presence was claimed to be for the purpose of eliminating 'the vain weeds' that had sprung up among the bards. Henry IV, in addition to his punitive legislation against the Welsh in general, enacted a law to get rid of 'the many diseases and mischiefs which have happened before this time in the land of Wales by many wasters, rhymers, minstrels and other vagabonds which had become a burden on the country.'

With the loss of independence in 1282 and the consequent disappearance of the princes, the old bardic organisation came to an end, but the principle of patronage was continued by the nobility, and while the bards still retained a position in society, they no longer had the security of an office at court and their status was diminished. The distinction between *pencerdd* and *bardd teulu* had faded, and although some of the gentry kept house poets in the old manner, the bards generally had to depend on more than one patron and had to roam the countryside from house to house. The fourteenth century poet Iorwerth Beli reproached the Bishop of Bangor for failing to respond to the plea of the poets who, having lost the patronage of the prince, were now appealing to him, as a prince of the church, but he, though a Welshman, had turned a deaf ear, while at the same time bestowing honour and raiment upon 'young English minstrels whose songs were no better than the squealing of piglets.'

The bards revelled in disputations on matters related to their craft and status. Some were frivolous and some were scurrilous but, in the main, they consisted of serious discussion or debate. In a controversy between Gruffudd Gryg and Dafydd ap Gwilym, the former attacked Dafydd's slavery to courtly love. Less than a century later, Rhys Goch Eryri was involved in a lengthy dispute with Sion Cent and Llywelyn ap Moel y Pantri arising from a comment in Rhys's elegy to his bardic teacher, Gruffudd Llwyd ap Dafydd, which Llywelyn regarded as a slur on the princedom of Powys. The most celebrated of the bardic altercations was that which took place between Edmund Prys, archdeacon of Merioneth, and William Cynwal, a graduate of the 1568 Eisteddfod, which produced, between them, fifty-four *cywyddau* containing some five thousand lines. It began when Prys sent an *englyn* to William Cynwal, in 1580, reminding him that he had promised an archer's bow to Rhys Wyn of Maentwrog. This led to a poetic cut and thrust that lasted seven years, culminating in a bitter argument over bardic learning. Cynwal refused to recognise the archdeacon as a poet because he had not qualified in accordance with bardic tradition, thus typifying the attitude of the craftsmen-poets who had been initiated into the mysteries of bardism. Among those who were critical of this attitude was Dr Sion Dafydd Rhys, the eminent physician and grammarian, who censured the bards for keeping 'their art hidden without revealing it to anyone except to some disciple who will swear that he will not teach it to anyone else, or to an occasional gentlemen who promises upon his honour to keep it a secret.' He wanted to expose the glory of Welsh poetry 'to the sight of all Europe in a language that was common to all.'

The bards, however, clung to the rules governing their craft which were reiterated in a tract preserved in the hand of John Jones of Gelli-lyfdy in the early part of the seventeenth century, known as *Y Tri Chov* and which stated that:

> The office or function of the British or Cambrian Bards was to keep and preserve Tri Chov Ynys Prydain: that is, the Three Records or Memorials of Britain, otherwise called the British Antiquities ... for the preservation whereof, when the Bards were graduating at their Commencements, they were trebly rewarded:
>
> The first of the Three Cov is the history of notable acts of the Kings and Princes of Britain and Cambria.
>
> The second of the Three Cov is the language of the Britons, of which the Bards were to give an account of every word and syllable therein, when demanded of them, in order to preserve the ancient language and to prevent its intermixture with any foreign tongue, or the introduction of any foreign word in it, to the prejudice of their own whereby it might be corrupted or extirpated.
>
> The Third Cov [is] of the pedigrees or descent of the nobility, their division of lands, and the blazoning of arms.

There is no authentic record of an eisteddfod being held after Cardigan until the middle of the fifteenth century, and reports of any festivals during that period cannot be supported historically. One such report states that Rhys Meigen lampooned Dafydd ap Gwilym at an eisteddfod held at Llanfihangel Afan, and that Dafydd responded with such effect that Rhys Meigen fell dead. This was the time of the 'three Renaissance Eisteddfodau', so called because they represented a revival of Welsh poetry after the depression that had followed the disappearance of the princes. The first was said to have been held at Gwern-y-clepa under the patronage of Ifor ap Llywelyn, lord of Bassaleg, whom Dafydd ap Gwilym, for his generosity, had dubbed 'Ifor Hael'. The second, at Dol-goch by Llywelyn ap Gwilym, constable of Newcastle Emlyn, and uncle and tutor of Dafydd ap Gwilym who won the birchen garland for the best love-poem. The third, Eisteddfod Maelor, was held in 1330 with Roger Mortimer, Earl of March, as its patron.

Although none of these events took place, and despite the gloom that hung over the bards after the loss of independence, there arose, in the middle of the fourteenth century, a great burgeoning that produced poets of the calibre of Gruffudd ab Adda and Madog Benfras and above all, Dafydd ap Gwilym. Dafydd brought a concept of courtly love and romance into the bardic tradition and breathed new life into Welsh poetry.

Around 1450, the poet Llawdden, a native of Loughor, went to see his kinsman Gruffudd ap Nicolas at Abermarlais. While he was there, a wandering minstrel called and recited some verses in English. Llawdden, an accomplished poet, denounced the verses in abusive terms, and when asked how things could be improved, he appealed to Gruffudd to promote an eisteddfod, but he was reminded that this could only be done with royal consent. Llawdden argued that the king could hardly withhold his consent if approached by a nobleman of the calibre of Gruffudd, and under such persuasion, Gruffudd made application to Henry VI, and obtained his agreement to hold an eisteddfod at Carmarthen in 1451.

Gruffudd described at one and the same time as 'the most powerful political figure in west Wales' and 'the greatest rogue of his time in Wales', was lord of Dinefwr and sheriff of Carmarthenshire and was appointed Deputy Justiciar of South Wales in 1447. Eulogies were addressed to him by Lewis Glyn Cothi, Gwilym ab Ieuan Hen, Dafydd ab Edmwnd and other leading poets, especially for his role in organising the eisteddfod.

Although there is no contemporary account of the event extant, it is recorded in transcripts by Robert ab Ifan, in 1587, and by John Jones of Gellilyfdy, in 1636. Robert ab Ifan states that it was held at Dinefwr Castle and that it lasted three months, but recent evidence indicates that the venue was Carmarthen Castle, and it is more likely to have lasted a week, or perhaps, a fortnight.

The prize for the best harpist, a silver harp, was awarded to Cynwrig Bencerdd of Holywell, and a silver tongue for the best singer to the accompaniment of the harp, went to Rhys Bwting of Prestatyn. Gruffudd, who was sufficiently steeped in bardic tradition to be accepted as the adjudicator, awarded the silver chair, which he is said to have designed himself, to Dafydd ab Edmwnd, a gentleman-poet of Hanmer in Flintshire, of whom it was said that 'he touched a word as though it were the leaf of a rose, or the string of a harp.' He won the chair for a *cywydd* to the Trinity, but of far greater importance was his revision and systematization of Welsh prosody. He rearranged the Twenty-four Metres, a classification usually attributed to Einion

Offeiriad (fl. 1330). He made some of the metres more difficult and introduced new ones, of such extreme complexity that they were said by Sir John Morris-Jones to 'engender nonsense rather than poetry.' It has to be remembered, of course, that they were specifically designed to make entry into bardic orders more difficult so as to safeguard the status and livelihood of professional poets by getting rid of poetasters and lesser minstrels. Apart from a requirement in order to qualify for the degree of *pencerdd*, some of the metres were hardly ever used, except in exemplary poems written to display a poet's skill in all Twenty-four Metres. Even this number was exceeded by Dafydd Llwyd Mathew in 1611 when he wrote an 'Ode in Twenty-four Metres, and more conjectured by the Author' addressed to George Owen of Henllys, lord of Cemais.

Although Llawdden is said to have been awarded a gold axe as a prize for his classification, which led to the saying that a masterly poetic work bore *ôl bwyell Llawdden* (the mark of Llawdden's axe), he is also said to have accused Gruffudd ap Nicolas of having been bribed by Dafydd ab Edmwnd. There was, in any case, considerable dissatisfaction among the poets of south Wales at seeing most of the prizes go to north-east Wales, and the bards of Glamorgan were said to have refused to accept Dafydd's revisions. His innovations were generally adopted, and they were incorporated in the Bardic Grammar written by Gutun Owain, his disciple and friend, who accompanied him to the Carmarthen eisteddfod.

The Bardic Grammars were largely adaptations of the Latin Grammars to which were added the rules governing the Welsh metres that had evolved from the sixth century onward. The earliest extant Grammar dates from the first half of the fourteenth century and is ascribed to Einion Offeiriad and they continued to be produced in augmented forms culminating, in about 1570, in a definitive work, *Pum Llyfr Cerddwriaeth* (The five Books of Minstrelsy) by Simwnt Fychan, a native of Llanfair Dyffryn Clwyd who had studied under Gruffudd Hiraethog.

CAERWYS AND AFTER 1523-1819

THE MAIN purpose of the Carmarthen Eisteddfod was to safeguard the privileges and status of the professional poets, and the aim was the same in 1523, when certain gentlemen of North Wales obtained a commission from King Henry VIII in the following terms:

> Let it be known to all gentlemen and common men that an eisteddfod for craftsmen in poetry and music will be held within the town of Caerwys in Flintshire the second day of the month of July in the fifteenth year of the crowning of Henry VIII before Richard ap Hywel ap Ieuan Fychan Esquier with the collaboration of Sir William Gruffudd and Sir Roger Salusbury and with the personal counsel of Gruffydd ap Ieuan ap Llywelyn Fychan and Tudur Aled a chaired poet, and many gentlemen and wise men besides in order to bring order and government to the craftsmen in poetic art and their art according to the words of the Statute of Gruffudd ap Cynan, Prince of Gwynedd, namely to certify and confirm master craftsmen and those who were previously awarded a degree and to award [a degree] to whoever deserved it and to give space [of time] to others to learn and meditate as deeply as conscience allows and by the Statute of Prince Gruffudd ap Cynan.

Richard ap Hywel ap Ieuan Fychan, of Gloddaeth and Mostyn, had fought at Bosworth alongside his kinsman, Henry Tudor, and was the father, by his wife Catherine, daughter of Sir Thomas Salusbury of Llewenni, of Thomas Mostyn, the first of the Mostyn family to be known by that name. Sir William Gruffudd, of Penrhyn, was Chamberlain of North Wales and a hero of the French campaign during which he was knighted at Tournai. Sir Roger Salusbury, the son of Sir Thomas, had fought at the battle of Blackheath and had been knighted by Henry VII. These gentlemen sat as commissioners, with Richard ap Hywel presiding. They were assisted in the grading of the bards by Gruffudd ap Ieuan ap Llywelyn Fychan, gentleman-poet and son-in-law of Richard ap Hywel, and the master-poet Tudur Aled, nephew and pupil of Dafydd ab Edmwnd.

The gentry were interested in promoting standards because they wanted their patronage to extend only to those who had qualified in the intricacies of Welsh verse, and particularly in the associated subjects of genealogy and heraldry. As Gruffudd ap Ieuan ap Llywelyn Fychan had warned in one of his poems: *Nac aed mwngler i glera* (Let no bungler seek patronage).

The Statute of Gruffudd ap Cynan was concocted before, and possibly in preparation for, the 1523 Eisteddfod to reinforce the plan to bring order and discipline to the craft and to eliminate 'the vainglorious weeds' that had grown among the bards and minstrels. It divided the bards into various classifications beginning with the lowest degree of *disgybl ysbas heb radd* (a bardic apprentice without a degree). He had to serve for a probationary period of three years before he was accepted as a *disgybl ysbas graddol* (a graduated pupil), and had to master six of the twenty-four metres of poetic art before proceeding to the grade of *disgybl disgyblaidd* (an amenable apprentice) who had to be proficient in twelve of the metres. He then became a *disgybl pencerddaidd* and would have to master the twenty-four metres, the whole system of *cynganeddion*, the eight parts of speech, the rules of grammar, and all there was to know about Welsh prosody, before he could qualify as a *pencerdd* (a master of poetry). A *pencerdd*, it was said, 'should know everything.'

A code of behaviour for the bards was also laid down in the Statute. They were not to get drunk while attending feasts, and they were not to make unseemly advances to the ladies of the houses they visited. They were not to go into hidden corners to play cards, or dice, or any other game, for profit. In the absence of a gathering of bards, or an eisteddfod, a bard could receive his degree at the marriage feast of a royal person, or of someone descended from one of the royal tribes. Tudor Aled, for example, had his first degree conferred upon him at a marriage feast in the hall of Ieuan ap Dafydd ab Ithel Fychan at Northop in Clwyd. It was preferable, however, for a degree to be awarded at 'a warranted eisteddfod' which should be held every three years at an appointed place, after being proclaimed at fairs and markets at least a year and a day in advance.

The Statute referred to the three main circuit festivals during which the bards could visit the homes of the gentry. The first was from

Christmas Day to Candlemas; the second from Easter to Ascension Day, and the third from Whitsun to Relic Sunday, which is the seventh after Trinity. They could also go on circuit on the feast day of the parish saint, or when a virgin got married. Only one poet was allowed to visit a nobleman whose income did not exceed ten pounds; two where the income was twenty pounds, and one more for every additional ten pounds. There was a scale of payments by which a *pencerdd* received 3s.4d. (17p), and lower grades had less, down to a *disgybl ysbas* who got 1s.6d (7d).

Among other minutiae is an instruction of the method of dealing with a silver chair if, through the death of its holder, or for any other reason, it should lie idle. Any *pencerdd* wishing to do so could issue a challenge to his fellows, but if he won it, he would still have to compete at the next eisteddfod. Tudur Aled had won a chair by such a challenge and, at the next eisteddfod, which was the one at Caerwys, he won it again, so that Lewys Môn was able to describe him as 'a double bard who bore two [silver] chairs upon his gown.' The silver harp was won, by Dafydd Nantglyn, and twelve musicians received their various degrees. There is no record of bards graduating, but this may be because the list has been lost.

The earliest known text of the Statute is in the hand of Gruffudd Hiraethog (d. 1564), a herald bard of whom Edmwnd Prys said that he was more learned than any two men together, and a fuller version was compiled by the physician and grammarian Sion Dafydd Rhys (1534–1609).

Although the Statute stipulated that an Eisteddfod should be held every three years, forty-three years went by before the next was held at Caerwys, nor is there any evidence of any other eisteddfod being held elsewhere, which is difficult to explain when so much importance was attached to the award of a recognised degree that would serve as a licence by which a bard could earn his living. The Commission for that Eisteddfod was issued, on behalf of Queen Elizabeth, by the Earl of Pembroke. President of the Council of Wales and the Marches, and was given at Chester on 23 October of the ninth year of the Queen's reign (1567):

> Elizabeth by the grace of God of England, France and Ireland Queen Defender of the Faith, &c. To our trusty and right wellbeloved Sir Richard Bulkeley Knight, Sir Rees Griffith Knight, Ellis Price esquire Doctor in Civil Law and one of our Council in the Marches of Wales,

William Mostyn, Ieuan Lloyd of Yale, John Salusbury of Rug, Rees Thomas, Maurice Wynn, Wm Lewis, Piers Mostyn, Owen John ap Howell Vaughan, John William ap John, John Lewis Owen, Morris Gruffydd, Simon Thelwall, John Griffith, Ellis ap Wm Lloyd, Robt Puleston, Harry Apharry, William Glynne and Rees Hughes esquires and to every of them, Greeting. Whereas it is come to the knowledge of the Lord President and other our said Council in our Marches of Wales that vagrant and idle persons naming themselves minstrels rhythmers and bards are lately grown into such an intolerable multitude within the principality of north Wales, that not only gentlemen and other by their shameless disorders are oftentimes disquieted in their habitations, but also the expert minstrels and musicians in tongue and cunning thereby much discouraged to travail in the exercise and practice of their knowledge and also not a little hindered in their livings and preferments. The Reformation whereof and the putting of those people in order the said Lord President and Council have thought very necessary and knowing you to be men of wisdom and upright dealing and also of experience and good knowledge in the science, have appointed and authorized you to be Commissioners for that purpose. And forasmuch as our said Council of late travelling in some part of the said principality had perfect understanding by credible report that the accustomed place for the execution of the like Commission hath been heretofore at Caerwys in our county of Flint and that William Mostyn esquire and his ancestors have had the gift and bestowing of the silver harp appertaining to the chief of that faculty, and that a year's warning at the least hath been accustomed to be given of the assembly, and execution of the like Commission, our said Council have therefore appointed the execution of the Commission to be at the said town of Caerwys the Monday next after the feast of the blessed Trinity which shall be in the year of our Lord God 1568. And therefore we require and command you by the authority of these presents not only to cause open proclamations to be made in all fairs, markets, towns and other places of assembly within our counties of Anglesey, Caernarfon, Merioneth, Denbigh and Flint, that all and every person and persons that intend to maintain their livings by name or colour of minstrels, rhythmers or bards, within the Talaith of Aberffraw comprehending the said five shires, shall be and appear before you the said day and place to show forth their learnings accordingly, but also that you ... repair to the said place the day aforesaid, and calling to you such expert men in the said faculty of the Welsh music as to you shall be thought convenient to proceed the execution of the premises and to admit such and so many as by your wisdoms and knowledge you shall find worthy into and under the degrees ... giving straight monition and commandment in our name and on our behalf to the rest not worthy that they return to some honest labour and due exercise, such as they be most apt unto for maintenance of their living upon pain and to be taken as sturdy and idle vagabonds and to be used according to the Laws and Statutes provided in that behalf ...

The commission referred only to the silver harp and made no mention of the chair which is known to have been awarded. The chair, like the harp, was a silver brooch, and was worn by the successful bard on the shoulder. There was also a silver *crwth* awarded to the best fiddler, and a silver tongue given to the best singer. They were all returned to Mostyn Hall after the Eisteddfod, where the silver harp is still kept.

There has been a good deal of argument as to the date of this Eisteddfod, especially since 1968 when a Gorsedd ceremony was held at Caerwys to celebrate its quatercentenary. The commission was given at Chester on 23 October 1567, and the Eisteddfod was to be held on the first Monday after the Feast of the Trinity, namely 14 June, 1568. It is known, however, that it was held on 26 May which was the date of the first Monday after Trinity in 1567, and there is other evidence to indicate that it was held in that year. The commission may well have been prepared early enough to give the required notice of at least a year and a day, but it could not have been signed, as required, by the Lord President of the Council of the Marches, the Earl of Pembroke, as he was in Ireland from the beginning of 1566 until his return in October 1567.

Among the gentlemen named in the commission were Sir Richard Bulkeley of Baron Hill, Beaumaris, who was a friend of the Queen; Sir Rhys Griffith of Penrhyn, who had fought in Ireland; Elis Prys of Plas Iolyn, chancellor of Bangor and known, from the colour of his red robe as Doctor of Common Law at Cambridge, as *Y Doctor Coch*; William Mostyn of Mostyn Hall, grandson of Richard ap Hywel who had presided over the Eisteddfod of 1523; John Salusbury of Rug; Maurice Wynn of Gwydir; Piers Mostyn of Talacre, William Glynne of Glynllifon, Ieuan Lloyd of Yale, and Simon Thelwall of Plas y Ward, judge and poet and patron of Simwnt Fychan.

Some of these gentlemen were competent to judge and to admit those who were worthy of a bardic degree. William Mostyn, Simon Thelwall and Sion William ap Sion of Ysgeifiog had either written poetry or had adjudicated the work of other poets, and took their task seriously, but some of the others were less zealous. Ieuan Lloyd played cards, until he was interrupted by William Cynwal who urged him to practise archery instead. Dr Elis Prys, who had a reputation as a womaniser, was paying attention to a pretty wench when Cynwal interfered again, and sent her away before 'the Red Doctor' had got beyond a kiss. Cynwal was thus accusing two of the judges of behaving contrary to the code laid down by the Statute of Gruffudd ap Cynan.

The chair was awarded, according to one report, to Simwnt Fychan, while another states that it went to William Llŷn. It is certain that they, together with Lewis ab Edward and Owain Gwynedd, all four pupils of Gruffudd Hiraethog, graduated in the degree of *Pencerdd*. Seven other poets, including William Cynwal, were admitted to the rank of *Disgybl pencerdd*, three to that of *Disgybl disgyblaidd*, and three apprentices as *Disgyblion ysbas*.

Those who did not qualify for a degree were to be given 'straight monition and commandment' to return to 'some honest labour and due exercises, such as they be most apt unto for maintenance of their living upon pain to be taken as sturdy and idle vagabonds and to be used according to the Laws and Statutes provided in that behalf.' Most of the commissioners were magistrates and under a duty to administer the law relating to 'sturdy and idle vagabonds.'

In 1594 a petition was signed by a number of gentlemen of north Wales, including Sir John Wynn of Gwydir and Tomos Prys of Plas Iolyn, calling for another eisteddfod for the purpose of safeguarding the privileges of the professional bards and to get rid of the 'loiterers and drones,' to be held 'at a convenient place,' but nothing came of the petition. At about the same time, Sion Mawddwy addressed a poem to George Owen of Henllys, lord of Cemais, in north Pembrokeshire, asking him as 'the brave, the wise and generous lord of Cemais, the keeper of the silver harp, who knows the true fountain head, the Queen, to go to her, and to her counsellors, and bring an eisteddfod to Henllys.' The lords of Cemais also claimed to be the hereditary keepers of a silver harp which, during the absence of the lord, was kept by the Prior of St Dogmael's Abbey.

The 1567 eisteddfod was the last of its kind and when the festival appeared again, two centuries later, it was a different kind of affair altogether.

Sion Dafydd Rhys could say, in 1592, that no longer were there any eisteddfodau 'worth mentioning,' and the only one of which there is a reliable account was the bardic gathering that took place, some time before 1590, at the house of William Evans, chancellor of Llandaff and so generous a patron of the bards that he was known as 'Ifor Hael Llandaf.' Those who were present wrote poems in competition, and composed extempore *englynion*, which were adjudicated by the good chancellor and Thomas Lewis of Van.

There are few references to any gatherings of bards during the seventeenth century. Edward Morris of Perthi Llwydion, Cerrigydrudion, drover and household bard to Thomas Mostyn of Gloddaeth, described a meeting of bards at Bala in 1663 as an eisteddfod, and it was reported that Sion Prichard Prys of Llangadwaladr had composed *englynion* at another eisteddfod held at the town in 1680, in which he sought the aid of Sir Roger Mostyn and the Bishop of Bangor 'to obtain a patent to hold an eisteddfod without delay.'

In 1701 an eisteddfod was held at Machynlleth 'to begin to revive and bring order to the Eisteddfod of the Bards (as it was in former times), to reprove false *cynghanedd*, to explain the dark and difficult things, and to verify that which is correct in the art of poetry in the Welsh language.' By then, however, the quality of Welsh poetry had degenerated and Sion Prichard Prys complained that 'metres have been shattered, the *cynghaneddau* have been emasculated, the art has languished.' Sion Rhydderch, the grammarian and almanack publisher, bemoaned the fate of the language and its literature and held the view that in the eisteddfod lay the best hope for its salvation. In his *Grammadeg Cymraeg*, which he published in 1728, he gave an outline, based on the Statute of Gruffydd ap Cynan, of the procedure that should be taken in promoting an eisteddfod:

> When the assembly is gathered, in response to a summons or call, at a particular town or village, they firstly choose twelve men knowledgeable in the Welsh language and also in poetry and in verse. If there will be judges among them, they shall set the subjects for the composition of the bards, either for an *englyn unodl union* or a *cywydd* or any of the twenty-four measures, but not for a lyric or carol or some poor verse which the chief bards will not as much as acknowledge because there are no established rules attached to them. The adjudicators shall warn the competitors that they must not satire or revile, one the other, and give them time to compose an *englyn* or *cywydd* as would seem appropriate. The names of competitors are taken so that each may be called by name and in the right order to the Chair to recite his poem.

And those who do not win the Chair must concede defeat on paper and deliver it to the Chief Bard or to the Chaired Bard, and they must drink the health of the Chief Bard and place six pence each in the cup for him.

Early in the eighteenth century, eisteddfodau began to be advertised in almanacks, and they gradually became known as *Eisteddfodau'r Almanaciau*. Thomas Jones of Tre'r Ddôl, near Corwen, had obtained letters patent granting him the sole right of 'writing, printing and publishing an almanack in the British Language' in 1679, and had published the first one in the following year, containing, in addition to a calendar, a list of fairs, astrological prophecies and a number of poems. Jones had spent some years in London, first as a tailor and then as a bookseller and publisher, before settling in Shrewsbury in about 1695, and establishing that town as the leading centre for the publication of Welsh books.

Other almanack makers followed to meet the demand, including Sion Rhydderch, Gwilym Howel of Llanidloes and John Prys (Philomath).

These eisteddfodau consisted of small groups of poets and rhymesters who met in a tavern to enjoy a verbal battle by composing extempore verses in competition. Such gatherings attracted the scorn of people like William Wynn, antiquary and vicar of Llanbrynmair, who condemned their frequenters as 'our contemptible set of smatterers in *barddoniaeth* [poetry] that make a figure in our Welsh almanacs.' Sion Rhydderch, and others like him, however, travelled widely to attend the meetings in the belief that they were the successors of the Caerwys eisteddfodau, and Rhydderch publicised them in his almanack, the 1719 issue of which contained a notice stating:

> Be it known to all Poets and men of Letters and other merry men of Wales that an Eisteddfod of the Poets of Wales will be held at the Cat Inn, Llandegla-in-Yale in Denbighshire on the 14th day of May 1719.

In his introduction to the 1735 issue, however, he complained that an eisteddfod held at Dolgellau the previous year had been a disappointment. He had travelled from Carmarthen, though now over sixty of years of age and in reduced circumstances, hoping to have 'the company of the majority of the Welsh bards who had some talent in poetry, but not half a dozen came in all', and he saw there 'only signs of apathy, faintheartedness and cowardice' and put it down to the deterioration that had set in following the withdrawal of the patronage which the nobility had extended at Caerwys.

An eisteddfod held at Cymer on St David's Day in 1735 was attended by not more than half a dozen poets, which drew some satirical verses from Wil Hopcyn, the thatcher-poet from Llangynwyd and reputed author of the popular song *Bugeilio'r Gwenith Gwyn* (Watching the Wheat). Wil is also said to have been at a gathering of bards at Pyle in 1740.

A gathering of bards at Bala on Whit-Monday 1738, included a woman, Sian Evans of Llanfaircaereinion, and Edward Wynne, vicar of Gwyddelwern, who presided, sang an *englyn* to each person present. The chair was won by Ellis Cadwaladr of Llandrillo for an eulogy to Sir Watkin Williams Wynn, and there were *englynion* sung in praise of Squire Price of Rhiwlas, and poems to the family of William Lloyd of Rhiwedog.

There was another eisteddfod at Bala in 1740, and others are said to have been held at Llansantffraid Glyn Ceiriog in 1743, at Selatyn in 1748 and at Llansannan in 1769. A notice in Philomath's almanack, *Dehonglydd y Sêr* (Interpreter of the Stars), for 1759 stated that :

> 'An Eisteddfod of the Poets and Musicians of Wales will be held at the Bull in Bala town on Whit-Monday and Whit-Tuesday in 1760 ... under the same rules and in the like manner as the ancient Eisteddfod at Caerwys in the days of Queen Elizabeth and at the same time and place there will be an eminent Master of Art (of Poetry) to pass judgement as is the right of a man who has that honourable rank.'

Gwilym Howel complained, in his almanack, *Tymhorol Newyddion o'r Wybren* (Seasonal News from the Firmament), in 1773, that he had received no support for an eisteddfod he had arranged at the Red Lion, Llanidloes, the previous year, and 'only one skilled bard turned up, John Jenkin (Ioan Siengcyn) from Cardigan.' Siengcyn, a cobbler turned schoolmaster at Nevern in north Pembrokeshire, nonetheless, arranged for an eisteddfod to be held at Cardigan in that year and was also prominent at another held on Whit-Monday 1774 'at the house of John Davies under the sign of the Ship and Castle' at Newport in Pembrokeshire

The 'almanack eisteddfodau' were paltry affairs held in lowly taverns, yet they were national events in that poets from various parts of

Wales were able to attend and compete against one another, and though they may not have been important in themselves, they kept alive the eisteddfodic tradition during a dark period, and provided a link between the royally commissioned event at Caerwys and the eisteddfod in its revivified form.

An eisteddfod held at Llangollen on 6 January 1789, to which the bards of north Wales had been bidden, was very poorly attended, but there was present an exciseman of Corwen, Thomas Jones, who saw in the eisteddfod a medium for the promotion of the arts and approached the Gwyneddigion Society for support.

The Gwyneddigion was one of two learned societies founded by prominent Welshmen in London. The Honourable Society of Cymmrodorion had been established in 1751 under the patronage of Richard Morris, who had left his native Anglesey at the age of eighteen and became chief clerk to the Comptroller of the Navy, and when that Society ceased to exist, in its first phase, in 1787, its role as patron of Welsh learning was taken over by the Gwyneddigion, founded in 1770 by Owen Jones (Owain Myfyr) and Robert Hughes (Robin Ddu o Fôn).

Jonathan Hughes of Llangollen wrote to the Gwyneddigion to ask for a prize to be awarded at an eisteddfod to be held at the Owain Glyn Dŵr Hotel at Corwen in May 1789 and his application was supported by Thomas Jones, as the promoter of the eisteddfod, who also asked for the Society's advice as he wanted 'to do the thing well.' He received an encouraging reply from the secretary, William Owen Pughe, who stated that the most effective way for the Society to assist the bards would be by promoting an eisteddfod at which the Society would give the prizes, including a chair provided it were offered for the best heroic poem on a subject that would be announced a year and a day in advance. Poems would be submitted under a pseudonym and would be adjudicated by fit persons who would consider 'purity of language and regular composition of the poems to be among their chief merits.' In the event of any disagreement, the Society would be the final arbiter. The name of the victorious poet would be announced on the first day of the eisteddfod when he would be hailed as *Pencerdd* and would not be allowed to take part in the impromptu verse competitions. The winner of that competition would be given the rank of *Disgybl pencerddaidd*. The Society would not be able to provide prizes for the Corwen eisteddfod, however, as the notice was too short, but, even so, Jones announced that the event was held under the patronage

of the Society, although he had paid for advertisements in the newspapers and for a broadsheet that he sent to the local nobility and
clergy, and to bards and musicians throughout north Wales and also
for the accommodation at the Owain Glyn Dŵr Hotel. Sir Robert
Williams Vaughan of Nannau provided a prize for the best poem in the
form of a silver breastplate, but the adjudicators failed to agree which
of three poems, submitted by Gwallter Mechain (Walter Davies: 1761-
1849), Twm o'r Nant (Thomas Edwards: 1739-1810) and Jonathan
Hughes, deserved the prize. The poems were sent for adjudication to
the Gwyneddigion in London, who decided in favour of Gwallter
Mechain, but Dr David Samwell, the naval surgeon who had accompanied Captain Cook on the *Resolution* and the *Discovery*, and was a
prominent member of the Gwyneddigion, felt so strongly that Twm
should have received the award that he sent him a silver writing pen as
a consolation prize.

Thomas Jones arranged another eisteddfod at Bala at Michaelmas
that year and, this time, the Gwyneddigion undertook to promote the
event at its own expense, but also under its own control. The subject
chosen for the *awdl* was *Ystyriaeth ar Oes Dyn* (Consideration of the Life
of Man), which attracted twelve entries. When these were sent to
London for adjudication, the Gwyneddigion members were disappointed to find that they were mostly of the exemplary type, containing all the twenty-four measures of Dafydd ap Edmwnd, whereas
the Society based its standards on the *awdlau* of Goronwy Owen and
urged the poets to select the measures that suited their artistic purposes.

The Bala Eisteddfod formed a landmark in the history of the
development of the festival in that this was the first time for the public
to be admitted to an Eisteddfod, and that on the presentation of a
ticket bearing the legend *Publica concordia nihil utilis*. This was the first
time, also, for the subject of the *awdl* to be announced in advance, and
for a drama, in the form of an *anterliwt*, by Twm o'r Nant, to be performed during an eisteddfod.

Owain Myfyr had realised that in these bardic meetings he had a
ready platform for the Society's ideals which, at the time, were
heavily influenced by the French Revolution. This is to be seen in the
notice he published of the meeting that was to be held at the Rose Inn
at St Asaph the next year:

> Be it known that the Gwyneddigion Society will give a Silver Chair
> for the best poem on the subject for 1790, namely Freedom, and that

they will also give a Silver medal for the best essay in prose to the same effect.

Above the notice was a paragraph that gave an indication of the nature of the treatment of the subject the Society would expect, stating that 'Freedom is the most valued treasure on the face of the earth; for from it there emanates, and upon it there rests, the greater part of the happiness of mankind this side of the grave – Freedom bridles Oppression and Tyranny: – it casts aside the darkness of Ignorance and Superstition, the which torment and enslave every good quality that pertains to the nature of Man'.

On 20 May 1790 Owain Myfyr sent a message to 'the Bards and others who wrote on Freedom' to inform them that 'the Gwynedd-igion Society adjudicates the best of the Songs the work of Phil-eleutheros, and of the Essays that of Gildas o Wynedd.' Phileleutheros the winner of the silver chair was Dafydd Ddu Eryri (David Thomas: 1759-1822) who had been wise enough to abandon the illustrative *awdl* and had written in selected measures to suit his subject.

Dafydd Ddu had relinquished his job as weaver in order to keep a school at Llanddeiniolen. As a corresponding member of the Gwyneddigion, he had heard from Robin Ddu yr Ail o Fôn about the tavern meetings of its members in London and he wrote a poem inviting the poets in his neighbourhood to meet at Betws Garmon on Lady Day 1784. He felt that Welsh poets should be given more freedom but that 'this freedom should be sparingly used lest a way should be opened for unworthy rhymesters to break into the realms of poetry.' Among those who responded to his invitation were Gutyn Peris (Griffith Williams: 1769-1835), Gwilym Peris (William Williams: 1769-1847), Gwyndaf Eryri (Richard Jones: 1785-1848), Gwilym Padarn (William Edwards: 1786-1857), Ieuan Lleyn (Evan Prichard: 1769-1832) and Cawrdaf (William Ellis Jones; 1795-1848). They formed a progressive school of bards, and became known as *Cywion Dafydd Ddu* (Dafydd Ddu's chickens).

The silver medal for the essay went to Gwallter Mechain, who saw himself journeying to Paris, where the French were fighting for the kind of freedom enjoyed by the British. Owain Myfyr was so impressed that he published the essay at his own expense and offered to pay the fees for a full course at Oxford University for its author. The medal was the work of M Dupré, the official engraver to the French Republic. It bore Freedom's head on the obverse and the inscription:

'The Society to Walter Davies for his Essay on Freedom. Exergue. 1790' The reverse showed Freedom slaying Tyranny, and was inscribed 'Justice overcomes tyranny. St Asaph Eisteddfod, Exergue. Dupré. F.'

Dafydd Ddu won the chair again at Llanrwst in 1791, for his *awdl* on *Gwirionedd* (Truth), but by the following year, at Denbigh, the eisteddfod had reverted to its previous tavern standards and a contemporary critic expressed the view that Bacchus, and not the Muse, had taken possession of the minds of the bards.

A notice that appeared that year made it 'known to the Welsh people that an Eisteddfod will be held, under the patronage of the London Gwyneddigion, upon bards and musicians, in accordance with the custom and usage of the Bards of the Isle of Britain in former times, at the Dadleudy (or Hall), Bala, on Tuesday and Wednesday next Whitsun 1793. As many as would wish to write on the subject, namely, *Y Pedwar Amser, neu Dymhorau, y Flwyddyn* (The Four Seasons of the Year) are requested to send their poems without a name, but only a pseudonym, and written in a different hand, by post from where they live to Mr Owen Jones, 148 Upper Thames Street, London, by the first Monday in March 1793.' Gwallter Mechain and Dafydd Ddu Eryri were not allowed to compete so that other poets may have an opportunity, but they were asked, nonetheless, to write a poem each on the subject so that 'the country would not be the poorer because of this temporary sanction on their muse.' The eisteddfod suffered on account of the religious fervour that, in the words of Thomas Charles, 'put an end to all the merry meetings,' and Thomas Jones maintained that it had been a mistake to hold it 'among the saints of Bala.'

Two chairs were offered at the Dolgellau eisteddfod in 1794, one for the winner of the Society's medal and the other for the impromptu verse competition. In 1796 Dafydd Ddu Eryri, who was ruffled at not being allowed to compete, held an eisteddfod a Y Wern, Penmorfa near Tremadoc, without consulting the Gwyneddigion, at Whitsuntide.

The eisteddfod returned to Caerwys at Whitsuntide in 1798, for which the Gwyneddigion published a notice stating that the event would be held at the expense of the Society and 'under the guidance of the Reverend gentlemen Robert Thomas, Peter Whitley, Robert Williams, Llywelyn Llwyd and Walter Davies, and also Dafydd Ddu Eryri, Chaired Bard, and many others of the sages of Wales. The subject: *Cariad i'n Gwlad drwy Adgyfodiad yr Hen Eisteddfod a Defodau Cymru'* (Love for our Country through the Revival of the Old Eisteddfod and the Customs of Wales). It was noted that the eisteddfod would be held in the Old Hall 'where the magnificent Eisteddfod, by command of the Queen Elizabeth, was held in the year 1567' and the notice ended with the significant couplet:

Dowch chwithau a'ch hymnau heirdd,
Ddiwair, addfwyn Dderwyddfeirdd

(Come, with our beautiful hymns, ye chaste and gentle Druidbards).

Dafydd Ddu was prominent in founding Cymreigyddion Bangor in 1810 and, in 1813, he re-established Cymdeithas yr Eryron which he had set up at Betws Garmon in 1784.

The Society's silver medal offered at the Llangefni Eisteddfod in 1816 was awarded to Gwyndaf Eryri, although there was a strong feeling that it should have been given to Gwilym Morganwg (Thomas Williams: 1778-1835) and that had been denied it because he came from south Wales. He got the second prize.

When the pseudonym 'Plorator' was called out at the St Asaph Eisteddfod in 1818, there was no response and no one knew for another two years that the winner of the chair and the Society's medal for an *awdl* to *Y Dywysoges* (The Princess) was Ieuan Glan Geirionydd (Evan Evans: 1795-1855).

The adjudicators, William Owen Pughe, Dewi Silin (David Richards: 1738-1826) and Bardd Nantglyn (Robert Davies: 1769-1835) caused a controversy that has lasted to this day by awarding the chair, at the Denbigh Eisteddfod in 1819, to Y Dryw (Edward Hughes: 1772-1850) for his poem to *Elusengarwch* (Charity) in preference to the poem submitted by Dewi Wyn o Eifion (David Owen: 1784-1841) with its memorable lines.

In that same year, an Eisteddfod was held at Carmarthen at which the Gorsedd of Bards was to become an integral part of the festival, by the action of an artful genius, Edward Williams, known to history as Iolo Morganwg.

IOLO MORGANWG

EDWARD WILLIAMS (Iolo Morganwg) was born on 10 March 1747 in the hamlet of Pennon in Llancarfan parish, the son of Edward Williams, and his wife, Ann, a daughter of Edward Matthews of Ty'nycaeau in the parish of Llangrallo, who were married in the church at St Athan on 8 November 1744. Iolo states that his father was the son of Thomas Williams, 'an industrious farmer' in the parish of Llandough, and that he had been 'brought up in the trade of a mason' who also practised as a stone-cutter, tiler, plasterer, carpenter and joiner. His mother was descended from the gentry Mathew family of Llandaff, Radyr and Castell-y-Mynach on the one hand, and from a Glamorgan dynasty of poets on the other. She was, he states, 'a woman of uncommon mental abilities.' While he maintained that he did not seek noble ancestry he, nevertheless, professed that he was descended on the paternal side from Bleddyn ap Cynfyn and added, for good measure, that 'Oliver Cromwell and myself are legitimately descended from him.'

By 1756 the family had moved to Flemingston, to the cottage that Iolo regarded as his home for the rest of his life. It comprised 'only one small room below, and divided above into two very small bedrooms, never finished unceiled and only the bare thatched roof at each side about 4 feet above the floor so that it is only in or near the middle that a grown person can stand upright.'

The language of the hearth was English, as his mother had been brought up in an English-speaking home though, Iolo states, 'the vernaculum of the Country was Welsh.' He claimed to have been able to read both languages equally well from a very early age, but his contemporaries remarked that, in conversation, he was better in English than in Welsh, and he certainly wrote in English with consummate ease. He did not attend school, save for a few days during which he was so 'sullen and stubbornly silent', that he was sent home. He claimed that he 'first learned the Alphabet about 4 years of age by observing my father inscribe Tomb and other gravestones, and soon after began to attempt cutting letters in stone.' It has been aptly said that 'the hearth (and his mother in particular) and the graveyard were his first colleges.'

Iolo maintained that he had been taught the elements of Welsh poetry by Edward Williams of Middle Hill in the parish of Llancarfan, and that he had been a pupil of Sion Bradford, a weaver descended of an armigerous family in Bradford-on-Avon who had settled in Betws Tir Iarll. Bradford was a keen student of the bardic system and a collector of Welsh manuscripts in which, Iolo maintained, he had found matters relating to the bardic *gorsedd* that had survived in Glamorgan and, in particular, in Tir Iarll. He also claimed that Bradford had bade him 'step into the garden with him and taking out of his pocket a blue ribbon invested me with the insignia of the Primitive Order of the Bards of the Isle of Britain in [the] Chair [of] Glamorgan and Tir Iarll.'

Iolo had come under the influence of the Glamorgan poets Lewis Hopkin and Rhys Morgan who were masters of the bardic craft and had arranged eisteddfodau, similar to those in north Wales, in Glamorgan. He stated he had been able to borrow Dr Sion Dafydd Rhys's Welsh Grammar, *Camrobrytannicae Cymraecaeve Linguae Institutiones et Rudimenta* (1592) and he was fortunate to come into contact with two scholarly clerics and lexicographers, Thomas Richards, vicar of Coychurch, and John Walters, rector of Llandough, who gave him access to their libraries and collections of manuscripts. He profited from their erudition, for Richards taught him how to write good Welsh and, in helping Walters with the production of his English-Welsh dictionary, he had experience of coining new words, and it was at their encouragement that he learned some Latin and French. All this had to be undertaken during his leisure time as he, like his brothers Thomas, Miles and John, along with several other journeymen and apprentices, was employed by his father at 1s 4d (60p) per day.

His mother died of the consumption in August 1770. 'For seven weeks,' he claimed, 'I sat up with her without ever taking a moment's rest in bed.' After her death, his grief was such that he no longer wished to remain at home and, according to him, he wandered all over the country. In fact, he did not leave the neighbourhood until 1772 when he went to north Wales to gather subscriptions for a work that was never published. In the following year, he and his brothers set off for London and Kent in search of work. Iolo, undoubtedly, had an ambition to go to London as he had heard, during his sojourn in north

Wales, of Owain Myfyr and other members of the Society of Gwyneddigion. He later claimed to have been 'one of the very first members' of that Society, although he was not yet in London when it was formed in 1770, but he attended some of its meetings, as a guest, and was given access to the manuscripts that were in the possession of the Society. In 1785 he was admitted a corresponding member which, in itself, was a rare privilege for a south Walian.

Iolo left London in 1776 for Bristol, where he stayed for a few months, and then went to Ross-on-Wye, where he worked on the memorial to John Kyrle, 'the Old Man of Ross.' On his way to Bristol he visited Avebury and came to the conclusion that 'there is nothing more evident to me than that this was the grand seat of the Druids before the Roman invasion.'

On 18 July 1781, at St Mary Church, Llanfair, he married 'her that from a child I dearly lov'd,' Margaret (Peggy) the daughter of Rees and Eleanor Robert of that parish. In a letter he addressed to Owain Myfyr in May 1782, he stated that he was now married to a woman about three years his junior (although he said elsewhere that she was born in 1748) and that she had brought, as her dowry, thirty acres of land with a house and a barn and other outbuildngs at Rumney, near Cardiff, and 'between that and that which I earn at my craft, I hope, by God, that it will never be necessary for me to leave Glamorgan again.' A year later, however, he wrote complaining 'that what an ingenious Welsh author has observed I find to be in fact very true: *Bedd yr Awen yw Gwely Priodas* (the marriage bed is the Muse's grave). The married life with all its advantages, has too many cares and anxieties, too much bustle and business, to allow a man, especially a man of narrow circumstances, to attend much to the Muses.' It did not prevent him from wandering, however, and his wife's letters, charging him with neglecting his family, reveal that she was a person of considerable, and even classical, education.

Iolo was no business man. He tried his hand at several ventures but each one failed miserably. In 1785, he and his family had to flee from his creditors, but the law caught up with him on 7 August 1786 with only threepence in his pocket and he was comitted to the debtors' prison at Cardiff, where he was detained for a whole year. His wife was allowed to share his room, for a charge, but when she became pregnant, he refused to pay rent for an additional chamber and quarrelled so violently with the gaoler that she had to leave immediately in her night clothes and move to a lodging house near the prison, where their son, Taliesin, was born. Iolo complained that he was being un-justly held, as the amount for which he had been committed was only £34, whereas his proven assets exceeded £600. An arrangement was eventually made and he was released in August 1787.

Iolo began writing under the bardic name Iorwerth Gwilym, which is an exact translation of his baptismal name, but when he got to London and found Owain Jones from Llanfihangel Glyn Myfyr calling himself Owain Myfyr, and Robert Hughes from Anglesey being known as Robin Ddu o Fôn, he felt that he, too, should have a pseudonym with a territorial connotation and changed to Iorwerth Morganwg, which he retained until 18 April 1784. On his way home, rather late that night, he was obstructed by the Reverend James Evans, vicar of Marshfield, who wanted to know who he was and where he had been, and as he gave no satisfaction, he was struck by one of the vicar's men. In retaliation he wrote a defamatory poem and called it 'The Clerical Shepherd, a Monmouthshire Pastoral,' though claiming that it was a translation 'from the ancient British of Iolo Morganwg, a Bard that flourished about the Year 1285.' This name appealed to him, and he used it from that time forth.

Iolo's literary career spanned the years 1770 to 1826 during which time he adapted the ideas of romanticism, that were sweeping across Europe, for the benefit of his own people by providing them with lyrical poetry and a romantic history.

The revived interest in the Welsh heritage aroused as a result of the researches of antiquarians like Edward Lhuyd had a profound in-fluence on Iolo. His nimble mind envisaged a future that would be greater even than the past, having as its intellectual core the eisteddfod of the bards, and this induced him to invent a past upon which he could build a future. That imaginative past he enshrined in his *Cyfrinach Beirdd Ynys Prydain* (The Secret of the Bards of the Isle of Britain) which, he declared, had been written by the early bards of Glamorgan but it was, in fact, his own work, much of it written in Cardiff gaol. In it, he maintained that the Bards of the Isle of Britain, after the departure of the Romans, had revived *Cadair wrth Gerdd* (the Chair of Poetry) at Caerleon-on-Usk, where Merlin, Taliesin and others were the Masters of Poetry, and 'there, under the patronage of King Arthur and his Knights and the assembled wise men, was established the Order of the Round Table', which was a classification of the craft, ritual and privileges of the bards. The motto of this *Cadair* was *Y Gwir yn erbyn y Byd, yn enw Duw a'i dangnef* (the Truth against the world, in the name of

God and His peace). There was a *Cadair,* for which the terms *Gorsedd* and *Eisteddfod* are also used, in each of the Welsh kingdoms, Gwynedd, Powys, Deheubarth and Morgannwg, and there was also *Cadair Tir Iarll,* covering a district that is described variously but usually includes Margam, Pyle, Betws and Llangynwyd.

Iolo claimed that the Glamorgan bards had held *Cadeiriau* in an unbroken tradition down the centuries, such as the one held at Cardiff Castle in 1520 under the patronage of William Herbert, Earl of Pembroke, at which the presiding bard was Lewys Morganwg, the family poet of the Herberts. The list of those present contained the names of poets that were then unborn, and the patron, William Herbert, was not to receive his earldom for another thirty years.

In July 1780, he wrote to Owain Myfyr stating that 'a few bards that are in Glamorgan (I mean those who know anything of our old poetry) have established "a yearly association" at Llantrisant. We (for I am one of the meanest) intend to make some new regulations in our Barddoniaeth,' and he refers to the association as *Brodoliaeth Beirdd Morganwg,* (the Brotherhood of the Bards of Glamorgan). Reports of small eisteddfodau and other meetings held at Llantrisant were greatly exaggerated by him, although there was a group formed there in 1771 to promote the Welsh language, and calling itself the Anti-Hengist Society. There is no other reference to the *Brodoliaeth* and the likelihood is that it did not exist outside Iolo's imagination, but that it was invented by him to create the impression that there were bards in Glamorgan who had clung to the older regime that had been lost in the rest of Wales. In order to uphold this fiction, he devised his own set of twenty-four metres, complete with examples of each, and contended that the Glamorgan bards had never forgiven Dafydd ab Edmwnd for his rearrangement and modification of them at the Carmarthen Eisteddfod of 1451.

He wrote to *The Gentlemen's Magazine* in 1785 explaining the mysteries of bardism as disclosed in *Cyfrinach y Beirdd,* by Llywelyn Sion (1540-1615) whom he credited with having preserved and reduced into systematic form 'the secrets of the Bards of the Isle of Britain.' In the introduction that he had prepared for that book Iolo stated that 'some assert, perhaps under the impulse of jealousy, that it was at the Carmarthen Eisteddfod, *circa* 1450, that *Barddas Morganwg* [the bardic system of Glamorgan] and its associated literature was first devised, but that is merely the outpouring of ignorance, proving the lack of knowledge of such spurious dreamers, who have understood nothing

of the works of the ancient bards or, if they have read, do not comprehend the teeming references therein to the *Hen Ddosbarth* [the Old
Order], which has been known for ages as *Dosbarth Morganwg*, [the
Glamorgan Order], as opposed to *Dosbarth, nay Annosbarth, Caerfyrddin*
[the Disorder of Carmarthen].'

Iolo referred to the classification of the Welsh metres, which, he
claimed, had been retained by the bards of Glamorgan even after the
bards in the rest of Wales had adopted the metres of Dafydd ab
Edmwnd, as *Y Pedwar Ansawdd ar Hugain* (the Twenty-Four Qualities).
He claimed that it had been confirmed as the original and true
classification of the Bards of the Isle of Britain at a Gorsedd held at
Beaupré on the Monday, Tuesday and Wednesday of Whitweek in
1681, under the patronage of Sir Richard Bassett, who had been
knighted that year, after notice had been given, a year and a day in
advance, throughout Glamorgan, Gwent and Ewyas. The chief poets
there were Charles Button, Esq., Dafydd o'r Nant and Edward
Dafydd of Margam, and with them were thirteen named bards, 'by
privilege and custom of the Bards of the Isle of Britain', but most of
whom are not otherwise known to have existed.

Sir John Morris-Jones, in his *Cerdd Dafod*, dismissed Iolo's claims to
the exclusiveness and antiquity of the bards of Glamorgan. The 'Chair'
at Carmarthen, Sir John maintained, made Dafydd ab Edmwnd 'the
pencerdd of all Wales and it was he that "led" the chair as long as he
lived. After him came his nephew, Tudur Aled, and then Lewys
Morgannwg' who, as he was recognised as *Pencerdd y Tair Talaith* (Chief
Bard of the Three Provinces), provided proof that there was none of
the discord that Iolo alleges.

Gwallter Mechain, who had accepted Iolo's classification unques-
tioningly, and won a prize at the Carmarthen Eisteddfod in 1819 for an
essay demonstrating the superiority of 'the Twenty-four Qualities,'
referred to the practice among naturalists of 'classifying trees and
plants as families' and maintained that a 'measure', in 'the Old Order'
corresponded to such a 'family'. Sir John pointed to Iolo's claim that
'all the principles, all the varieties, all the combinations of verse that
exist in nature belong to one or other of these measures,' and compared it with the classification of plants by Linnaeus into '24 Classes
that comprehend every known genus and species.'

The second half of the eighteenth century was a period during
which efforts were being made to collect, and translate, early Celtic
poetry. Ieuan Brydydd Hir (Evan Evans: 1731-88), in *Some Specimens of*

the *Poetry of the Ancient Welsh Bards* (1764), provided the first substantial selection of early Welsh verse. He had been urged to produce 'an elegant translation of some curious pieces of ancient Welsh poetry' by Thomas Percy, the English ballad collector and, later, Bishop of Dromore, and he also agreed to do some translation for Daines Barrington, at whose expense his volume was published and who had brought his work on early Welsh literature to the attention of Thomas Gray and Dr Samuel Johnson. While admitting the difficulty he had experienced in translating early Welsh poems, Ieuan expressed the opinion that they formed part of 'the Druids' Caballa', a point which Iolo Morganwg was not slow to pursue in his *Poems, Lyric and Pastoral*, where he maintained that the poems of Taliesin revealed that 'ancient British Christianity was strongly tinctured with Druidism.'

In 1788, William Owen Pughe wrote to Iolo to seek his assistance in the publication of a volume of poems by Dafydd ap Gwilym. Iolo had previously sent him a selection of *cywyddau* which, he alleged, had been written by Dafydd and which, he claimed, he had found in a hitherto undiscovered manuscript. He now supplied more poems and even when the book was ready for publication, he sent a further batch which had to be inserted as an appendix. Iolo's contributions were of such excellence that they were accepted as the genuine work of Dafydd ap Gwilym up to the present century.

It was an age of literary forgeries. In Scotland, James Macpherson had published his *Fingal, an Ancient Epic Poem, in Six Books,* in 1762, purporting it to be a translation of the work of Ossian, son of Finn, a Gaelic bard of remote Scottish history, and it was widely acclaimed. Reynolds painted his portrait and Joseph Banks, when he discovered the 'cathedral of the seas', was moved to name it Fingal's Cave. The poem sold well and it was translated into a dozen foreign languages, but when Dr Johnson undertook his *Journey to the Western Isles* in 1775, he declared that he looked 'upon McPherson's *Fingal* to be as gross an imposition as ever the world was troubled with.'

Thomas Chatterton, while still a schoolboy at Bristol, began to write verse that he passed off as the work of a fifteenth century monk, Thomas Rowley, and fabricated correspondence between Rowley and a Bristol merchant. He then went to London, while still only eighteen years of age, and had not been there long before, reduced to despair by poverty, he committed suicide.

When Iolo was asked by Daniel Walters, a boyhood friend and, by then, a teacher at Norwich, to enter into a literary correspondence,

Walters, by a strange coincidence, chose as subject 'the Chatterton controversy,' and Iolo advanced a strange argument claiming that the poems had been written by a third person. In a footnote to his *Poems, Lyric and Pastoral*, he had no compunction in condemning the deception of both Chatterton and Macpherson.

Iolo published his English poems, *Poems, Lyric and Pastoral*, in two volumes, in 1794. The subscription list was an impressive one and included the Prince of Wales, to whom the work was dedicated, George Washington, President of the United States of America, Horace Walpole, Earl of Oxford, William Wilberforce, William Cowper, Joseph Priestley, and Tom Paine. To avoid offending his subscribers he had tempered his more extreme poems with explanatory and apologetic notes. Even so, he claimed that he had been summoned to appear before the Privy Council, and also before the Prime Minister, William Pitt, but Pitt had invited him to tea.

In November 1798 he sent some poems to the editor of *The Gentlemen's Magazine*, along with the following letter which he, inexplicably, signed 'J.D.':

Cowbridge, Oct 10

MR URBAN,

The pieces you herewith receive were written by *Edward Williams*, of Flimston, near Cowbridge.

He is absolutely self-taught, and was never at school; and it may be observed, that, in those parts, the Welsh is the general language of common conversation, the English being very little known, and very little understood. His first poetical productions were in the Welsh language. About the age of twenty he was admitted a *Bard* in the ancient manner; a custom still retained in Glamorgan, but, I believe, in no other part of Wales. This is by being discipled to a regular Bard, and afterwards admitted into a Congress of Bards assembled for that purpose, after undergoing proper examination; and being also initiated into their Mysteries, as they are pleased to call them. Besides Edward Williams, there is, I believe, now remaining only one regular Bard in Glamorgan, or in the world; this is the Rev Mr *Edward Evans*, of *Aberdare*, a Dissenting Minister. These two persons are the only legitimate descendants of the so-long-celebrated *Ancient British Bards*; at least they will allow no others this honourable title. Not that but there are excellent poets in considerable numbers in many other parts of Wales, who write both in Welsh and English; but they have never been qualified as above; and what knowledge they have of the ancient laws and rules of Welsh poetry they derive from books ...

Edward Williams is now about forty years of age and lives by the humble occupation of a *journeyman mason.* He is remarkably sober and temperate, very seldom drinks any strong liquour, and, if he sometimes tastes them, it is in very small quantities, and was never seen in liquor. His food is almost entirely vegetables; and he is a professed Pythagorean with respect to his opinion of animal food. He has other singularities: none of them, however, to my knowledge, of a vicious cast. Though not in the least given to wastefulness or extravagance, he is but a poor oeconomist; and when was a poet known to be otherwise! Some, that are but little acquainted with him, suppose him not sufficiently industrious; the charge is unjust: but he has certainly been in other respects very inattentive to his interests ... *Edward Williams* lives the life of a hermit ... He is naturally reserved, very bashful and has been very unfortunate in his little concerns through life hitherto; yet he is cheerfully contented with his lot, diffident to a fault, and too inoffensive to thrive in such a world as we live in. He is, however, respected by some gentlemen of learning and genius. – He is never seen walking without a book in his hand. – In his religious opinions he seems to be inclined to Quakerism, though he professes himself of the Established Church. He has acquired considerable reputation in his trade.

He intends publishing proposals for printing some of his pieces by subscription: he has written an incredible number, both in the Welsh and English languages. Whether the pieces I send you have any considerable merit; I will not pretend to say; but if they have, the insertion of some of them in your valuable Magazine will much oblige your constant reader.

J.D.

Mr Urban, responded by promising that 'a specimen of them shall be given in the Poetry of this month' and included Iolo's 'Ode, imitated from the Gododdin of Aneirin Gwawdrydd, a Welsh bard that flourished about the year 550.'

Among those who read the letter, and the poem, was Joseph C. Walker, the Irish historian and author of *Historical Memoirs of the Irish Bards,* who told the editor that he would like to have 'a particular account of the congress of bards mentioned in J.D.'s letter.' It may be that it was the response to this letter, together with the realisation that he had at his bidding the gentlemen of the Gwyneddigion Society, who had grown to regard him as the greatest living authority on Welsh poetry, that led him into a new field of fantasy and inventiveness that was to bring a colourful ceremonial into the grey mould of Welsh life in the form of 'the Gorsedd of Bards of the Isle of Britain'.

Iolo had studied the writings of William Stukeley and, in particular, Henry Rowlands' *Mona Antiqua Restaurata*, which portrayed Anglesey as the home of druidism. Rowlands, who was the vicar of Llanidan, had never been beyond Aberconway but he had read about 'the stupendous works' the Druids had 'left' at Avebury and Stonehenge

Iolo had read in the ancient laws that courts of justice were held in the open air and came to the conclusion that the bards, too, held their meetings 'in the eye of the sun', on prominent hill-top sites such as Garth Maelwg, Twmpath Diwlith on Margam Mountain, and Bryn Owen, or Stalling Down, to which they made their way in colourful, banner-bearing processions. He maintained that eisteddfodau had been held at Llancarfan and at Llantwit Major, at the monastery on Penrhys 'under the patronage of Owen Glyn Dŵr' and, in 1417, at Neath Abbey, and on Garth Maelwg in 1460, when objection had been made to the classification of Dafydd ab Edmwnd.

In 1791, he returned to London leaving his father to look after his family, and there he earned a meagre living by writing articles for magazines and journals. He took with him the manuscript of a book he had written on his hypotheses regarding the bardic tradition, under the title *The History of the Bards*, and its contents impressed the members of the Gwyneddigion. William Owen Pughe, who was in the process of writing his *Heroic Elegies and other Pieces of Llywarch Hen*, inserted a section of nearly sixty pages, under the heading 'Bardism', in the introduction to his book and, in it, he disclosed the nature of the Bardic Order. Its foundation, he stated, was 'the doctrine of Universal Peace and Good Will; for so entirely was a bard to be a votary to it, that he was never to bear arms, or in any manner to become a party to a dispute, whether political or religious, nor was any naked weapon to be held in his presence, for he was recognised Herald of Peace, under the title of Bardd Ynys Prydain.' A maxim of the Order was 'the perfect equality of its members ... A man cannot assume authority over another; for if he may over one, by the same reason he may over a million, or over a world. All men are necessarily equal; the Four Elements in their natural state, or everything not manufactured by art, is the common property of all.'

During the time he was in London, Iolo came in contact with men whose sympathies lay with the French Revolution, including Prince Talleyrand, Lord Stanhope, Dr Benjamin Franklin, Thomas Paine and Dr Joseph Priestley, and also with members of the Gwyneddigion, who were imbued with concepts of liberty. The Society's motto was 'Freedom in Church and State'. He became friendly with the poet Robert Southey, who had been expelled from Westminster School for starting a magazine called *The Flagellant* and had proceeded to Oxford with 'a head full of Rousseau and Werther', and with Samuel Taylor Coleridge and other English writers of Radical tendencies. They called him 'The Bard', while he called himself 'The Bard of Liberty'.

He admired the struggle for independence in America, 'where first since the world began, appears of, apparently, Human Institution, a government founded on the true principles of Liberty, Justice, and the Rights of Humanity.' He planned to go there, in 1792, in search of 'the Welsh Indians' descended from Madog ab Owain Gwynedd and his men who, it was believed, had sailed from Abercerrig, near Abergele, and landed in Mobile Bay in 1169. To prepare himself for the rigours of the journey, he followed the teaching of Rousseau by reverting to nature. He went to live in the fields and the forests, eating grass and sleeping under trees, with the result that he got rheumatism and had to abandon the expedition. John Evans, of Waun-fawr, whom he had planned to accompany, went on his own and made his way up the Missouri, but found no trace of the Welsh Indians.

It is considered that Iolo's greatest contribution to Welsh scholarship was in his role as one of the editors of *The Myvyrian Archaiology of Wales*: 'collected out of Ancient Manuscripts' and published in three volumes between 1801 and 1807. In the introductory 'General Advertisement' the editors, Owain Myfyr, at whose expense it was published and after whom it was named, William Owen Pughe, and Iolo, state that their aim was to preserve 'the ancient manuscripts in the Welsh tongue' which are described as 'venerable monuments of enlightened periods of literature among the Britons, while scenes of barbarity were acted over Europe and darkened the light of our island: a literature whose origin was not borrowed, but matured at home, under that extra-ordinary system, the Bardic institution; concerning which, under the name of Druidism, much has been written, much misunderstood, and of which the world yet knows but very little.' The purpose was to draw the attention of scholars to the existence of the manuscripts, which contained some of the most important works in early Welsh literature, including the poetry of the *Cynfeirdd*, of the sixth to the eleventh centuries, and of the *Gogynfeirdd* to the twelfth to mid-four-teenth centuries, the Law of Hywel Dda, historical documents, collec-tions of aphorisms, proverbs, triads, old music notation and other mis-cellanea.

Elijah Waring, in his *Recollections and Anecdotes of Edward Williams, the Bard of Glamorgan*, commented on the untidy profusion of Iolo's manu-scripts and stated that 'to find a desired paper, it was necessary to make a long voyage of discovery amongst a crowded archipelago of documents scattered about his tables, shelves and floor.' After Iolo's death, the papers were removed by his son, Taliesin, from the cottage at Fleming-ston and taken to his home in Merthyr Tudful, and when Taliesin died, they were offered to the British Museum, but the offer was declined and they found their way to the library of Sir Benjamin Hall at Llanover, where they were made available to students of Iolo's works until they were transferred to the National Library of Wales in 1916.

Taliesin spent years arranging the manuscripts and in selecting ones for publication. He had helped his father to prepare *Cyfrinach y Beirdd*, which appeared posthumously in 1829, and the selected papers were published by the Welsh Manuscripts Society in 1848, as the *Iolo Manu-scripts*. These contained, among a great corpus of fake mediaeval poetry, a collection of twenty poems which Iolo had attributed to Rhys Goch ap Rhiccert, of whom little is known except that he appears in the pedigrees as the grandson of Einion ap Collwyn. Iolo maintained that he had found the poems in a manuscript that was in the possession of Sion Bradford, that Rhys Goch had retained the use of the original Welsh metres and that, under the influence of the trouba-dours that the Normans had brought with them, a romantic school had arisen in Glamorgan early in the twelfth century. The poems puzzled Welsh scholars up to the middle of the present century, when it was shown that Iolo had refurbished five old poems and had himself written the other fifteen.

Iolo, and his son Taliesin, embraced Unitarianism soon after it began to be espoused in south Wales. Tomos Glyn Cothi (Thomas Evans: 1764-1833) the first Unitarian minister in Wales, began to preach the doctrines set forth by Joseph Priestley to such an extent that he became known as 'little Priestley'. Iolo was a leading spirit in establishing the Unitarian Association of South Wales in 1802, and it was he who drew up the rules and regulations of that body. He wrote nearly three thousand hymns of which more than four hundred were published, some of them in a collection for use by Unitarians.

Tomos Glyn Cothi's sympathy with the French Revolution brought him twice to the stocks in Carmarthen and, in August 1801, he was arraigned before Judge Lloyd at the Court of Great Sessions and sentenced to two years' imprisonment in Carmarthen gaol for sedition. It was alleged that, at a *cwrw bach*, 'a bid-ale', at Brechfa, he had committed treason by singing an English song composed by Iolo which contained verses such as:

> And when upon the British shore
> The thundering guns of France shall roar,
> Vile George shall trembling stand,
> Or flee his native land
> With terror and appal –
> Dance Cormagnol, dance Cormagnol.

Iolo composed a number of freedom poems, both in English and Welsh. Many of them were in praise of the French who had set out to establish a regime based on freedom and equality and he saw the Revolution as the dawn of the day when their dreams would be realised.

When he went to visit William Winterbotham, a Baptist minister who had been imprisoned at Newgate for his seditious sermons, Iolo signed the visitors' book as 'Edward Williams, Bard of Liberty.' On his next visit, he was asked by Kirby, the governor of the gaol, whether he was 'The Bard of Liberty,' and upon saying that he was, Kirby told him: 'Then you had better know that there is no liberty for you here, except to get out as swiftly as you can.' 'Thank you,' said Iolo, 'and I hope that I shall never receive worse treatment than to be thrown out of gaol,' and went off to compose his 'Newgate Stanzas,' which he sent to Kirby.

Iolo also wrote verses denouncing John Reeves who had established the Crown and Anchor Society 'for protecting Liberty and Property against Republicans and Levellers.' His attitude to kingship and to the church was influenced by Voltaire, to whose works he had been introduced in London.

In 1796, when he kept a shop at Cowbridge, he displayed a book in the window that was marked, on its cover, *Rights of Man*. Government officers, believing that they had caught him in possession of Tom Paine's publication, came in and bought the book, only to find that it was, in fact, a copy of the Bible. He took advantage of the shop to display his views on slavery by placing a notice on the confectionery:

'East India sweets, uncontaminated with human gore.'

If one can rely on the gentle and gullible Elijah Waring, it is pertinent to note his opinion, 'that Iolo had for many years abandoned his republicanism, except as a theoretic model for a free government,' but he is probably nearer the truth when he states that it was Napoleon's absolutism and ambitions that had 'kindled a latent spark of military heroism in the Bard's bosom,' and caused him to compose 'a warlike song for the Cowbridge Volunteers.' He also composed songs to the Glamorgan Volunteers and the Neath Volunteers, but he was being anti-Napoleon rather than expressing any opposition to the Republic.

About the only contemporary voice to doubt the authenticity of Iolo's theories was that of Edward Davies (1756-1831), known, from his *Celtic Researches* (1804) as 'Celtic Davies.' In his *Mythology and Rites of the British Druids* (1809) he stated that there was no historical foundation for the belief that the bards and the Druids had any knowledge of the doctrine outlined by William Owen Pughe in his *Heroic Elegies of Llywarch Hen*, and added: 'I do not recollect to have seen this doctrine, in its full extent, promulgated by any code, before a certain period of the French Revolution, when the meek Republicans of Gaul, and their modest, partizans in other countries, joined the indefeasible right of equality with the inviolable duty of peace, and impressed them upon the orderly subjects of every state; whilst they themselves were preparing for every species of injury to civil society.'

Iolo's ideas were generally accepted throughout the nineteenth century until Sir John Morris-Jones, in a series of articles in the magazine *Cymru*, in 1896, and again in *Y Beirniad*, of which he was editor, in 1911, revealed that the Gorsedd of Bards was an invention of Iolo's. Then, in 1916, Griffith John Williams, began to examine Iolo's manuscripts, which had recently been acquired by the National Library of Wales, and he was able to demonstrate in his *Iolo Morganwg a Chywyddau'r Ychwanegiad* (1926), that the *cywyddau* provided by Iolo for the volume of poems by Dafydd ap Gwilym published by the Gwyneddigion in 1789 had been written by him.

Griffith John Williams, professor of Welsh at University College, Cardiff, who is described in *The Oxford Companion to the Literature of Wales* (1986) as 'perhaps the most versatile Welsh scholar of all time,' spent most of his life investigating the work of Iolo Morganwg. He came to the conclusion that Iolo was a scholar, 'far more familiar with the learning of the old master poets than any other scholar of the eighteenth century,' but that he was, as well, 'probably the most successful and the most marvellous forger – if that be the correct term to use – in literary history, a forger of genius.'

The *Oxford Companion* saw Iolo as 'the most brilliant child of the antiquarian revival, the greatest interpreter of Romantic enthusiasm in Wales and, although a Unitarian and a political Radical, one of the greatest influences on Welsh letters and culture in his day ... he believed that the Welsh were the most important people of the Isle of Britain and that Welsh tradition could be traced back without break to the Druids.'

Iolo not only created the Gorsedd of Bards: he converted the old bardic gatherings into a body corporate that developed into a national cultural foundation. His interpretation of history inspired the literary clerics to take an initiative in founding the eisteddfodic movement, and Ab Ithel to undertake the task of arranging the Llangollen Eisteddfod of 1858, from which the present festival has grown. 'It is not too much to say,' stated Griffith John Williams, 'that he owned the Eisteddfod of the Welsh people, and that he was one of the spiritual fathers of the national movement.'

'I am giving you the Patriarchal religion and theology, the Divine Revelation given to mankind and these have been retained in Wales until our own day,' Iolo told his audience on Primrose Hill in 1792. He was, as Gwyn A. Williams, professor of History at University College, Cardiff, has stated:

> announcing to the Welsh the rediscovery of their ancient Druidic tradition; he was giving them, for the first time in two centuries, a coherent vision of their own past, to inform and direct the re-creation of their nation. He was offering them, in his newly minted gorsedd, or Order of Bards of the Isle of Britain, a democratic organization for their intelligentsia, a cadre of people's remembrancers, as its instrument.

Benjamin Heath Malkin, whose wife came from Cowbridge, knew Iolo and devoted close on four pages to him in his *Scenery, Antiquities and Biography of South Wales*, published in 1804. He described him as 'a man who is capable of doing the world more service than the world seems willing either to receive or to return. He stands unrecommended by external rank in society; yet are his mental powers of a superior order.' He proceeded to give an account of Iolo's life, up to that date, and concluded that 'the proverb of a prophet in his own country is but too much verified in him; for while Mr Williams the antiquarian is mentioned elsewhere with the respect due to the attainments, without the estate, of a gentleman, there are few in Glamorganshire who know him by any other name than that of Ned Williams the stonecutter.'

In assessing Iolo's character, it is difficult to know the effect his addiction to laudanum may have had upon him. He states that 'about 26 years of age I fell into the habit of taking Laudanum in which I continue to this day. I took it at first [to] relieve a very troublesome cough, and that often in very large doses even 300 drops at a time, which is I think more than half an ounce.'

He complained of poor health throughout his life. 'My mother was consumptive,' he wrote, 'and I inherited her disorders. I was thro' childhood so very sickly and weak that my death was almost daily expected.' He wrote to his father from Sandwich in 1774 complaining that he had 'had a smart stroke of the palsy which quite disabled me for some time', and when he was visiting the British Museum in the 1790's he informed his wife that the disorder that had 'greatly tormented and weakened me for some months turned out to be a stone' which, he reckoned, had been caused by sitting for eight or nine hours at the Museum without rising, 'and retaining the urine.' In a letter to Edward Williams, the London publisher, in 1809, he states that his 'asthmatic complaint has been such that I have not been able to lie down on a bed for more than two years', which had debilitated both body and mind, and he was no longer able to pursue his studies with his former perseverance. For the last eighteen years of his life he slept sitting upright in a chair, and frequently was awakened by the cramp. He asked Edward Williams to find him a room in a garret somewhere near the Strand: 'a bed will not be wanted – I cannot make use of it.' In 1813 he was suffering 'a sensation in my hands and feet chiefly as if coals of fire fell on my skin', and was unable to write or 'do anything in my trade.' Before he was seventy-five, he wrote to Elijah Waring stating that his eyes were extremely weak, he could hear but very little, and was 'obliged to use a crutch under one arm and a staff in my other hand, and I endeavour to walk a little in my garden.' He remained a cripple for the last three years of his life.

The Iolo the world knew was an irritable, case-hardened romancer, an inveterate fabulist, a drug addict, a hypochondriac, a mythomaniac who imagined, invented, fabricated, forged, contrived at will to fit the occasion. Yet, he was not only the finest scholar of his time in Welsh history and Welsh literature, but also extremely knowledgeable in other fields, including music, geology, agriculture, horticulture, botany, theology, political theory, architecture and industrial development, in addition to his craft as a stonemason.

THE FIRST GORSEDD

IOLO MANAGED TO persuade the members of the Gwynedd-igion Society that the Welsh bardic tradition derived from the Druids and had survived in *Gorsedd Beirdd Ynys Prydain* (The Gorsedd of the Bards of the Isle of Britain). Prominent Gwyneddigion expressed a desire to become members of the Gorsedd, but Iolo informed them that they could only do so at a ceremony held 'in the face of the sun, the eye of light.' He prepared a proclamation, in rather archaic Welsh, which he issued in the early part of June 1791, and which may be translated:

> When the age of Christ is one thousand seven hundred and ninety one, the sun being at the summer solstice, and at the hour of nine in the forenoon, an invitation is given, in the hearing of country and king, under notice of a day and a year, and with protection for all who might seek to obtain Grade and Licence in Poetry and Verse by privilege of the Bards of the Isle of Britain, to repair to Primrose Hill, near London, in a day and a year, at nine o'clock in the forenoon, where there will not be a naked weapon against them; and there will be present Iolo Morganwg, a Bard by privilege and custom of the Bards of the Isle of Britain, and with him, Daniel Dafydd, and Gwilym Owen [William Owen Pughe], and Glan y Gors [John Jones: 1766-1821], and Dafydd Ddu Feddyg [David Samwell: 1751-98], and Sion Penllyn [Edward Jones, Bardd y Brenin: 1752-1824], and Y Bardd Cloff [Thomas Jones: 1768-1828], and Hywel o'r Eryri [Hugh Evans: 1767-1841], and Dafydd Ddu Eryri, – they all being Licensed in the privilege of the Bards of the Isle of Britain, to deliver the Judgement of the Gorsedd, in the eye of the sun, and in the face of light, upon everyone concerning Poetic Gift and Faculty, who may seek Grade and Licence in Poetry and Verse in the privilege of the Bards of the Territory of Glamorgan, and Gwent, and Erging, and Ewyas, and Ystrad Yw. And this in the name of God and all Goodness.

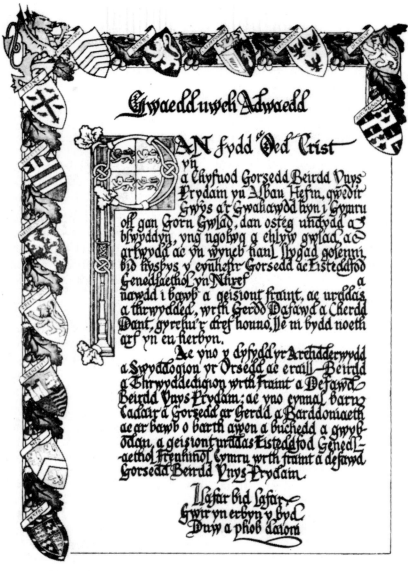

The Proclamation Scroll used by the Recorder to announce the next Eisteddfod, to be held at least a year and a day hence.

The gentlemen named were all members of the Gwyneddigion Society with the exception of Hywel o'r Eryri, who had recently gained prominence as a *cywydd* poet, and Dafydd Ddu Eryri, who later became a corresponding member of the Society.

Iolo defined a 'Bard by privilege and custom' as one who had studied under a graduate Gorsedd Bard until he was fully conversant with the rules of prosody and 'knew the mystery and the privilege and custom of the Bards of the Isle of Britain, and also had knowledge of the three memorials and the three symbols of the Bards of the Isle of Britain.'

In choosing Primrose Hill as the venue of his first Gorsedd, Iolo must have had in mind the meeting held there at the autumnal equinox in 1717 by John Toland, and the subsequent foundation of the Ancient Druid Order. He laid out a circle of twelve stones, and another in the middle to serve as the Maen Llog, on Primrose Hill on Alban Hefin, 21 June, 1792, and within it he held the first ceremony of the Gorsedd of Bards of the Isle of Britain. The ceremony opened with the placing of the sword upon the Maen Llog, and then Iolo read his English poem, 'Ode on the Mythology of the Ancient British Bards', in which he hailed the goddess of Liberty and called for an end to slavery. William Owen Pughe, and some others, were initiated members of the Gorsedd, and it also appears that Iolo admitted his son, Taliesin, who was only six years of age at the time.

Gorsedd ceremonies were held, according to Iolo, at the solstices and the equinoxes and he invented the word *alban* to signify 'the high quarter of the year', and coined for each quarter a name: *Alban Eilir*, the vernal equinox; *Alban Hefin*, the summer solstice; *Alban Elfed*, the autumnal equinox, and *Alban Arthan*, the winter solstice. He associated each with seasonal plants: clover for *Alban Eilir*, 'the blessed oak' for *Alban Hefin*, ears of corn for *Alban Elfed*, and mistletoe for *Alban Arthan*.

A second ceremony was held at the same place on *Alban Elfed*, that year, an account of which appeared in the *Morning Chronicle*:

> Saturday, Sept. 22, being the day on which the autumnal equinox occurred, and consequently, in the phrase of Bardism, a Solemn Bardic Day, some Welch Bards, resident in London, assembled in Congress on Primrose Hill, according to ancient usage, which required that it should be in the eye of public observation, in the open air, in a conspicuous place, and whilst the sun is above the horizon. The wonted ceremonies were observed. A circle of stones was formed, in the middle of which was the Maen Gorsedd, or altar, on

which a naked sword being placed, all the bards assisted to sheathe it. The ceremony was attended with a proclamation, the substance of which was, that the Bards of the Island of Britain, for such is their Ancient title, were the heralds and ministers of peace, and never bore a naked weapon in the presence of anyone: nor was it lawful for any person to bare one, on any pretence, in their presence. On this occasion the Bards appeared in the insignia of their various Orders. The presiding bards were David Samwell of the Primitive, and Claimant of the Ovation and Primitive Orders: William Owen [Pughe], of the Ovation and Primitive Orders; Edward Jones, of the Ovation, and Claimant of the Primitive Order; Edward Williams [Iolo Morganwg], of the Primitive and Druidic Orders. The Bardic Traditions, and several Odes were recited. Two of the Odes, one by David Samwell, on the Bardic Discipline, the other by Edward Williams, on the bardic Mythology, were in English and the first that were ever in this language recited at a Congress of Ancient British Bards. This was an intention to give the English reader an idea of what, though very common in Wales, has never yet been properly known in England. The Bardic Institution of the Ancient Britons, which is the very same as the Druidic, has been from earliest times, through all ages, to the present day, retained by the Welsh... The next meeting is to be held in the same place on the day when the next winter solstice occurs ... The subject proposed for an English Ode is The resurrection of Rhitta Gawr... a famous chief of the Ancient Britons who extermined so many despots that he made himself a robe of their beards.

Among those who were enrolled as Ovates were Sarah Elizabeth the wife of William Owen Pughe, and their eight week old child, Aneurin. Gwallter Mechain, a student at All Souls College, Oxford, Dr David Samwell, who had been surgeon on board *The Discovery* with Captain Cook, Edward Jones (Bardd y Brenin), and John Jones (Jac Glan y Gors) were also admitted at one or other of the ceremonies, and so were Edward Charles and Thomas Jones, secretary and recorder, respectively, of the Gwyneddigion Society.

Iolo emphasized that, although the Gorsedd meetings had been held in London, the ceremonies had been carried out in the tradition of the 'Ancient Welsh Bards' whose secrets had survived in Glamorgan, as stated in the Proclamation. 'The North Wales Bards,' he wrote, 'have nothing at all of the ancient and genuine Bardism.' It was 'the Brotherhood of Bards in Glamorgan' that had nurtured the bardic tradition, and had kept alive *Cadair Morgannwg*, the bardic institution of the province of Glamorgan, Gwent, Erging, Ewyas and Ystrad-yw. The *Cadeirau* of the other three provinces, Dyfed, Powys and Gwynedd, he maintained, had long disappeared. The object of *Cadeiriau* was to maintain standards among the bards, and those who were admitted into membership had a duty to hold such gatherings in the lost provinces, and to enroll worthy poets as Bards of the Isle of Britain.

In the Proclamation Scroll that Iolo devised for the Gorsedd on Primrose Hill, he stated that there would be present, in order 'to give Gorsedd Judgement, in the eye of the sun, and in the face of the light,' apart from himself, a number of other bards, all Licence-holders by privilege and custom of the Bards of the Isle of Britain. In a scroll that he prepared for a ceremony to be held on Bryn Owen (Stalling Down) in March 1796, however, the list begins with 'Plennydd, Alawn and Gwron, and with them Iorwerth Gwynfardd Morganwg [Edward Evans, Aberdare], and Gwilym Fardd Glas o'r Gadair [Edward Williams, Cowbridge], and Thomas Glyn Cothi' and others. Plennydd, Alawn and Gwron were, according to Iolo, 'the three Primitive Bards', of the time of the Druids, if not Druids themselves, who, when the Britons settled in the Isle of Britain, had instructed novitiates in the art of poetry-making, and had licensed them as Bards of the Isle of Britain, 'in the eye of the Sun, and the face of Light', or, as otherwise given, 'in the face of the Sun, and the eye of Light'. He presumably wished to convey that their spirit was present at a bardic gathering at all times, and they were included in proclamation scrolls from that time until the early part of the present century. From time to time Iolo included, after the Primitive Bards, the names of fictitious Glamorgan bards such as Ieuan Fawr ap Y Diwlith and Edeyrn Dafod Aur.

In the preface to his *Poems, Lyric and Pastoral* Iolo propounded that 'God created the world by the melodious threefold utterance of his Holy Name, and that the form and figure of that Name was /|\, being the rays of the rising sun at the equinoxes and solstices conveying into focus "the eye of light".' He made little use of this *nod cyfrin* (mystic mark), however, and it appeared only on the frontispiece of his hymn book for Unitarians, published in 1812. After his death, his son, Taliesin, placed it on the Proclamation Scroll of the Cardiff Eisteddfod of 1834, and it was widely used by Myfyr Morganwg and Ab Ithel. It was inserted on the Gorsedd admission certificate in 1860, and on the notice of the Chester Eisteddfod in 1866, after which it appeared with greater frequency until it became adopted as the emblem and badge of the Gorsedd of Bards.

It is also embodied in the lay-out of the Gorsedd Circle at its entrance, where *Maen y Cyfamod* (the Covenant Stone), which marks the east cardinal point, and the two Portal Stones, of which the one to the north faces the rising sun on the longest day and that to the south, sunrise on the shortest day, are so placed that their alignment in relation to the Maen Llog is in the form of the mystic mark.

Iolo invented an alphabet which, he maintained, in the same preface, was based on 'the three shafts of light' of the mystic mark and which he claimed to have been the alphabet of the Druids, and of the ancient Britons, that had been preserved by the bards of Glamorgan. It has twenty characters, and twenty more variations to represent elongated vowels and mutations. Each is composed of straight lines so that, as with ogham, the letters are more easily carved. The characters were often cut on each face of a square strip of wood and thus a four-lined stanza or, more regularly, an *englyn*, could be carved on each strip. These strips could have their ends rounded and fitted into a pair of upright battens so as to form a gate-like frame that could carry a number of verses or *englynion*. The frame was known as a *peithynen*, a word coined by Iolo, possibly from the Latin *pectinum*, meaning a comb or a rake. Occasionally, the strips would be three-sided to accommodate three-line verses, or *englynion milwr*.

As a mason and stonecutter Iolo would have been interested in the art of lettering and he may have got the idea of the *peithynen* from the 'clog almanack', which was a square piece of wood with characters carved on each face, a picture of which appeared in *The Natural History of Staffordshire* (1686) by Robert Plot, Keeper of the Ashmolean Museum and Secretary of the Royal Society.

The Gorsedd members met on 8 November 1792 to consider the situation arising from a problem presented by Edward Jones who had been admitted in the grade of Ovate, but described himself publicly as a Bard. A native of Llandderfel, he had gone to London in 1775 and had become a teacher of the harp to several persons of rank, and was eventually appointed harpist to the Prince of Wales and made constant use of the title *Telynor*, or *Bardd y Tywysog* from about 1790 onward. On the prince's accession to the throne, as King George IV, in 1820, he became known as *Bardd y Brenin*. Following the meeting, a notice was sent to him stating that at 'an Ovation of the Bards of the Isle of Britain it was resolved that the Bards of the Primrose Hill Gorsedd shall be summoned to meet on the day of the New Moon next ensuing'

COELBREN Y BEIRDD

The Bardic Alphabet reproduced in Celtic Researches on the Origin, Traditions and Language of the Ancient Britons (1804) *by Edward Davies, 'as I was favoured with them by the ingenious antiquary', William Owen Pughe.*

at Lamb's Conduit Fields, behind the British Museum, 'there to produce poems and orations on given subjects as testimonials of the several claims to the Bardic degrees and titles, or to give up their claims.' A selection of subjects was then given to the harpist 'to lecture on there, or in default of his acquiescence in this requisition to renounce his claim to the title and character of Bard.' History does not record whether Jones submitted himself to this inquisition, but he continued to use his Bardic title. It is not even known whether the inquisition was held.

The next Gorsedd was notable as the one at which Iolo Morganwg delivered his English 'Ode on Converting a Sword into a pruning hook. Recited on Primrose Hill at a meeting of Ancient British Bards Resident in London 22 Sept 1793.' It is said that the Prince of Wales was present at the ceremony. Anna Seward, 'the Swan of Lichfield', who was a great admirer of Iolo, was initiated an Ovate.

On his return to Flemingston in 1795 Iolo held a series of Gorseddau, beginning with one on Bryn Owen, which he had proclaimed to take place at the spring equinox that year. Its purpose, according to the proclamation scroll, was 'to hold a Gorsedd upon poetry in accordance with the ancient customs observed by the Bards of the Isle of Britain in the early ages.' Poets were adjured to master the old metres and the *cynganeddion*, and to compose in them regularly, as they alone could save the Welsh language from sinking into the depths of corruption and oblivion; to practice the free metres, so as to provide education for the public; to know the Grammar of Sion Dafydd Rhys; not to write verse that would corrupt morals, and to renounce all impurities of language that would mar their work.

The authorities, who suspected that the Gorsedd meetings may have some connection with the French Revolution, and knew that their promoter paraded as 'the Bard of Liberty', decided to put a stop to these mountain-top gatherings. A report in the *Cambrian Register* in 1796 stated that:

> a silly attempt was lately made in Glamorganshire to hold something like a poetic session upon a hill, preceded by a ridiculous advertisement or handbill, which the magistrates, knowing the harlequin of the farce to be of democratic principles, apprehended might endanger the peace of the kingdom; they therefore very properly prevented his rising in the world, least [sic] he got to the summit he might beckon to Buonaparate, and bring him over the British Channel to the top of Garth.

This did not prevent Iolo from holding Gorsedd meetings but it is significant that, for the next two years, he varied the locations. In June 1797, a Gorsedd meeting was held on Mynydd y Garth, in the parish of Llantwit Fardre, at which Iolo read his new poem on the state of religious knowledge among the early Welsh, and delivered an address on the procedures adopted by the Bards of Cadair Morgannwg in practising their art as an effective measure to preserve the Welsh language.

Iolo admitted that the proceedings at the Gorsedd held on Forest Mountain, north of Cowbridge, in September that year, were 'of novel character, in that the bards busied themselves with inventing a coat of arms for Napoleon Buonaparte. The arms they selected were those of Ritta Gawr', and they hardly expressed surprise to notice that no less than twelve magistrates and a troop of Cowbridge Volunteers had kept watch on them lest they should act 'in any way anti-royalist.' He seemed to taunt the authorities, however, at the Gorsedd held at Glyn Ogwr, in the parish of Llandyfodwg, in March 1798 by reciting his poem *Breiniau Dyn* (The Rights of Man), for which he had used the title of the book by Tom Paine.

A Gorsedd proclaimed to be held on Forest Mountain in June 1798 had its venue changed to Mynydd y Garth but, even so, the Glamorgan Yeomanry were soon on the scene ordering the bards to disperse in case they should 'attract the French invader.'

In response to a notice proclaiming a Gorsedd to be held on Mynydd y Garth in September, Tomos Glyn Cothi wrote to Iolo to say that he was not certain whether he could 'come to the Eisteddfod (alias Gorsedd) Alban Elfed or not' as he might have to attend a meeting of Unitarian ministers. He later wrote inviting Iolo to arrange a Gorsedd at Carmarthen the next winter solstice, but nothing further was heard.

Meanwhile, the Gwyneddigion Society was proclaiming meetings of bards to take place at the summer solstice in 1798 and inviting:

> all who might seek for Privilege and Graduation in Science and Bardism, to repair to the London Meeting, upon Primrose Hill, to the Chair of Glamorgan, upon Tyle y Gawl, and to the Chair of North Wales at Caerwys, where there will not be a naked weapon against them.

The Proclamation, for so it is described, goes on to state that there will be present at the 'Meeting', Y Meddyg Du (Dr David Samwell), who was the president of the Society, Gwilym Fardd Glas (Edward

Williams, Cowbridge) and Iolo Morganwg. Iolo had not been consulted in the matter, and he does not appear to have taken any interest in what went on and, on that account, he missed a great opportunity to hold his first Gorsedd outside Glamorgan, at the Eisteddfod held at Caerwys in 1798.

In 1799, while he was travelling through north Wales collecting material for the *Myvyrian Archaiology*, Iolo arranged for a Gorsedd to be held on Bryn Dinorwig, in the parish of Llanddeiniolen. He had for some time been trying to persuade Dafydd Ddu Eryri to be installed as *Bardd Cadeiriog Gwynedd*, and he must have seized on this opportunity to do so. Dafydd Ddu wrote, in a letter to his pupil and friend, Sion Lleyn (John Roberts: 1749-1817):

> that an Eisteddfod had been held in accordance with the order and custom of the Bards of the Isle of Britain on Pen Bryn in Arfon (Bryn Dinorwig) on October 16 1799, where Ieuan Lleyn, Gutyn Peris and Dafydd Ddu were enrolled as graduate bards of the Chair of Gwynedd. It is a secret, and yet not a secret. I know that you would like to be a member and this you shall be if you live until Tuesday following next Whitsun, when it is planned to hold an eisteddfod on Bryn Dinorwig, near Llanddeiniolen in Arfon, to meet in the morning at high noon.

The terms *eisteddfod* and *gorsedd* were used interchangeably by Dafydd Ddu, and the event that he arranged to take place on Whit-Tuesday in 1802 on Bryn Dinorwig had the semblance of a Gorsedd but was described as *Eisteddfod Cadair Dinorwig*. A second Eisteddfod was held, not on the hill, but in the village of Llanddeiniolen, and the chair offered for a poem on *Barddoniaeth* (Poetry) was won by Dafydd Ddu Eryri. There was no Gorsedd ceremony, and none was held in Gwynedd for another twenty years.

It was at the Bryn Dinorwig Gorsedd, in 1799, that Iolo read his poem *Gorymbil am Heddwch* (Prayer for Peace), an extract from which appears in the Gorsedd programmes for the Proclamation and for the Eisteddfod each year.

Dafydd Ddu Eryri soon lost his enthusiasm for the Gorsedd and distanced himself from Iolo and his beliefs, and when he heard that the Gwyneddigion Society had invited Iolo to select the subjects for the Eisteddfod the Society planned to hold at Harlech in 1804, he announced that neither he, nor any of the bards of Arfon, would compete. He was critical of the Society for advocating the use of free, that is, non-strict, metres, and for allowing Iolo to promote the twenty-four Glamorgan measures to the exclusion of those of Dafydd ab Edmwnd, to which the bards of north Wales had adhered. He furthermore objected to the Society's insistence on adjudicating the *awdlau*, for which it provided the prizes. He rallied the poets of Gwynedd behind him in resenting the Society's interference, and when Sion Lleyn was asked by the Gwyneddigion to arrange an Eisteddfod in 1804, he declined. The Gwynedd poets willingly agreed, however, to take part in an Eisteddfod held at Tremadoc in September 1811 to celebrate the completion of the great embankment, the Cob, by W. A. Madocks.

As soon as Paris fell, and Napoleon retired to Elba, Iolo inserted a notice in *Seren Gomer* announcing that 'a *Cadair* and Eisteddfod' would be held at 'Y Maen Chwŷf, by Pont-y-tŷ-pridd, in Glamorgan ... on the day of the full moon, on the 1st August next, to write verse on various subjects, and especially on the Restoration of Peace, and to grant a degree and honour in Poetry to all who may deserve it.'

Y Maen Chwŷf, which Iolo regarded as an early Gorsedd site, and which is marked *Carreg Siglo* on the Ordnance Survey map, and is commonly known as 'The Rocking Stone', stands on the mountainside at Pentre Bach in the parish of Eglwys Ilan. Myfyr Morganwg (Evan Davies: 1801-88) later named it *Maen Arch* because he considered that it 'rocked like *Arch Noah* (Noah's Ark) on Mount Ararat,' and as the Welsh were descended from his grandson, Gomer, it was fitting that it should be so called. The Stone is so poised that it is said to sway at the touch of a finger, and Gwilym Morganwg recounted that Iolo sat on the stone, after a Gorsedd ceremony, busily writing regardless of its rocking in response to the curious bystanders that had gathered around it.

Gwilym Morganwg, poet and penillion singer, at whose hostelry, the New Inn, the bards met, was initiated a Bard at the ceremony, and his poem *Heddwch* (Peace) was 'declaimed at the Gorsedd of Morganwg upon the Maen Chwŷf.'

Gwilym placed a notice in *Seren Gomer* stating that the next Gorsedd would be held in the Maen Chwŷf on Alban Arthan (21 December) 1814, and the bards and poets of the Principality were invited to attend 'a *Cadair* and *Eisteddfod*'and to compete on a choice of nine subjects that included 'The Excellence of Brotherly Love', 'The Excellence of the Welsh Language', 'A View of a Wicked Heart', 'The Burial of the

Y Maen Chwŷf, 'the Rocking Stone', at Pentre Bach, Pontypridd, where Iolo Morganwg held a Gorsedd in 1814. Myfyr Morganwg enclosed the stone with two stone circles and a 'serpent' avenue.

Sword', 'Y Maen Chwŷf' and 'The Fall of the Miserly'. He sent a pressing invitation to Iolo to be present, and to bring his son, Taliesin ab Iolo, with him, and it would appear that the invitation was accepted, for Taliesin, having been made a child Ovate on Primrose Hill, was now raised to the rank of Bard. In the introduction to Gwilym Morganwg's volume of poetry, *Awen Y Maen Chwŷf*, Taliesin states that he and Gwilym were 'initiated into the arcana of Druidism by my father,' and refers to Gwilym as 'my only brother Druid'.

At a Gorsedd held on the site on Alban Eilir (21 March) the next year, Gwilym recited his poem *Twyll y Melinydd* (The Miller's Deceit). He kept regular meetings of *Cymdeithas y Maen Chwŷf*, that were also known as Gwilym Morganwg's Meetings, at his inn, one being held there at Alban Hefin (21 June) 1825, at which the set subject was 'Pont y Tŷ Pridd, the biggest single-arch stone bridge, maybe, in the world.' There is no account of another Gorsedd being held on the Maen Chwŷf, except for a brief reference to one that may have taken place in December 1817, until 1827, at which Taliesin ab Iolo presided and Gwilym read poems, some of which were written in memory of Iolo, who had died the previous year.

The next ceremony at the Maen Chwŷf took place in connection with the Gwent and Dyfed Royal Eisteddfod held at Cardiff in 1834. Taliesin had forgotten to give the necessary notice of a year and a day and he, therefore, arranged for a Gorsedd to be held on the Maen Chwŷf on 22 September, '(the 21st, the exact time of the autumnal equinox, and one of the four annual bardic festivals, having fallen on a Sunday).' The bards assembled at the New Inn and, having formed a procession, began to climb the mountainside, led by a harpist. Gwilym Ddu Glan Cynon (Richard Williams, Merthyr) followed, carrying the sword by its point, and then came the 'Druid-Bards Taliesin ab Iolo and Gwilym Morganwg', and after them, the other Bards, including Gwilym Ilid (William Jones, Caerffili) and Myfyr Morganwg. Taliesin, presiding, unsheathed the sword with the help of some of the licensed Bards and, bearing it by its point, mounted the Maen Chwŷf. He then declared the Gorsedd open, and read some of the Triads devised by his father. The first of several Ovates to be admitted into membership of the Gorsedd was Mrs Augusta Waddington Hall, the future Lady Llanover, who had won the essay prize at the Cardiff Eisteddfod under the pseudonym Gwenynen Gwent, which also became her bardic name.

Gwilym Morganwg read his *awdl* on *Derwyddon Ynys Prydain* (The Druids of the Isle of Britain) from the Maen Chwŷf, and Taliesin announced that Gorseddau would be held at Merthyr and at Pontypridd 'after the expiration of a year and a day', but neither took place.

At a ceremony held at the Spring equinox earlier that year Taliesin had admitted Evan Davies, a native of Pencoed, who had referred to himself as Ieuan ap Dafydd, Ioan Morganwg, Ieuan Morganwg and Ieuan Myfyr Uwch Celli before settling on Myfyr Morganwg as a bardic name. He had received no formal education but, by his own efforts, he had gained a mastery of the rules of Welsh bardism, together with a proficiency in mathematics. In 1845, he settled at Pontypridd as a watchmaker.

After Taliesin's death, in 1847, Myfyr claimed to be his successor as 'Archdruid of the Bards of the Isle of Britain', although there is no indication that Taliesin, or his father, ever used such a title. In 1850 he revived *Cadair Morgannwg* that had been dormant, according to *Seren Gomer*, for sixteen years, that is, since the last ceremony at *Y Maen Chwŷf*, and that journal was able to report that:

> on Alban Hefin (22 June) an Eisteddfod was held on the old, primitive and honourable Gorsedd of *Y Maen Chwŷf* within the charmed circle

of the court of Ceridwen, and the revealers of the coiled Serpent, on the banks of Taf, near Pontypridd. At ten o'clock, the bards, and many friends of the cause, from near and far throughout Gwent and Morganwg, gathered together before the New Inn and the Market Place, and a procession was formed to commence towards the Gorsedd-place. At the head was a white banner, gilded and inscribed with the motto of *Cadair Castell y Rhaglan*, namely *Deffro mae'n ddydd* [Awake, it is day], then a carriage bearing the harp ... There followed the broad banner of the Gorsedd of Bards of the Isle of Britain, of azure hue, bearing the mystic sign in gold and the motto *Y Gwir yn erbyn y byd*, and then the licensed bards, among them Ieuan Myfyr bearing a sheathed sword by its point, along with other eminent personages ... The Gorsedd was opened in the form of the 'ritual of the Primitive Bards of the Isle of Britain' by Ieuan Myfyr; then, after offering the Gorsedd Prayer, he sang 'A song of Praise to the Bards of the Isle of Britain.'

It was one of Myfyr Morganwg's nonsensical notions to refer to the Gorsedd Circle as *Llys Ceridwen* (Ceridwen's Court). The goddess Ceridwen was the mother of Taliesin, in Welsh mythology. She lived at Bala, with her husband Tegid Foel, after whom Llyn Tegid was named, where she brewed a potion in her magic cauldron to imbue her son, Morfran, with the gift of poetry, but this was swallowed by Gwion Bach and, by a complicated process of metamorphosis, he is reborn as Taliesin, the poet. Another version states that she gave rebirth to him on the shores of Llyn Geirionydd, and that her cauldron was there. The 'coiled serpent' was a symbol of deity and eternity from earliest times. Myfyr enclosed Y Maen Chwŷf with two concentric stone circles and built a winding avenue of stone pillars in the form of a serpent, with a small circle to represent its head, an idea that he may have got from Dr William Stukeley's description of Avebury in which he envisaged the Sanctuary forming the head, and the avenue the body, of the Solar Serpent.

When Dewi Wyn o Essyllt (Thomas Essile Davies: 1820-91) was publicly chastised from Y Maen Chwŷf for having accepted a money prize with the chair that he won at Dowlais in 1851, he was 'excommunicated through the tail of the serpent, and driven to the brook, and from the brook to the river Taf, and from the river Taf to the sea to the state of evil, and from the state of evil to Annwn [the nether world], and from Annwn to the water closet of Lucifer.'

Among the Ovates admitted at the ceremony in 1850 were Evan James (Ieuan ap Iago), the author of *Hen Wlad Fy Nhadau*, and his son, James James (Iago ap Ieuan), who composed the air. At the close of the ceremony, Myfyr Morganwg announced that the next Gorsedd would be held at the Maen Chwŷf in September, at the autumn equinox. The bards and the gentry then dined at the New Inn, and, at six o'clock, retired to the Market Hall where the competitions were taking place.

Myfyr held a Gorsedd on King's Castle Hill at St Bride's Major at the summer solstice in 1857 at which Yr Estyn (Thomas Richard Lloyd: 1820-91) and Glasynys (Owen Wynne Jones: 1828-70), having made application, were admitted as a Druid and a Bard respectively. Glasynys, in his letter of application, had addressed Myfyr as '*Hybarch Archdderwydd*' (Venerable Archdruid), which appears to be the first time for that mode of address to be used.

Myfyr continued to hold ceremonies regularly at the Maen Chwŷf despite the fact that his peculiar ideas caused some revulsion among the other poets. Talhaiarn (John Jones: 1810-70), in an address that he delivered from the platform at an eisteddfod at Morriston in 1855, declared that before he would 'walk bare-footed through the tail of this imaginary coiled serpent, and be guilty of the other puerilities of this Gorsedd, I would eschew strong drink and take to small beer for the rest of my life,' and he reproved Eben Fardd (Ebenezer Thomas: 1802-63) for having written to Myfyr to ask whether he considered him worthy of receiving a bardic degree from the Maen Chwŷf as he did not think that any other Gorsedd was 'sufficiently authoritative and proper to award such a degree.' This, despite the fact that he had been made a Bard at the Liverpool Eisteddfod in 1840. Eben was admitted *in absentia*, and so was Ab Ithel (John Williams: 1811-62) who had also made an application to be received at the Maen Chwŷf.

By now, Myfyr was describing himself as *Archdderwydd Ynys Prydain* (Archdruid of the Isle of Britain) and, although he was strong in his criticism of the 'National' Eisteddfod and of the Gorsedd of Bards, he was present at the Carmarthen Eisteddfod in 1867, where he was invited to take part in the ceremony from the Maen Llog, and at the Eisteddfod held at Cardiff in 1883 he was introduced from the platform by the Archdeacon of Llandaff, himself a member of the Gorsedd, as 'the Archdruid of Wales.'

Myfyr's eccentricity in religious matters brought him into disrepute with his contemporaries. He made out that Christianity was based on Hinduism which was, in itself, an aspect of Druidism that had spread to India after Noah's Ark had rested on Mount Ararat. At a ceremony held on Y Maen Chwŷf in 1878 he excelled himself when he made supplication to Kali, the Hindu goddess of destruction and death, to whom the Thugs, her worshippers, offered their strangled human victims.

A ceremony was held on Y Maen Chwŷf in December 1879, but Myfyr was not there, and most of his followers were unable to reach the stone on account of the cold and the frosty weather.

On the death of Myfyr Morganwg, in 1888, the title of 'Archdruid' was assumed by Morien (Owen Morgan: 1836-1921), a journalist working on the *Western Mail*, and he continued to hold ceremonies on the Maen Chwŷf for the rest of his life.

THE PROVINCIAL EISTEDDFODAU

IN 1818 a group of Anglican clergy in mid-Wales, motivated by a desire to preserve the Welsh from the growing influence of Methodism, set out to foster the Welsh literary traditions and, in so doing, they helped to lay the foundation of the Eisteddfod as a national festival.

The group had its origin at the vicarage at Kerry, in Montgomeryshire. The vicar, John Jenkins (Ifor Ceri), a native of Llangoedmor who, after graduating at Oxford and serving as a chaplain in the Royal Navy, had been rector at Manordeifi until 1807, when he was offered the living of Kerry by the Bishop of St David's, Thomas Burgess. A new vicarage was built for him, at a cost of £890, at which he kept open house during the first week of each year to 'all comers provided only that they could compose an *englyn*, sing a song, or play the harp.' The vicarage became known as *Llys Ifor Hael o Ceri*, with reference to the generous patron of Dafydd ap Gwilym.

Thomas Burgess was an Englishman, born at Odiham, in Hampshire. He was educated at Winchester and entered Corpus Christi College, Oxford, as a scholar in 1775. Soon after his appointment as Bishop, in 1803, he began to institute reforms within the diocese. He licensed four grammar schools, and founded St David's College, Lampeter, to prepare young men for Holy Orders. He made it a rule that incumbents in his diocese should be able to speak Welsh, and took a general interest in Welsh life. He gave his patronage to the group of literary clergy which included Walter Davies (Gwallter Mechain), vicar of Manafon, David Rowland (Dewi Brefi) of Carno and Llanwnnog, William Jenkins Rees of Casgob, near Presteigne, Rowland Williams of Meifod, David Richards (Dewi Silin) of Llansilin and Thomas, his brother, who was curate at Montgomery. In correspondence between themselves, the members of the group referred to the meetings which they held regularly, as 'clerical eisteddfodau.'

Llys Ifor Hael o Ceri, the vicarage built for John Jenkins (Ifor Ceri) in 1810-11 at which 'the literary clergy' met. The house, in picturesque style and with Gothic windows throughout, was built when John Nash was the diocesan architect. It is sited beneath the Kerry castle earthworks and was, on that account, known as The Moat.

After a meeting held in January 1818, Dewi Brefi, who had been away for eight years as a missionary in Newfoundland, put forward the suggestion that Welsh prosody should be taught to the clergy so that 'bardism may be revived in South Wales and a new era formed.' He then wrote to Ifor Ceri asking, 'as you are the Ifor Hael of the present day, will you revolve in your mind my proposal for the revival of Bardism?' and repeated the request to the bishop. The bishop visited Kerry in August of that year in order to discuss the matter with Ifor Ceri and Gwallter Mechain, and a decision was made to 'attempt to rekindle the bardic skill and ingenuity of the principality ... by holding eisteddfodau in different places in the four provinces.'

An inaugural meeting was held at the White Lion at Carmarthen in the following October, with Lord Dynevor, a descendant of Gruffudd ap Nicholas, the patron of the Carmarthen Eisteddfod of 1451, presiding. The bishop was present, along with a number of clergy, including Ifor Ceri, Dewi Brefi, W. J. Rees and Thomas Beynon, Archdeacon of Cardigan. Iolo Morganwg, whom the bishop had invited, was the only Nonconformist present. The meeting decided to form 'The Cambrian Society in Dyfed', with the object of promoting 'the preservation of Ancient British literature, poetical, historical, antiquarian, sacred and moral and the encouragement of national music.'

Iolo had been invited by the bishop to stay at the Bishop's Palace at Abergwili, and had been provided with a horse for the journey, but he adhered to his precept that there were three things he did not require: a cellar, as he did not drink, a purse, as he had no money, and a horse, as he had strong legs. Despite his age, he led the horse all the way from Flemingston to Abergwili.

Thomas Burgess, Bishop of St David's (1803-25), who gave his patronage to 'the literary clergy'.

In a letter that he wrote subsequently to W. J. Rees at Cascob, Ifor Ceri made a point of referring to the bishop's contribution in the establishment of the Society. 'The first suggestion,' he stated, 'was certainly that of Rowland [Dewi Brefi] at Kerry in January 1818, which he shortly afterwards communicated to the Bishop. No notice was taken of it at the time, but when the Bishop came to Kerry in the following August, he was most intent on a plan of that nature, and in travelling towards the Hay reduced it into form and fixed on the name of the Cambrian Society.'

On the day following the meeting at the White Lion, the promoters met again at the Bishop's Palace to draft a programme of activities for the Society, which included the preparation of a complete catalogue of Welsh manuscripts, with a view to publishing the important ones and depositing copies of the others at the British Museum. A collection of all books published in the Welsh language was to be made and placed for safe keeping in the library of the Honourable Society of Cymmrodorion in Gray's Inn Lane in London. Iolo was appointed to supervise any editing work, and to provide tuition for young poets, for which he would receive some remuneration.

A committee was formed, its members all churchmen, and including such notables as the antiquary William Lewes of Llwynderw, Edward 'Celtic' Davies, Benjamin Millinchamp, the Orientalist, of Plas Llangoedmor, Dr Thomas Bowdler, editor of the 'Family Shakespeare', and the Bishop. Dewi Brefi acted as its secretary and, on his death in 1820, David Lewis, curate of Cynwyl Elfed, took his place. The committee met on 25 November and decided that an eisteddfod would be held at Carmarthen on 8, 9 and 10 July 1819. Iolo Morganwg was made an honorary member of the committee and his influence is apparent in most of the decisions taken although his suggestion that 'a Grand Gorsedd' should be held in London every fifth year did not find favour. Particulars of the competitions were published in a pamphlet that was widely distributed:

> The following prizes are proposed by the Cambrian Society for the year 1819, viz. Five Guineas for the best *Englyn* on 'The Harp New Strung'; Ten Guineas for the best *Awdl* on 'The Death of Queen Charlotte', and Twenty Guineas or a medal of not less than twenty guineas for the best poem in any one or all the four and twenty metres on 'The Death of Sir Thomas Picton.' Also Ten Guineas for the best English essay on each of the following subjects, viz.

On the Language and Learning of Britain under the Roman Government, with a particular reference to the testimony of Martial (*Dicitur et nostros castare Britannia versus*) and Juvenal and to the influence of Agricola's Schools.

On the Distinct Characters and Comparative Advantages of the Bardic Institutions of Carmarthen and Glamorgan and on the Notices which remain of each.

Also a Silver Harp will be given with a gratuity to the best proficient on the Harp and other gratuities to the several competitors to defray their expenses. The Verses and Essays to be delivered into the Secretary, at the Vicarage, Carmarthen, on or before the 1st May, 1819, on or before which day the candidates for the Silver Harp must send their names to the Secretary.

Iolo issued a Proclamation inviting those who wished to seek 'the dignity and licence' granted by the Bards of the Isle of Britain to gather in 'an open place near the town of Carmarthen in the province of Dinefwr, where, to pass judgement on any applicants, there would be present Eleaser, Gwynfardd Glan Deifi, [Eliezer Williams: 1754–1820] and Dafydd, Gwynfardd Glyn Ceiriog [otherwise Dewi Silin], Robert [Bardd] Nantglyn and Iolo Morganwg, all of them Chief Poets and Licensers according to the Privilege and Custom of the Bards of the Isle of Britain.' The term *Gwynfardd* is used to indicate a privileged bard, or a member of the highest bardic order. There, at Carmarthen, would be held 'a *Cadair* and a *Gorsedd* and a Judgement upon poetic art and verse' so as to ascertain who should be considered worthy of receiving 'honour and dignity and licence under the privilege of the Bards of the Isle of Britain and of *Cadair Talaith Dinefwr* (the Chair of the Province of Dinefwr) through the patronage of Pendaran Dyfed and of the Crown of George, the Third of that name, King of the Island of Britain and the other islands.' The description of the province as Dinefwr rather than Dyfed, is a blandishment to please Lord Dynevor, and the euphemism Pendaran Dyfed is additional flattering unction.

The Eisteddfod was held at the Ivy Bush Inn at Carmarthen. The Bishop presided, in the absence of Lord Dynevor and, according to a report in the *Carmarthen Journal*, 'the General Meeting of the members of the newly instituted Cambrian Society commenced with the sound of a trumpet at the Green Room' of the inn. Iolo Morganwg then delivered an address, in English, in which he said that 'one of the principal objects of the Cambrian Literary Society is the cultivation of our national poetry and the restoration of it to its ancient character, that of being the guardian and teacher of truth.' He expressed his delight at being present on 'the resurrection-day of learning in our greatly beloved native language', and proceeded to read the adjudication on the *awdl* on the death of Picton. The winner, Gwallter Mechain, was conducted to a chair that had been specially made 'of indigenous oak ... in the pure gothic style', which had been placed on a table in the centre of the room. As soon as he was seated, 'that learned and venerable bard, Mr Edward Williams [Iolo], despite his seventy-two years, leapt on to the table and tied a blue ribbon round the poet's right arm to indicate that he had been admitted a member of the Gorsedd of Bards of the Isle of Britain.' Iolo then approached the Bishop and said that he was authorised to install him in the Order of Druids, to which the Bishop replied that he would submit to anything that was proper, whereupon Iolo tied a white ribbon round his arm.

Gwallter Mechain then read his *awdl* and the ceremony ended with a rendering of *Morfa Rhuddlan* played on two harps, by Thomas Blayney, harpist to the Earl of Powis, and Henry Humphries of Welshpool.

Gutyn Peris was awarded the prize for the *awdl* to commemorate Queen Charlotte and, as he was not present, Eliezer Williams read it for him. Gwallter Mechain wrote the best *englyn*, and he also had the prize for the best essay on the Bardic institutions of Carmarthen and Glamorgan. Blayney won the Silver Harp and was paid thirty guineas for his services as official harpist. He and Humphries 'sang sweet songs between the readings.'

Iolo's great ambition was that the Gorsedd of Bards should become a component part of the Eisteddfod or, even preferably, that the Eisteddfod should be merged in the Gorsedd of Bards. His opportunity came, perhaps unexpectedly, on the Saturday morning, when he arranged a Gorsedd ceremony, in order to confer degrees on deserving bards, in the garden of the Ivy Bush. He began by marking out a circle with small stones, and placed a larger one at the centre of the circle. There were seven other bards, constituted 'by privilege and custom', present: Gwallter Mechain, Dewi Silin, Daniel Ddu o Geredigion, Gwilym Morgannwg, Bardd Nantglyn, Taliesin ab Iolo and Eleaser, and they elected Iolo as the Officiating Bard. He took the sword from the Sword-Bearer, Gwilym Morgannwg, which he partly unsheathed, and asked each of the bards to place a hand on its hilt while he held the scabbard by the point. He proceeded to explain the qualities expected in a candidate for the degree of Bard, emphasizing that it would not be possible to admit anyone other than on the recommendation of a Bard who was present, or by examination of his skill in poetic composition. 'The ceremony of admission,' stated a contemporary account, 'after suitable commendation and approval, was performed by the Officiating Bard, who held the sword with its point towards him while the entrant held the hilt, the former observing to the latter that, once admitted, he would be under an obligation not to show violence towards any man with the sword. After receiving him, the Officiating Bard tied a blue ribbon about his right arm. When all the Bards had been admitted, the sword was placed upon the stone at the centre of the circle.' Candidates were then admitted 'to the degree of Druid' and Iolo tied white ribbons on their arms. The admission of others to the degree of Ovate was similarly carried out, with a green ribbon being tied round the arm of each. Elizabeth Jones, who was initiated an Ovate, was erroneously believed, in *Y Gwyddoniadur Cymreig*, to have been the first woman to receive the honour 'since The Flood.' She was the daughter of Edward Jones, vicar of Berriew, although she spent most of her early life at Trawscoed Hall, in Guilsfield, where her brother was married to Martha Price, step-daughter of Gwallter Mechain. She sang, and wrote poems, and it has been suggested that Gwallter had put her name forward for admission to the Gorsedd so as to gain the support of the Trawscoed family and other gentry of Montgomeryshire. Ifor Ceri, in a letter to Dewi Brefi, had said that he considered 'it to be very essential to its establishment to have a full assemblage of Gentry of the first Rank at the Primary Eisteddfodau.' He himself, a fifty year old bachelor, espoused the gentry by marrying Elizabeth Jones, at Kerry, where an ox was roasted for the wedding feast, and the bells of the churches around were rung.

When the next Eisteddfod was held at Carmarthen, in 1823, the Gorsedd met 'in a field on the edge of the town.' Cawrdaf (William Ellis Jones: 1795-1848) presided, and he was assisted by Daniel Ddu o Geredigion (Daniel Evans: 1792-1846) and Ioan ap Hywel (John Howell of Abergwili: 1774-1830). The Bishop had, by now, changed his attitude towards Iolo and the Gorsedd of Bards. He may have taken umbrage because Iolo, when he asked him to curtail the Gorsedd ceremony in 1819 had refused to do so, but he also resented an intrusion upon the Eisteddfod, which he regarded as an Anglican institution, by an organisation which had, as its founder, a Unitarian.

The subject set for the chair poem that year was 'St David's

College', the foundation stone of which had been laid by the Bishop at Lampeter the previous year. The winner was Daniel Ddu o Geredigion, a native of Llanfihangel Ystrad, who had graduated at Oxford and had been appointed chaplain at the Royal Military Museum at Northampton. He also won a silver medal for an ode to commemorate the recent victory of the Greeks over the Turks following the massacre of thirty thousand Greeks at Chios.

Bishop Burgess was translated to Salisbury in 1825, and his successor, Bishop Jenkinson, showed no interest in the Society or its work. Thomas Beynon, Archdeacon of Cardigan, became its patron and did his best to promote its interests. Arrangements were made for an Eisteddfod, the first for ten years, to be held at Carmarthen in 1833, but

Ifor Ceri (John Jenkins), vicar of Kerry who, with Bishop Burgess,
'rekindled the bardic skill and ingenuity of the principality.'

Elizabeth Jones, who was admitted a member of the Gorsedd at Carmarthen in 1819
as 'Eos Bele', and who became the wife of Ifor Ceri.

the Archdeacon died that year, and no further attempts were made to
hold a provincial eisteddfod in Dyfed.

The ranks of the literary clerics had been swollen with the addition
of men of similar sentiments, such as Ab Ithel, Carnhuanawc (Thomas
Price: 1787-1848) and Ieuan Glan Geirionydd and they continued to
foster Welsh culture for a period of forty years, up to 1858. Dr R. T.
Jenkins has made out that they were the guardians of the Welsh
literary tradition and that they bridged the gap between the Gwyneddigion Society in London and the new scholarship of the Universities
of Oxford and Wales. Between them they had a hand in the formation
of the Cambrian Archaeological Association, the Welsh Manuscripts
Society, and the foundation of Llandovery School and Lampeter
College. In all their endeavours they were motivated by a zealous

desire to counter the growing influence of Methodism. They had to face, on the one hand, opposition from the anti-Welsh elements within the Anglican Church and, on the other, a charge of being snobbish in the way they adorned the Eisteddfod platform with bishops and gentry, and of converting the Eisteddfod into a musical and Anglicised festival in return for their patronage.

The pioneer work of the Cambrian Society in Dyfed inspired the other provinces to establish similar societies that were dedicated to the promotion of the Welsh literary tradition. The Society soon felt, however, that there was a need for a central body that would co-ordinate the activities of these bodies and, for this, they turned their eyes towards London. W. J. Rees, acting on behalf of the literary clerics, took advantage of the endeavours that were being made to revive the Honourable Society of Cymmrodorion, that had ceased to exist in 1787, but there was little co-operation between the Cymmrodorion and the Cambrian Societies, particularly over matters of finance.

The Powys Cymmrodorion Society, which chose to be so named as its formation coincided with the revival of the Honourable Society of Cymmrodorion, held its first meeting at the Eagles Inn at Wrexham in October 1819 under the Chairmanship of Sir John Evans. Iolo Morganwg, Gwallter Mechain, Dewi Silin and W. J. Rees were among those appointed to serve on a committee that met at Welshpool the following February, with Sir Watkin Williams Wynn in the chair and, among those present was the Viscount Clive of Powis Castle. The committee decided to hold an Eisteddfod at Wrexham in September 1820.

Bardd Nantglyn received the prize for an elegaic ode to King George III, and the chair, for an *awdl* on *Hiraeth Cymro am ei Wlad* (A Welshman's yearning for his Homeland) was awarded to Ieuan Glan Geirionydd who had the unique experience of being chaired twice at the same Eisteddfod. It had only recently become known that he was the winner of the chair at the Denbigh Eisteddfod the previous year for his poem *Y Dywysoges* (The Princess), as he was indisposed and unable to attend the festival. He was first installed for this poem, and when Lord Mostyn asked him whether he would prefer to receive a medal or some money, he chose the latter as he wished to help his impoverished parents. After he had been installed for the second time, Angharad Llwyd, the antiquary from Caerwys, invested him with a green ribbon.

Gwallter Mechain had intended holding a Gorsedd ceremony at

Ruabon during the Wrexham Eisteddfod but he had to abandon it, according to a letter he sent to Angharad Llwyd, owing to the onset of rain. Taliesin ab Iolo wrote to his father, however, stating that he had been told that Bishop Burgess had prevented it, 'objecting to the ceremonies', and added that 'the Bishop is more your enemy than friend.'

Dewi Silin, in obedience to Iolo's exhortation to spread the custom of holding Gorsedd ceremonies in other parts of Wales, had held a ceremony in his churchyard at Llansilin, at which Ifan Ceri, Gwallter Mechain and Bardd Nantglyn were present. He had also proposed to Ifor Ceri, may be as a result of the prohibition at Ruabon, that a Gorsedd ceremony be held at Bron Aran in Kerry on Alban Arthan (21 December) 1820. Gwallter Mechain made an effort to prevent it happening, again making the weather an excuse, but when it did take place, belatedly in January, he was present and taking a leading part. 'We were 12 in all at Kerry,' Taliesin ab Iolo reported to his father, 'from different parts of Wales ... We had an Eisteddfod and held a Gorsedd. Walter Davies (Gwallter Mechain) presiding ... Two Bards and 5 or 6 Ovates were graduated after the manner of Carmarthen.' The Bards were Y Bardd Cloff and Ioan Tegid (John Jones: 1792-1852), and among the Ovates was Angharad Llwyd.

An Eisteddfod was held at the Guildhall, and at the Leeswood Arms, at Mold in 1823, when Alun (John Blackwell: 1797-1840) was awarded the chair for his *awdl* on *Maes Garmon*, as a result of which a fund was raised in the town, of which he was a native, to pay for his education at Jesus College, Oxford. He won the chair at the Ruthin Eisteddfod in that same year for a poem on the 'Birth of Edward II.' An Eisteddfod was also held at Caerwys in 1823.

The Powys Cymmrodorion Society's Eisteddfod at Welshpool in 1824 opened with 'a procession through the town with the bards each wearing round his arm the colour of the rank he held, whether of Bard, or Druid or of Ovate, and several of them distinguished by the honorary medals which previous Eisteddfodau had awarded to their respective talents.' The chair was won by Eben Fardd for his *Dinistr Jerusalem* (The Destruction of Jerusalem).

On 24 November 1827, a Gorsedd ceremony was held on the vicarage lawn at Llangynyw, in Montgomeryshire, to which Thomas Richards had recently been instituted as vicar. Gwallter Mechain appears to have presided and among others present were William Owen Pughe, Rowland Williams, vicar of Meifod, and three of Richards's four brothers: Richard, rector of Caerwys, John Lloyd, vicar of Llanwddyn, and Lewis (Llywelyn Powys), curate of Rhuddlan. David (Dewi Silin) had died the previous year and had been buried at Llansilin where he had been vicar. The ceremony was held for the purpose of honouring Lord Ashley, son and heir of the Earl of Shaftesbury, who was learning Welsh and was on visit to the neighbourhood. He was initiated a Druid under the name of Lleon Llew Gyffes.

The bards met at the Golden Lion at Llansanffraid Glyndyfrdwy on 6 November 1829, the second morning of the Eisteddfod held there, and conducted a Gorsedd ceremony on Bryn Maesycarchardy at which four Bards and six Ovates, three of whom were women, were received into the Gorsedd by Bardd Nantglyn.

At a Gorsedd ceremony held during the Bala Eisteddfod of 1836, among the initiates admitted was Talhaiarn, the poet and architect who was to join Sir John Paxton in the building of the Crystal Palace. Some years later, he wrote to Ioan Madog (John Williams: 1812-78), reminding him of the occasion when they 'had both been honoured together on the shore of Llyn Tegid', where there were present a mere 'wheel barrowful of onlookers and a waggon-load of bards.'

The Mold Cymreigyddion Society, formed in 1848, held an Eisteddfod in the town in 1851. On the opening day, a great procession made its way to the Bailey Hill where a Gorsedd ceremony was held. Lord Mostyn took his rightful place in the procession, as a member of the Gorsedd, along with the other Gorseddogion and representatives of local organisations, among whom, prominent in their regalia, were representatives of the Ancient Order of Druids and the Ancient Order of Foresters who, with their bows and arrows, looked like clones of Robin Hood. Iorwerth Glan Aled (Edward Roberts: 1819-67), who won the chair, reflected that 'bards and harpists, in days gone by, were kept by the nobility to compose or play at their leisure, but the world has changed for the worse; instead of bards, the gentry keep race horses! Instead of harpists, they keep hounds!'

The Gwynedd Cymmrodorion Society held its first meeting in December 1820 with the aim of preserving 'the Remains of Ancient British Literature and for the Encouragement of the Remains of National Music.' Its president was Sir Robert Williams Vaughan of Nannau and its patrons included the Marquess of Anglesey, Viscount Bulkeley and the Bishop of Bangor. Neither Dafydd Eryri nor any of the bards of Gwynedd were invited to sit on its committee, nor was Iolo Morganwg, and it is small wonder the Society should experience some difficulty in arranging for an Eisteddfod to be held in September

1821. A Proclamation Scroll, on the lines of that used at Carmarthen in 1819, was issued, stating that a Gorsedd would meet 'on an open site on the edge of the town of Caernarfon' under the patronage of the Marquess and of King George IV. Posters described the event as an 'Eisteddfod or Congress of Bards and Minstrels. Grand patron: The King.'

The Eisteddfod opened at eleven o'clock in the morning of 12 September with an address by the Marquess, a Welsh summary of which was given by Dafydd Ddu Eryri, who had been asked to conduct the proceedings. The Marquess was supported on the platform by his son, the Earl of Uxbridge, and his daughters, the Ladies Georgiana and Agnes Paget, the Bishop of Bangor and Mrs Majendie, Lord Newborough, Sir Charles Morgan, Sir Thomas Love Parry and other members of the local nobility. The Marquess's party dined each evening at the Uxbridge Arms, now the Royal Hotel, while the bards fed on broth and ale at the Goat Inn and, on the last night, they went to a *noson lawen* at *Sein Delyn*, as the Harp Inn was known locally. The nobility had to rely on the Goat, however, for the use of boot-jacks to remove their footwear so that they could enter the Gorsedd Circle barefoot. The Eisteddfod was held at the County Hall, 'a low, mean-looking building, although it was neat and fairly commodious within,' and when the Marquess saw that there were hundreds of people outside, unable to gain admission, he opened the window and announced that they would adjourn to the castle, across the road from the County Hall. A platform was hastily erected within the castle walls but, in no time, it came to rain, and the crowd dispersed. They met there again next morning and were, no doubt, amused to see that, high on the battlements, there 'stood an old goat with a long grey beard: for some hours he stood motionless on his perch and, to all seeming, deeply interested in what was going on.'

Dafydd Ddu Eryri, as Presiding Bard at the Gorsedd ceremony, admitted new members, including Caledfryn (William Williams: 1801-69) and Cawrdaf (William Ellis Jones: 1795-1848).

It was largely at the instigation of Cawrdaf that a Cymreigyddion Society was formed at Dolgellau, in which he was appointed *Bardd y Gymdeithas* (the Society's Bard), a title that was later changed to 'Archdruid'. In May 1824, it held a Gorsedd ceremony on Cader Idris at which three new Bards and an Ovate were admitted.

Cymreigyddion Caernarfon held an eisteddfod at the Crown Inn in that borough in the same year, under the auspices of an obscure *Gorsedd o Feirdd*, but there were no admissions.

Neither Cymreigyddion society had any connection with the Gwynedd Cymmrodorion,

The Gwynedd Society held an Eisteddfod at Denbigh in 1828 at which Sir Edward Mostyn presided. A procession was formed at the Town Hall and it progressed, led by the Denbigh Militia Band, to Denbigh Castle, where the bards assembled for a Gorsedd ceremony. Alun read the proclamation scroll in Welsh, and it was then read in English by Aneurin ap Gwilym who, with his father, William Owen Pughe, had recently come to live at Nantglyn. Carnhuanawc gave a stirring address, and messages of greeting were read from William Wordsworth, Sir Walter Scott and Robert Southey. Ieuan Glan Geironydd was awarded the prize for his *awdl* on 'Belshazzar's Feast' and he was installed in a chair adorned with oak leaves and blue ribbons. Some of the bards were involved in quarrels after over-indulging at a local hostelry and appeared, the following morning, bearing the scars of a bout of fisticuffs.

A Gorsedd ceremony was also held at Selwrn, near Llandderfel, Meirioneth at which 'several ladies and gentlemen of literary talent were admitted to the degrees of ovates, disciples and bards.'

Great preparations were made for the Gwynedd Society's Eisteddfod held at Beaumaris in 1832, as it was visited by the Duchess of Kent and her daughter Princess, later Queen, Victoria, who were the guests of the Eisteddfod's president, Sir Robert Bulkeley, at Baron Hill. On Tuesday, 28 August, Sir Robert led a procession from the Town Hall to Beaumaris Castle where, after a trumpet call, Alun once more proclaimed the Eisteddfod to be open by reading the scroll in Welsh, which Aneurin ap Gwilym, again, read in English. The prize for an *awdl* on the wreck of the *Rothesay Castle* was awarded to Caledfryn, and he was chaired and invested with a silver medal by Lady Bulkeley. On account of the inclement weather, the royal ladies were unable to leave Baron Hill and the prizewinners in the various competitions were taken to the house to receive their prizes from the Duchess. The Princess was presented with a length of homespun material woven in the herring-bone pattern by the master weaver and man of letters Gweirydd ap Rhys (Robert Pryse: 1807-89).

The Eisteddfod was an unparalleled success from a literary point of view, with no fewer than three hundred entries received, but financially it was a failure. The weather was blamed, and so was 'the prevalence of cholera at Beaumaris', and also the expenditure of £600 incurred in the attendance of choirs and musicians. There was a deficit of £89, which was cleared by the local nobility.

The Eisteddfod held at Llannerch-y-Medd in June 1835 opened with a Gorsedd ceremony held on Llwydiarth farm land, with Clwydfardd (David Griffiths: 1800-94) acting as Presiding Bard, and another ceremony was held on the following day when Gwalchmai (Richard Parry: 1803-97), the chaired bard, was admitted a member, among several others. For some unexplained reason, a third ceremony was held six weeks later, on 23 July, at which the runner-up in the chair competition, Owain Llwyfo (Owen Roberts, Pentraeth) was made a member of the Gorsedd. Aotrou de Pothonier was also admitted, under the bardic name 'Orpheus o Ffrainc,' and was the first Breton to be so honoured. The eight year old harpist Joseph Tudor Hughes, who had been admitted earlier as an Ovate under the name 'Blegwryd ap Seisyllt', was now given the superior rank of Bard.

The Ordovician Society of Liverpool and Birkenhead, established in 1839 under the presidency of Lord Mostyn, immediately set in motion the arrangements for an Eisteddfod to be held at Liverpool the following year. A proclamation ceremony took place in a field off Brunswick Road, on 17 June 1839, after which the assembled company retired to the Brunswick Hotel in Hanover Street for a luncheon. On the same date in June the following year, a grand procession was formed and, led by a brass band and comprising members of the Gorsedd and of numerous organisations and local societies, it progressed towards 'the Old Hospital Court, where St George's Hall stands today'. Among the banners carried in the procession, 'the flag of the Ancient Druids bore a gilded harp on a green field', and the members of that Order wore 'white cloaks or gowns, with hoods or caps in one covering the heads and long beards. The superiors wore coronets or crowns, and each appeared like a venerable priest of the time of yore.' The appearance of these gentlemen caused confusion in the public mind and the *North Wales Chronicle* found it necessary to distinguish between the members of the Gorsedd and the representatives of the Ancient Order of Druids by referring to Ieuan Glan Geirionydd, who presided over the Gorsedd ceremony in the stone circle, as 'the Bardic Druid.'

Eben Fardd was awarded the chair for an *awdl* on *Cystudd, Amynedd ac Adferiad Job* (The Suffering, Patience and recovery of Job) and, afterwards, he attended a Gorsedd ceremony where he 'took the sword in his right hand while [Ioan] Tegid tied a blue ribbon round his arm above his elbow.'

A Gorsedd was held during Eisteddfod Llifon at Bryngwran in the parish of Llechylched in Anglesey in 1842, at which Clwydfardd presided and admitted new members.

The Gwynedd Society's next Eisteddfod, after 1835, was held at Aberffraw in August 1849. At the opening Gorsedd ceremony, on Bryn Llywelyn, Clwydfardd read the Proclamation Scroll and Hugh Owen, vicar of Trefdraeth, read an English version, According to the *Transactions of the Aberffraw Royal Eisteddfod*, 'the ceremony of conferring degrees was conducted by the Rev. D. James, FSA, of Kirkdale, Liverpool, [Dewi o Ddyfed] who officiated as Archdruid.' The use of the term 'Archdruid' in this instance is likely to have been a borrowing from one of the friendly societies, such as the Ancient Order of Druids. Dewi o Ddyfed, a native of Manordeifi, had been admitted by Iolo at Carmarthen in 1819, when he was sixteen years of age, and had been elevated to the grade of Druid at Liverpool, where he was the vicar of Kirkdale, in 1840.

Twenty-one Bards were admitted at Aberffraw, among whom were Hwfa Môn (Rowland Williams: 1823-1905) and Gweirydd ap Rhys, and seven Druids, that included Carn Ingli (Joseph Hughes: 1803-63) and Llallawg (Thomas James: 1817-79), who was Dewi o Ddyfed's brother.

The three adjudicators, Eben Fardd, Iocyn Du (John Richards: 1795-1864) and Chwaneg Môn (Joseph Jones: 1787-1856) failed to agree which of the competitors for an *awdl* on 'The Creation' should be awarded the chair. Eben Fardd considered that the poem submitted by Emrys (William Ambrose: 1813-73) was the best, but Iocyn Du favoured the work of Nicander (Morris Williams: 1809-74). Chwaneg Môn wanted to give the prize to Bardd Du Môn (Robert Williamson: 1807-52), but he was persuaded by Iocyn Du to cast his vote for his candidate. It was generally considered that Emrys had been unfairly treated and the controversy was pursued in the press and it reached a new intensity when it was realised that Nicander and the adjudicators who voted for him were Anglicans, while Eben Fardd and Emrys were Nonconformists.

An insight into the procedure for awarding bardic degrees is given by Gweirydd ap Rhys, who wrote that when he 'arrived at Aberffraw on 15th August 1849, the first day of the Eisteddfod,

> 'I told Clwydfardd, the Gorsedd Bard, that I had composed some shape of Awdl containing the Twenty-Four Measures, and that I

wished to obtain consent to read it at the Gorsedd ceremony to be held on the third day in a bid to obtain the Order of Pencerdd! Clwydfardd laughed heartily and asked if I did not know that the Bardic Degrees had, for a long time, been Bard, Ovate and Druid … He said that all that was now needed, in order to obtain one of the three degrees, was to get a Bard to propose the candidate. 'But as for you,' he said, 'your work is sufficiently known; on that account it will not be necessary for anyone to propose you.' I hesitated after hearing this, (and I wanting to be a Pencerdd!) as to whether I should accept the important Order offered to me; but I was dragged away by two friends to the Gorsedd where I was solemnly exalted by Dewi o Ddyfed and Clwydfardd as B.B.D. *Bardd Braint a Defod.*' [Bard by Privilege and Ordinance].

A Gorsedd Circle had been erected in the grounds of Rhuddlan Castle in preparation for the opening ceremony of the Eisteddfod held there in September 1850. Dewi o Ddyfed, described as *Prif Fardd* (Chief Bard), rather than as 'Archdruid' as he was at Aberffraw, presided and admitted nine new bards, including Owain Alaw (John Owen: 1821-83), Idris Fychan (John Jones: 1825-87) and Gwyneddon (John Davies: 1832-1904), seven Druids and nineteen Ovates, among whom were Lord Mostyn (Ifor Mostyn) and the Patagonian pioneer Hugh Hughes (Cadfan Gwynedd).

The chair was offered for a *pryddestawdl*, a long poem in free or strict metre, which gave the poets the freedom to write as they wished. The set subject was *Yr Atgyfodiad* (The Resurrection) and the prize was awarded to Ieuan Glan Geirionydd for a pryddest of some three thousand lines, 'the whole poem a body of divinity' according to one of the adjudicators, in preference to an *awdl* by Caledfryn. The decision was not well received and the bards got together and ruled that 'the Eisteddfod Chair should only be awarded for an *awdl* and that no one would be considered a bard henceforth except that he had graduated "by privilege and custom".'

Meurig Idris, who was *Bardd yr Orsedd*, a deputy to the *Prif Fardd*, at Rhuddlan, acted in the same capacity at Tremadoc, where an Eisteddfod was held in 1852. Among those admitted at a Gorsedd ceremony there were Emrys, Elis Wyn o Wyrfai (Ellis Roberts: 1827-95) and Iolo Trefaldwyn (Edward Davies: 1819-87). One unfortunate candidate for honours was asked by Meurig Idris if he could recite an *englyn* of his own making, and when he admitted that he could not, Meurig promptly ordered him out of the Circle.

An attempt was made to hold an Eisteddfod at Bangor in 1853, but the patronage of the gentry was not forthcoming, which prompted Ioan Tegid to suggest that the people of Bangor should promote their own Eisteddfod without relying on others.

A Gorsedd Proclamation ceremony was held within the walls of Beaumaris Castle in July 1859, announcing that an Eisteddfod would be held in the town the following year, but it was eventually realised that this would clash with the Eisteddfod that was to be held at Denbigh that year.

During the Gwynedd Society's Eisteddfod at Caernarfon in September 1821, Sir Charles Morgan, of Tredegar Park, the Member of Parliament for Merioneth, announced that he proposed to promote the formation of a Cymreigyddion Society in Gwent. A meeting for that purpose was held, however, at Brecon, in the December following, when a decision was taken to hold an Eisteddfod in that town in September 1822. Iolo Morganwg and Dafydd Ddu Eryri were made honorary members of the Society.

Sir Charles delivered the opening address at the Eisteddfod, and Carnhuanawc gave his standard speech on 'Awakening the sympathy of the Upper Classes in the Principality for the character and pursuits of the native population'. Iolo, as adjudicator, awarded the Chair, for an *awdl* on 'Regency', to Cawrdaf, and he was invested with a medal by Lady Morgan. At a Gorsedd ceremony that followed, Iolo raised Cawrdaf to the grade of *Athraw Cadeiriog* (Chaired Teacher).

The Gwent Society's next Eisteddfod was held, again, at Brecon, in October 1826, with Lord Rodney, who had recently married Sir Charles Morgan's daughter, presiding. The chair, for an *awdl* on *Rhodd-iad y Ddeddf ar Fynydd Sinai* (The Giving of the Law on Mount Sinai), was awarded to Pedr Fardd (Peter Jones: 1775-1845), while his daughter, Edith Jones, wrote the best *englyn* out of over a hundred entries. An improvised Gorsedd ceremony was held at which John Blackwell, who had recently graduated at Jesus College, Oxford, was initiated an Ovate under the bardic name Ieuan Ddu Glan Alun, which he later curtailed to Alun. Three students from that college were also admitted, and so was the daughter of Gwallter Mechain.

The Gwent and Dyfed Societies got together in 1834 to hold the 'Gwent and Dyfed Royal Eisteddfod' at Cardiff, under the patronage of the Duchess of Kent and the Princess Victoria, which Their Royal Highnesses had promised during their visit to Beaumaris two years previously. The Marquess of Bute presided and the vice-presidential list comprised peers, bishops and Members of Parliament, and the nobility and gentry were present in force. Lady Charlotte Guest recorded that she and her husband 'got a very good place in the front row opposite the platform. After a pause, Lord Bute opened the Eisteddfod. His speech was miserable.' One of the Eisteddfod secretaries was John Montgomery Traherne of Coedrhiglan.

Taliesin ab Iolo had promised to prepare a Proclamation Scroll, but failed to do so in time to give the required notice of a year and a day. He, nevertheless, agreed to declare the Eisteddfod open with the reading of the Scroll, as long as the entrances to the marquee, erected in the grounds of Cardiff Castle, were thrown wide open so as to provide the nearest approximation to 'the face of the sun, the eye of light.' The Scroll had been amended to read that 'the Eisteddfod would be opened without the Gorsedd (owing to lack of full notice of a year and a day)'.

When it was announced that the winner of the chair, for an *awdl* on *Derwyddon Ynys Prydain* (The Druids of the Isle of Britain) bore the pseudonym 'Llawdden', the man 'led forward amidst deafening cheers from the large and elegant assembly, was found to be no other that our highly gifted and not less respected townsman, Taliesin Williams, – ab Iolo Morganwg.' The prize for an essay 'On the advantages resulting from the Preservation of the Welsh Language and National Costume of Wales' was awarded to Mrs Augusta Waddington Hall, later to become Lady Llanover, who had given, as her *non-de-plume*, Gwenynen Gwent, a name that she retained when she was admitted to the Gorsedd of Bards at Y Maen Chwŷf at the autumnal equinox.

There were some complaints that the Eisteddfod had more concerts than musical competitions. There were only three competitors for the best variations on a Welsh tune, and the winner was a fourteen year old boy from Carmarthen, Brinley Richards, who received the award for his variations on *Llwyn Onn* ('The Ash Grove'). The Duke of Newcastle, who was present, was so impressed with his performance that he became his patron and arranged for him to be educated at the Royal Academy of Music.

The Cardiff Eisteddfod turned out to be the last of the Provincial Eisteddfodau in South Wales, and their place was taken by Eisteddfodau arranged by Cymreigyddion y Fenni at Abergavenny.

At Merthyr Tudful, Cymdeithas Cadair Merthyr held an Eisteddfod at the Boot Hotel in that town on Christmas Day 1823, when the subject set for the chief poem was *Nos Olwg ar Weithiau Haearn Merthyr Tudful* (A Night Vision of Merthyr Tudful Ironworks). Carnhuanawc

did not miss the opportunity to remind the audience of the sad plight of
the Bretons who did not have the Bible in their own language, and
which he was helping to have translated. At the next Eisteddfod, held
in May 1824, the chair was awarded to Gwilym Ddu (Richard
Williams) for an *awdl* on *Y Goleuni* (The Light), and at another held in
September, Thomas Lewis, Dowlais, won the chair for his *Y Bedd* (The
Grave). There were two more eisteddfodau held, in the same months
in the following year. Taliesin ab Iolo, who was an active member of
the Society, along with other prominent Gorseddogion installed by his
father, decided to organise a Gorsedd to be held on Twyn-yr-odyn,
near Merthyr, on Alban Arthan (21 December) 1825. Taliesin was the
presiding bard at the ceremony and, according to him, only one person
showed sufficient proficiency to be admitted a member of the Gorsedd
of Bards.

Cymreigyddion y Fenni was formed at a meeting held at the Sun
Inn, Abergavenny, on 22 November 1833. Among its founding members were Carnhuanawc, who was then vicar of Llanfihangel Cwm
Du, near Crickhowell, and Benjamin and Augusta Hall, of Llanover
and Abercarn. The Society was set up to promote the Welsh language
and Welsh culture, and it held an Eisteddfod in November 1834 that
was the first of a series, known as *Eisteddfodau y Fenni*, held annually for
the next five years.

One evening, during the Eisteddfod held in 1836, after dining at the
Angel Hotel, the assembled company adjourned to a concert that was
being held at the Abergavenny Grammar School. M. Alexis Francois
Rio, who had recently married Appelonia Jones, of Llanarth Court,
near Raglan, was due to preside at the concert, but he had been
detained in his native Brittany, and William Williams, vicar of Llan-
gybi Fawr, took his place. Benjamin Hall and Carnhuanawc delivered
speeches and, following a suggestion by William Williams of Aber-
pergwm, the initial steps were taken to form the Welsh Manuscripts
Society, which took an active part in publishing such works as *Ancient
and National Airs of Gwent* by Maria Jane Williams, *The Literature of the
Kymry* by Thomas Stephens, Lewys Dwnn's *Heraldic Visitations* and *The
Iolo Manuscripts*.

Benjamin Hall presided over the Eisteddfod held in October 1837,
and among those present was Ioan Tegid, by now precentor of Christ
Church, Oxford, who had recently transcribed the Red Book of
Hergest for Lady Charlotte Guest and otherwise helped her in her
translation of *The Mabinogion*.

The 1838 Eisteddfod opened with a great procession, led by many banners and a carriage conveying a dozen harpists, followed by the Cymreigyddion, bards and members of the Ancient Order of Druids, with two of its 'archdruids' dressed in their ceremonial regalia. The quality brought up the rear, in their carriages or mounted on horseback.

Sir Charles Morgan, who presided, introduced a Breton deputation, sent by Louis Philippe of France, and led by le Vicomte Theodore Hersart de la Villemarqué, to collect information relating to old Welsh manuscripts. Villemarqué, in an after-dinner speech, made reference to the Anglo-French battle of St Cast, at which the Bretons in the French army came face to face with the Welsh in the British army and had refused to fight but had, instead, sung Welsh and Breton songs. The incident had inspired Lamartine to write a poem in which he envisaged soldiers of the two Celtic nations splitting a sword and tying the halves together as an emblem of peace. The poem was recited by Jacquelot du Boisrouvray, a member of the delegation, at dinner the following evening, along with an English translation by Carnhuanawc, and from it was taken the idea of the ceremony of uniting the half-swords whenever the Welsh and Breton hold a joint-Gorsedd.

A Gorsedd ceremony was held in an enclosure at the rear of the George Hotel in inclement weather. In accordance with the custom at that time, the bards stood bare-headed and in their stocking feet inside the circle, that had been hastily made of some pebbles and small stones. Cawrdaf was the presiding bard and he wore a loose gown trimmed with purple, a blue sash from which there hung a gold star, and a wide-brimmed hat of purple brocade. Ioan Tegid and Rhydderch Gwynedd brought Villemarqué before him to be admitted a Bard of the Bards of the Isle of Britain.

The procession at the opening of the Eisteddfod held in 1840 was led by a troop of mounted cavalry and, in addition to the bards and the members of Cymreigyddion y Fenni, there were representatives of the Ancient Order of Druids and of the Independant Order of Odd Fellows in full regalia and with banners flying. At the rear came the president, John Etherington Welch Rolls, of Hendre, in his horse-drawn carriage. Taliesin ab Iolo presided over a Gorsedd ceremony at which he admitted seven new members, among them John Evans (Ieuan ap Gruffydd), vicar of Llanover and chairman of Cymreigyddion y Fenni. He was a leading member of the Ancient Order of Druids which may have accounted for the prominence of that, and other, Friendly Societies, in the processions at Abergavenny and, afterwards, elsewhere. This was the last Gorsedd ceremony held at Eisteddfod y Fenni, although Taliesin was present at the Eisteddfod held in 1842 and delivered an address on the significance of *Gorsedd y Beirdd*.

By 1848, the Cymreigyddion, aided by Sir Benjamin Hall, Bart., as he now was, had provided themselves with purpose-built premises in which to hold their Eisteddfodau. The Halls had always invited notables, including foreign ambassadors and European scholars to be present; this year the Prince of Wales attended, and there were said to be no less than four hundred carriages in the procession on the opening day. The Eisteddfod is remembered, however, for the fact that the essay competition was won by Thomas Stephens, of Merthyr, whose work was published the following year under the title, *The Literature of the Cymry*.

The procession was two miles long again in 1853, when the last of the Abergavenny Eisteddfodau was held and, soon after, on 14 January 1854, Cymreigyddion y Fenni was abruptly dissolved.

THE NATIONAL EISTEDDFOD

AB ITHEL, the rector of Llan-ym-mawddwy, opened a Gorsedd ceremony held on Dolybont Common at Dinas Mawddwy, on 2 August 1855, with the following prayer:

Duw rho nerth;/Ac o nerth, pwyll;/Ac o bwyll,
gwybod;/Ac o wybod, y cyfiawn;/Ac o'r cyfiawn,
ei garu;/Ac o garu, caru pop beth;/Ac ynhgaru
pob peth, caru Duw.

The prayer is attributed to the mythical Talhaearn Tad Tanwyn and is one of several versions found in the Iolo manuscripts, one of which has been adopted as the Gorsedd Prayer:

Dyro, Dduw, dy nawdd;
Ac yn nawdd, nerth;
Ac yn nerth, deall;
Ac yn neall, gwybod;
Ac yng ngwybod, gwybod y cyfiawn;
Ac yn ngwybod y cyfiawn, ei garu;
Ac o garu; caru pob hanfod;
Ac ym mhob hanfod, caru Duw,
Duw a phob daioni.

(Grant, O God, thy protection;/and in protection, strength;/and in strength, wisdom;/and in wisdom, knowledge;/and in knowledge, knowledge of that which is just/and in knowledge of that which is just, its loving;/and from loving, love all existing things;/and in loving all existing things, love God. God and all goodness.)

Ab Ithel, who presided over the ceremony with the assistance of Glasynys, had hired a large marquee and had provided suitable prizes for the many competitions, as well as ribbons, white, blue and green, to tie round the arms of initiated bards, at his own expense. Although he had not, at that time, been admitted to the grade of Bard, he, never-theless, initiated a number of new members, including Mynyddog (Richard Davies: 1833-77) and Tafolog (Richard Davies: 1830-1904). They were both contestants for the Chair, offered for *Awdl y Gwylliaid Cochion a'r Barwn Owen* (Ode to the Red Bandits and Baron Owen), but it was awarded to Gwalchmai (Richard Parry: 1803-97).

Ab Ithel was educated at Ruthin School and at Jesus College, Oxford, where he graduated in 1835. He first adopted the bardic name 'Cynhaval' from his birthplace, Llangynhafal, but changed it to Ab Ithel when he later claimed descent, through his maternal grandfather, William Bethell, from Ithel ap Rhopert, archdeacon of St Asaph in the fourteenth century. He was given access to Iolo Morganwg's papers, then in the library at Llanover, and from these he extracted enough material to publish a work in two-volumes entitled *Barddas, or A Collection of Original Documents illustrative of Theology, Wisdom and Usages of the Bardo-Druidic System of the Isle of Britain.* He became an unreserved disciple of Iolo and claimed that he could 'unhesitatingly pronounce him to be incapable of perpetuating literary deceit or forgery, par-ticularly with the view of upholding a theory.'

In 1845, in association with H. Longueville Jones, he published the first issue of *Archaeologia Cambrensis* and, a year later, they founded the Cambrian Archaeological Association. In 1853, they quarrelled and Ab Ithel formed the Cambrian Institute, and edited its periodical, *The Cambrian Journal*, from 1854 until he died, in 1862. He also launched the journals *Baner y Groes* and *Taliesin*, and edited a number of texts for the Welsh Manuscripts Society, including *Y Gododdin*, *Brut y Tywysogion* and *Annales Cambriae*. He was regarded, rather misguidedly, as one of the leading scholars of the day, and his name was even considered for the proposed chair of Celtic at Jesus College.

He was a leading figure in the promotion of an Eisteddfod held at Llangollen in July 1857, where he presided over a Gorsedd ceremony, with the assistance of Taliesin o Eifion (Thomas Jones: 1820-76), poet and local inn-sign painter, and announced that he was arranging for an *Eisteddfod Fawr Freiniol* (a Great Royal Eisteddfod) to be held in the town at the autumnal equinox in the following year. This Eisteddfod had already been proclaimed by Myfyr Morganwg at a Gorsedd held on King's Castle Hill, St Bride's Major the previous summer.

The failure on the part of the local people to hold Eisteddfodau at Bangor and at Dolgellau, owing to the lack of patronage, had spurred Ab Ithel to attempt to arrange a festival in 'a manner different from the usual method, that is, without seeking first a president, grandiose in his pomposity, and as far as possible, in accordance with the old custom'. Thus motivated, he set about the gigantic task of organising an Eisteddfod on a national scale.

He was assisted in his venture by Carn Ingli, perpetual curate of Meltham in Yorkshire, and Môr Meirion (Richard Williams Morgan: 1815–89), perpetual curate at Tregynon, in Montgomeryshire, and later by Yr Estyn (Thomas Richard Lloyd: 1982–91), rector of Llanfynydd in Hope, Flintshire. He had realised the power of publicity and had advertised 'the Great Royal Eisteddfod' widely. He took advantage of the recently completed railway system in the area and came to an arrangement with the railway companies to run cheap excursions to Ruabon, the nearest railway station. A large marquee was erected near the Ponsonby Hotel, on the Ruabon side of the town, and a Gorsedd Circle not far away. He saw that the public, and the Gorsedd-ogion, were familiar with the procedure to be followed in the Gorsedd ceremonies by publishing a notice in the *Programme of the Grand National Eisteddfod, Llangollen, 1858* stating that 'when the procession reaches the Bardic Circle – Bards, Druids and Ovates will enter the enclosure, and occupy their various stations – the Presiding Bard on the central stone and others severally at the stones which form a circle. The minstrel of the Eisteddfod having played *Y Bardd yn ei Awen*, the Presiding Bard will give a brief explanation of Bardism and the ceremonies of the Gorsedd. A Druid will say the Gorsedd Prayer and the Congress will be opened in the usual form upon worthy candidates, who will be presented and their claims announced by members of the order'. Ab Ithel drew attention to the way in which the Friendly Societies appeared in the processions, wearing their robes and regalia, whilst 'the oldest brotherhood in the world' had none. He confided that an attempt had been made to produce a robe or dress for the Gorsedd-ogion, but it had not been possible to agree an appropriate design, and there was the problem that not everyone could afford to purchase one, although for such people a stole could be provided.

The band of the Royal Denbigh Rifles, and a large red dragon banner, led the procession from the Ponsonby Hotel to the Bardic Circle, and the Gorsedd Orders followed bearing banners of green, blue and white. Ab Ithel had appointed himself Presiding Bard, despite the protestations of the bards of Gwynedd that he was not a graduate Bard, and he appeared on the Maen Llog 'in his white robe as a Druid-Bard' and opened the proceedings by 'briefly reciting the history of

Bardism', following which Carn Ingli invited Môr Meirion to offer the Gorsedd Prayer. Ab Ithel then, with the sword partly unsheathed, called on those who wished to be considered worthy of membership to present themselves for scrutiny by himself, Carn Ingli, Môr Meirion, Myfyr Morganwg, Cynddelw (Robert Ellis: 1812-75) and Gwalchmai, all 'Bards by privilege and custom of the Bards of the Isle of Britain.'

Among the persons admitted to the degree of Bard were Ceiriog (John Ceiriog Hughes: 1832-78) and Glan Menai (Griffith Jones: 1836-1906), and Ovates included George Hammond Whalley (Madog), Owen Humphrey Davies (Eos Llechid) and James Kenward (Elfynydd), who had written *A Poem of English Sympathy with Wales* for the occasion, and was later to write a biography of Ab Ithel. Four women who were admitted were attired in the 'dress of the ancient Welsh, and on their heads ingeniously woven garlands of mistletoe, oak leaves, corn and leeks.'

The scene on the Eisteddfod platform, inside the marquee, was described by an English visitor as 'indescribably comic'. Myfyr Morganwg, the 'archdruid' of Y Maen Chwŷf, was wearing his white robe and 'bearing the mystic egg' round his neck. The mystic, or Druid's, egg was stated by Pliny to have been begotten of the spittle of angry serpents and it was kept buoyant by their constant hissing: any person who succeeded in grasping it without being fatally bitten by the serpents became invincible in any contest. Dr William Price of Llantrisant, who had established the legality of cremation after he had cremated his infant son, Iesu Grist, sat on the platform; although he was not a Gorsedd member he claimed direct descent from the Druids, and held ceremonies on his own at Y Maen Chwŷf, where he sang the 'Song of the Primitive Bards to the Moon'. He was 'dressed in a short velvet jacket or hunting suit, with an enormous foxskin cap, sword and flowing beard' and was accompanied by his daughter, 'the Countess of Morganwg', who wore 'a long scarlet robe with the paternal head dress of a foxskin'.

Eben Fardd was awarded the chair for his *awdl* on 'Bosworth Field', and Ceiriog won a prize for his love poem, *Myfanwy Fychan*. A 'bardic tiara in gold' was offered for 'the fullest illustration, from original sources, of the theology, discipline, and usages of the Bardo-druidic system of the Isle of Britain.' There was only one entry, which the three adjudicators considered worthy of the tiara. It was the work of Ab Ithel, comprising the writings that he had extracted from the manuscripts of Iolo Morganwg, and it was later publsihed, as the two volume *Barddas*.

At the close of the Llangollen Eisteddfod, the bards gathered in the 'Cambrian Tent' to consider the feasibility of establishing a national institution that would be lasting in its nature and useful in its purpose, and Glan Alun and Creuddynfab were asked to investigate ways and means of reorganising the festival. Their report, published in *Baner ac Amserau Cymru* in August 1860 recommended, *inter alia*, that the Eisteddfod be held annually, in alternate years in north and south Wales, and that 'the usual Gorsedd ceremonies be preserved undefiled, except that it was necessary to adopt a new method of determining the merit of those who sought orders at eisteddfodau.' Creuddynfab wanted to institute examinations in which the prospective Ovate would have to become proficient in 'the elements of grammar, logic an rhetoric.' The aspirant to bardic honours would have to be familiar with 'the principles that govern the structure of language forms' besides having mastery over all the free and strict metres. The degrees awarded to those who graduated would 'stand in the same rank as M.A. and B.A. Oxford and other places, and would give their holders the right to associate with the scholars of this country and of the Continent.' The Druids would be admitted without examination 'by virtue of their office as religious ministers.' Other reformers wanted to subject the candidates to a more rigorous test, and to include the Druids who, upon being successful in examination, should be given degrees that would rank with Doctor of Divinity or Doctor of Philosophy. Candidates were put to the test from 1861 onward, and it was sometimes carried to extreme, as when Nicander, who had been awarded the chair at the Aberdare Eisteddfod, was called upon to prove his ability before he could be admitted a Bard. 'I was placed under acute examination before I graduated,' he wrote in a letter to Eben Fardd, 'I had to compose I do not know how many *englynion* impromptu. The Gorsedd, from now on, is to be more than a pretence.'

It was generally agreed that the Gorsedd of the Bards should have complete charge of all matters relating to the Eisteddfod. It was, furthermore, to act as a court of appeal to which any person could turn for advice on any matter and, for that purpose, it was decreed that the Gorsedd would 'be open every day until Saturday, inclusive, and any one might give notice to the committee if he has any subject to bring forward.'

The reforms were accepted in principle at a meeting held at the Town Hall, Denbigh, on 9 August 1860, and an Eisteddfod Council was set up, with Creuddynfab as its secretary. The Council met at Shrewsbury in November, but it made slow progress until Gwilym Tawe (William Morris) produced a scheme upon which, with some amendments, the future conduct of the Eisteddfod was based. He recognised the contribution of the bards in preserving the language and in promoting the Eisteddfod, and made sure that they were granted privileges, such as free access to all Eisteddfod meetings, and given complete control on all matters relating to the Gorsedd. This did not satisfy Ab Ithel, however, who felt that there had been an infringement on the sovereignty of the Gorsedd.

The Eisteddfod was opened at a Gorsedd ceremony held on the green sward before Denbigh Castle, at which Clwydfardd read the Proclamation in Welsh, and Talhaiarn read it in English, and the town's welcome was conveyed in an address by Major Sir Hugh Williams, Bart., of Bodelwyddan. Twenty new Bards were initiated, among them John Evans (I. D. Ffraid) and William John Roberts (Gwilym Cowlyd), and sixteen Ovates and two Druids. Thomas Gee, who had been critical of the organisation of the Eisteddfod, was taken, seemingly reluctantly, to the Maen Llog to be installed a Druid. Ioan Madog, in an account of the incident that he gave to a local newspaper, stated that Gee had been 'made bard by compulsion. He was dragged by two bards, I presume, within the Gorsedd, as a drunken man is dragged by two members of the police force to the Bridewell. Mr Gee staggered, protested, and would not be a druid; but Clwydfardd shouted, "Get him in, let him be a druid." Mr Gee was got in, and made a druid.'

In addition to those who were admitted as Ovates, Bards and Druids, Meilyr Môn (Hugh Owen), vicar of Llannerch-y-medd, who had been initiated a Bard and a Druid at Aberffraw in 1849, was elevated to the degree of 'Archdruid', which gave him the right to wear a sash, and at the Llanerch-y-medd Eisteddfod in 1869 it was reported that he wore the 'archdruid's sash'.

Some of the Gorsedd members in north Wales objected to the holding of 'the reformed Eisteddfod' in its alternate venues and, in mid-August 1861, a fortnight before the Eisteddfod that was to take place at Aberdare, they held their own rival 'national eisteddfod' at Conway Castle. A procession led by the Royal Penrhyn Brass Band paraded through the town and, when they reached the castle gate, the men of the Llandudno Volunteer Regiment defiled and presented arms as the Bards passed through on their way to 'the Bardic Circle of

Federation' that had been erected in the castle grounds. Gwalchmai presided on the Maen Llog, assisted by Ab Ithel and Glasynys, and he admitted two Bards, seven Ovates, and sixteen Honorary Members. Gwilym Cowlyd was adjudged to have written the best *awdl* on *Mynyddoedd Eryri* (The Mountains of Snowdonia) and he was installed in a chair that was claimed to have 'been presented by Queen Elizabeth to the Bards of Britain'.

The Aberdare Eisteddfod, in 1861, was the forerunner of the festival as it is today in the sense that it was established as a national event to be held in alternate years in the north and south of Wales, and this was reflected in the subject for a series of *englynion* to 'The Union of North and South Wales in the General Eisteddfod, the first of which was held at Aberdare'. The prize of two guineas was awarded to Ifor Cwm Gwys (John Thomas: 1813-66), a self educated poet who admitted to being unable to write his name until he was past thirty years of age. The Chair was won by Nicander for his *Cenedl y Cymry* (The Welsh nation), and a medal was awarded to Ceiriog for his memorable pastoral poem, *Alun Mabon*.

Sir Hugh Owen, the educationist, arranged sessions during the Eisteddfod at which 'subjects calculated to elevate the moral and social character of the Welsh people' could be discussed, and went on to establish a Social Science section attached to the Eisteddfod.

Gwalchmai presided at the opening Gorsedd ceremony held on the Castle Square at Caernarfon on Tuesday, 26 August 1862. Several candidates presented themselves for bardic honours and were duly admitted after being examined, but it would appear that the method of examination was still not satisfactory for, in the following October, a panel comprising Clwydfardd, Nefydd (William Roberts: 1913-72), Hwfa Môn, Cynddelw, Ioan Emlyn and Gweirydd ap Rhys, was appointed to prepare 'a new code of procedure for awarding Gorsedd degrees.' There is no record of any recommendations by the panel and admission continued as hitherto for the next six years.

Hwfa Môn was awarded the chair at Caernarfon for his poem *Y Flwyddyn* (The Year) and Eben Fardd, one of the eight other competitors, was said to have been so disappointed that he suffered a premature death.

After the Gorsedd ceremony held on the Saturday morning, Ceiriog called at the office of *The Caernarvon and Denbigh Herald* where he met the composer Brinley Richards (Cerddor Tywi). The Eisteddfod Committee had decided to perform a choral work entitled 'The Prince of

Wales's Cantata', with words by Ceiriog, during the Eisteddfod in order to mark the coming of age of Albert Edward, Prince of Wales, (later King Edward VII), and his forthcoming marriage to Princess Alexandra of Denmark. During their conversation, the poet and the composer, who had never met before, decided that a special song should be written for the occasion, with Ceiriog providing verses that would be set to music by Richards. Ceiriog sent him two verses, the first beginning with *Ar D'wysog Gwlad y Bryniau*, which Richards, not being fluent in Welsh, asked George Linley to translate into English. Richards, even then, rewrote the first four lines, including the chorus line 'God bless the Prince of Wales'. It was sung for the first time by the famous baritone Sims Reeves in January 1863, and the song proved to be an immediate success and was highly acclaimed by the London papers and music journals, one of which stated that it 'may now fairly rank as a National Anthem'. Richards was complimented by the Prince and received £10 for his copyright. Ceiriog wrote that he 'never had a farthing … because we Welsh bards, though ridiculed to death, are as proud as we are poor'. He maintained that he simply 'happened to be the first to take the hint to write a suitable anthem, only to be intended for Wales … I never thought or intended it to be translated into English and still less into the languages of India.' The song was ousted from any place that it may have had as a national anthem by *Hen Wlad Fy Nhadau* (Land of My Fathers) that had been written in 1856 and had become popular following its inclusion in Owain Alaw's *Gems of Welsh Melody* in 1860.

It was announced at the Caernarfon Eisteddfod that the festival would be held, the following year, at Swansea, with an assurance that 'the divisions and dissensions between the people of the North and the South had been buried for ever.' The bards of Gwynedd felt, however, that it would be too far for them to travel to south Wales and so they arranged to hold a 'Chair Eisteddfod' at Rhyl at the end of August, 1863, a fortnight, again, before the 'National Eisteddfod' at Swansea. A Gorsedd ceremony was held, at which Gwrgant (William Jones: 1805-86) read the Proclamation Scroll, and, in a marquee, the president, Sir Watkin Williams Wynn delivered the opening address. The Chair was won by Robert Thomas, whose pseudonym 'Ap Vychan' was chosen because of his descent from the Vaughans of Caer-Gai, Llanuwchllyn.

Opposition to the reformed Eisteddfod also led to the formation of a rival Gorsedd in north Wales. Discontentment at the increasing practice of rewarding poems written other than in strict metre, in addition to the objection to the alternate venues, had driven Ab Ithel and Gwalchmai to invite those who were interested in 'the preservation of the ancient rights and privileges of the Gorsedd, Chairs and Eisteddfodau of the Isle of Britain, now threatened by a certain society which unjustly calls itself "Yr Eisteddfod",' to write to them. Gwilym Cowlyd, on his part, invited graduated Bards to an *Arwest Farddonol* (a Poetic Minstrelsy) on the shores of Llyn Geirionydd on 3 August 1863. He called it 'Gorsedd Taliesin' from the belief that the sixth century poet, Taliesin, had been born of the goddess Ceridwen beside the lake, and he gave himself the title *Pencerdd Pendant* (Chief Bard Positive). As he had been initiated a Bard at the Denbigh Eisteddfod in 1860, he had every right to hold a Gorsedd and to admit new members. In 1887 he became an Anglican, and appointed Penfro (William John Morgan: 1846-1918), vicar of Llansanffraid Glan Conwy, as Chief Druid. The Arwest prospered for a while but declined in the latter years of Gwilym Cowlyd's life, when he was declared bankrupt and became increasingly eccentric. He died in 1904, and all traces of Gorsedd Taliesin died with him.

Despite the efforts that had been made to bring order to the system of awarding bardic degrees, there were still anomalies. Glan Menai (Griffith Jones: 1836-1906) appeared at the Swansea Eisteddfod as a candidate for the degree of Ovate and was examined by Dewi o Ddyfed, Glan Alun and Tegai (Hugh Hughes: 1805-64), and they were so impressed with his abilities that they offered him a degree of Bard as well. Instead of feeling gratified, however, he complained that this was irregular and that the advanced degree had been forced upon him by the examiners.

Bishop Connop Thirlwall of St David's was 'invested with the badge of a Druid of the Isle of Britain' by Dewi o Ddyfed who, after he had tied a white ribbon round his arm, expressed the hope that the Bishop's 'life and doctrine will be as pure and spotless as the white ribbon.'

The Eisteddfod pavilion erected at Llandudno, for the Eisteddfod in 1864, was 'one of the most handsome and convenient buildings ever erected in Wales for any purpose,' according to the journal, *Yr Eisteddfod*, and a Gorsedd Circle, of tall pillars, with a massive Maen Llog as its centre, had been constructed near The Parade. Gwalchmai presided over the Gorsedd ceremonies and admitted, in addition to Ovates, Bards and Druids, Edward Stephens (Tanymarian) and Sarah Edith

Wynne (Eos Cymru) to the degree of *Pencerdd*, and three reverend
gentlemen to the degree of *Archdderwydd*, one of whom was John
Griffiths (Glan Aeron), rector of Neath and, later, Archdeacon of
Llandaff.

Talhaiarn, who was the stage conductor at the Eisteddfod, was said
to have spent most of the night holding court at the Royal Hotel and
was 'as jolly as Bacchus'.

An outsider's view of the Gorsedd held that year was given by
Matthew Arnold during a series of lectures he delivered at Oxford,
where he occupied the Chair of Poetry, in 1865, and which were
published in the following year in *The Cornhill Magazine* and, then, in
his book *On the Study of Celtic Literature and Other Essays*. He told his
audience that, when he and his family were on holiday at Llandudno,
he saw workmen:

> putting up a large tent-like wooden building, which attracted the eye of
> every newcomer, and which my little boys believed (their wish, no
> doubt, being father to their belief) to be a circus. It turned out, however,
> to be no circus for Castor and Pollux, but a temple for Apollo and the
> Muses. It was the place where the Eisteddfod, or Bardic Congress of
> Wales, was about to be held; a meeting which has for its object (I quote
> the words of its promoters) 'the diffusion of useful knowledge, the
> eliciting of native talent, and the cherishing of love of home and
> honourable fame by the cultivation of poetry, music and art.' My little
> boys were disappointed; but I, whose circus days are over, I, who have a
> professional interest in poetry, and who, also hating all one-sideness and
> oppression, wish nothing better than that the Celtic genius should be
> able to show itself to the world, and to make its voice heard, was
> delighted. I took my ticket, and waited impatiently for the day of
> opening. The day came, an unfortunate one; storms of wind, clouds of
> dust, an angry dirty sea ... First we went to the Gorsedd, or preliminary
> congress for conferring the degree of bard. The Gorsedd was held in the
> open air, at the windy corner of a street, and the morning was not
> favourable to open-air solemnities ... The presiding genius of the mystic
> circle, in our hideous nineteenth-century costume, relieved only by a
> green scarf, the wind drowning his voice and the dust powdering his
> whiskers, looked thoroughly wretched: so did the aspirants for bardic
> honours; and I believe, after about an hour of it, we all of us, as we stood
> shivering round the sacred stones, began half to wish for the Druid's
> sacrificial knife to end our sufferings. But the Druid's knife is gone from
> his hands; so we sought the shelter of the Eisteddfod building.

Arnold's lectures gave a prestige to the study of Welsh and other Celtic literature, and led to the establishment of a Chair of Celtic Studies at Jesus College, Oxford, in 1877. Its first incumbent was Professor (later Sir) John Rhys, who was present when Arnold delivered the lectures.

The Gorsedd ceremonies were held within the castle walls at Aberystwyth in 1865. Candidates for Gorsedd honours had to answer questions on the strict and free metres before admission, and it was recommended that certificates of proficiency should be provided for Gorsedd members. Prizes were awarded in two *pryddest* competitions, but no *awdl* to 'St Paul' was considered worthy of the chair. Prince Louis Lucien Bonaparte, nephew of Napoleon, who was studying the Celtic languages, had been expected to preside at the opening session but had been unable to do so, and his place was taken by Glan Aeron.

In response to an invitation from Sir Hugh Owen 'to read a paper on some topic of Celtic literature or antiquities' at the Eisteddfod held at Chester in 1866, Matthew Arnold apologised for his inability to do so in a reply that appeared in several newspapers and included the following paragraph:

When I see the enthusiasm these Eisteddfods can awaken in your whole people, and then think of the tastes, the literature, the amusements, of our own lower and middle classes, I am filled with admiration for you. It is a consoling thought, and one which history allows us to entertain, that nations disinherited of political success may yet leave their mark on the world's progress, and may contribute powerfully to the civilisation of mankind. We in England have come to that point when the continued advance and greatness of our nation is threatened by one cause, and one cause above all. Far more than by the helplessness of the aristocracy whose day is fast coming to an end, far more than the rawness of a lower class whose day is only just beginning, we are imperilled by what I call the 'Philistinism' of our middle class. On the side of beauty and taste, vulgarity; on the side of morals and feeling, coarseness; on the side of mind and spirit, unintelligence – this is Philistinism. Now, then, is the moment for the greater delicacy and spirituality of the Celtic peoples who are blended with us, if it be but wisely directed, to make itself prized and honoured. In a certain measure the children of Taliesin and Ossian have now an opportunity for renewing the famous feat of the Greeks, and conquering their conquerors. No service England can render the Celts by giving you a share of her many good qualities, can surpass that which the Celts can at this moment render England, by communicating to us some of theirs.

Arnold had also warned, in his letter, that one had 'to avoid the danger of giving offence to practical men by retarding the spread of the English language in the principality', which appeared to be unnecessary advice, for the festival was becoming increasingly anglicised. At Chester, the Proclamation had been read in English by Talhaiarn, who reminded Sir Watkin Williams Wynn, the president, and the gathered assembly, that the wars between the Welsh and the English were over, 'never to return ... we are now to all intents and purposes, one people.' Then again, the president of the Council, Glan Aeron in a letter of apology for his absence, stated that he was 'much attached to the old language and hope it will be long preserved, but I cannot sympathise with those amongst us who would exclude from profit or enjoyment everyone who cannot understand it.'

At the opening Gorsedd ceremony, that took place on The Roodee, during the Eisteddfod, the Gorsedd Prayer was read, in Welsh and in English, by Meilyr Môn. The silver medal offered for a *pryddest* on 'Arthur and the Round Table' was awarded to Llew Llwyfo (Lewis William Lewis: 1831-1901), and the chair, for an *awdl* on *Y Môr* (The Sea) was won, again, by Ap Vychan. Since the revival of the Eisteddfod, the chaired bard had been presented with a medal, sometimes referred to as the Chair-Medal, but at Chester, Ap Vychan was the recipient of a suitable oak chair.

'Regulations of the Eisteddfod', that were issued during the Chester Eisteddfod, appeared to vest all authority in the Eisteddfod Council, and made little reference to the Gorsedd of Bards. Peter Mostyn Williams read a paper during the festival entitled *Yr Eisteddfod*, in which he opened up the old argument by suggesting that the Chair should be awarded either for the *awdl* or the *pryddest*, and a sub-committee was appointed to give consideration to the suggestion. The sub-committee was unable to make any recommendation at the Carmarthen Eisteddfod the following year, and it was decided that the *status quo* should remain, except that a Crown be awarded for the best *pryddest*, the two awards to be of equal merit and distinction.

The language question was also under discussion at Carmarthen. The chairman of the local committee, the Rev. Latimer Jones, vicar of St Peter's, in his address at the opening session, claimed that 'the Eisteddfod does not desire a separate national language, a separate nationality, nor a separate and distinct existence' for Wales. This did not meet with the approval of the audience, who gave him a hostile reception. The local newspaper, however, congratulated him for introducing 'what was much required – an English element – into the meetings, to an extent far greater than has ever been attempted,' and his sentiments were echoed by a number of speakers, among them the Recorder of Carmarthen, Judge John Johnes of Dolaucothi who, shortly afterwards, was to be murdered by his Irish butler, and Glan Aeron, who felt that 'we cannot afford to spend all our time in the perpetuation of the Welsh language' and considered that 'the language is very well able to take care of itself.' There was also opposition to the engagement of professional singers from London 'to the exclusion of the Cambrian muse', for which Brinley Richards, himself a native of Carmarthen, was held responsible.

The Carmarthen Eisteddfod was described as 'a grand meeting of bards, literati and others interested in the prosperity of Wales and in its material and intellectual improvement.' A procession of some two thousand people was formed on the Tuesday morning and, led by the Mayor, it marched through the town, that was bedecked with banners and bunting. There were three *pryddest* competitions for which silver and gold medals were awarded, but only two entries for the Chair, offered for an *awdl* on *Y Milflwyddiant* (The Millenium), and the adjudicators being unable to choose which deserved the prize, Ceiriog was asked to do so. He awarded it to Gwalchmai and, as he was not present, Rhydderch o Fôn took his place for the chairing ceremony. The admission of eighteen new members to the various degrees excited *The Times* correspondent to refer to 'the puerile fopperies of making Druids in broadcloth and Ovates in crinolines.'

The Ivy Bush Hotel capitalised on its earlier connection and hung out a banner bearing the words: 'Home of the Bards, Old Ivy Bush.' The bards took the message to heart, and duly celebrated there, and one of them composed a suitable *englyn*:

> Nef y bardd yw'r Ivy Bws – ti gei fwyd,
> Ti gei fîr a ffwgws;
> O deui drwy drothwy'r drws,
> Nag amau gael lle cwmw's.

(The Ivy Bush is the poet's heaven: you get food and beer and tobacco.

As you come through the door, you are assured of finding a seemly place.)

Despite the decision to award a Crown to the winner in the *pryddest* competition, there was none available to place on the head of Llew Llwyfo at the Ruthin Eisteddfod in 1868 for his poem *Elias y Thesbaid* (Elijah the Tishbite), and he had to be content with a silver medal and twenty sovereigns. No one was considered worthy of the chair, offered for an *awdl*, uniquely, on the same subject. 'The elongated faces of the bards were a sight to see,' it was reported, and one of their number, Tudno (Thomas Tudno Jones: 1844-95), 'emitted an englyn which spoke of the coveted chair as so much timber for sale.'

There were still those who regarded the Crown as a sop, and felt that it was no match for the Chair. Gweirydd ap Rhys, supported by Llew Llwyfo, put forward a motion 'that the Chair should henceforth, and for ever, be awarded for the best verse, in whatever metre or metres the poet should choose,' but this was defeated by an amendment setting up a panel of the leading poets with a remit to study Welsh prosody and to recommend the most appropriate metres to use in a contest for the chair. There is no record that they made any recommendations.

The refusal of the local committee at Ruthin to hand over any of the proceeds to the Eisteddfod Council added to the parlous state of the Eisteddfod's finances and, despite contributions made by the President of the Council, Glan Aeron, and others, it was no longer possible to carry on, and appeals made to the nation fell on deaf ears. A request to hold the Eisteddfod at Brecon the following year was not considered by that town, which stated bluntly that it would have nothing to do with the Eisteddfod while it was in debt.

The Council was able to arrange for an Eisteddfod to be held at Holywell that year. It was described officially as the Holywell Crown Eisteddfod in order to emphasize that the winner in the chief poetry competition would be 'honoured by placing a crown upon his head rather that being installed in an oak chair' and, as it were to enhance the prestige of the Crown, there was no *awdl* competition. The Crown, 'a simple and narrow fillet of silver with a leek cut in front', was awarded to Mawddwy Jones, rector of Bagillt, for his *pryddest*, in the form of an elegy on the death of Hugh Pugh, the rector of Mostyn. He was escorted to the platform, to the sound of 'See the Conquering Hero Comes', and the Crown was placed on his head by a Miss Baker, of Holywell. There is no record of a Gorsedd ceremony and it may be that none was planned in view of the absence of a Chair competition.

The 'reformed' National Eisteddfod had come to an end and, in a letter that he wrote in July 1871, Glan Aeron was compelled to refer to it as 'an institution of the past', but he regretted that 'it was stopped just at the time when it was making its usefulness felt.'

An Eisteddfod was held at Llannerch-y-medd in August 1869 at which Meilyr Môn, the vicar of the parish, presided, wearing 'the archdruid's sash', as he had been admitted an 'archdruid' at the Denbigh Eisteddfod in 1860, and he was assisted by Clwydfardd and Gwalchmai in admitting more than twenty-five new members. Mynyddog was not present to receive the chief award and one John Jones took his place in the chairing ceremony. This was the first of a series of eisteddfodau, some describing themselves as 'national', that were held during the 1870's in north Wales.

The eisteddfod held at Tremadoc in 1872 was advertised as the Snowdonia Chair Eisteddfod, and the Gorsedd ceremonies were conducted by Owain Gwyrfai (Owen Williams, Waunfawr), who overslept one morning and was greatly taunted for keeping a crowd of bards and spectators waiting.

A proposal that was made to establish a Welsh Antiquarian Society met with widespread support and, by the time of the Mold Eisteddfod, in 1873, more than three hundred applications for membership of such a society had been received. The promoter of the idea, Y Thespiad (John Roose Elias: 1819-81), formally proposed the formation of the Society, but the proposition was overtaken by events that led to the establishment of a National Library.

The Honourable Society of Cymmrodorion, when it was formed in 1753, had expressed an intention to establsih a library that could be housed, in the first instance, at a school on Clerkenwell Green. The possibility of having a National Library in Wales, however, was first discussed at the Mold Eisteddfod in 1851, and again at the Eisteddfod at Llangollen in 1858, when George Hammond Whalley of Plas Madog, Llangollen, presented a petition to the Gorsedd of Bards in the following terms:

> That it is expedient to erect a building which shall be devoted to the maintenance and promotion of the interests of Wales, such building to combine the several purposes following: A museum and record office, for the preservation of MSS, books and relics relating to Wales and the ancient British Empire. An office for promoting the regular administration of the Gorsedd and the Eisteddfod; for preserving the pro-

ductions of the Eisteddfodau past and to come, as also the names of
those who have been distinguished therein, and of all patriotic Welshmen who may be deemed worthy of such honours, according to the
rules and regulations hereafter to be laid down by the authority of the
Gorsedd; that such building be erected in a conspicuous position and
that it be dedicated to the memory of Llywelyn, and the other princes,
heroes, and bards of Wales most distinguished in ancient times, as
having done honour to their country in establishing or maintaining its
immemorial renown.

He further proposed that the building should be transferred to the
care of a number of trustees who should hold it for the benefit of the
bards and literati of the Principality entirely, and offered to provide a
site on his estate at Plas Madog or, if that were not acceptable, to
purchase a suitable site elsewhere. The proposal was received and
carried unanimously and, although nothing came of it, it promoted
an idea that was raised again at the Eisteddfod held at Mold in 1873
following a suggestion by Sir Hugh Owen that a room be set aside at
the new College at Aberystwyth in which books could be stored so as
to form the nucleus of a library for Wales. The Gorsedd held two
meetings at Mold, at the first of which John Williams (Glanmor),
vicar of Ebbw Vale, stated that he had travelled specially to the
Eisteddfod from Monmouthshire to propose that steps be taken to
establish a National Library and that a committee be formed to take
the necessary action. At the second meeting it was reported that the
College authorities had agreed to earmark a room for the required
purposes and gentlemen possessing manuscripts and documents of
interest were asked to deposit them in that room. A committee of
eminent persons was formed, including Sir Hugh Owen, Sir John
Rhys, Sir John Puleston, Benjamin Thomas Williams, Recorder of
Carmarthen, Robert Ellis (Cynddelw), John Griffith (Y Gohebydd),
Thomas Richard Lloyd (Yr Estyn), Enoch Salisbury, Brinley
Richards and John Williams (Glanmor). The committee made little
impact, however, until 1896, when it was reconstituted and, three
years later, 'the Welsh Library' was set up in a room at the College,
and John Glyn Davies was appointed the first librarian at a salary of
£50 per annum. The matter was pursued at subsequent Eisteddfodau
and a Royal Charter was granted in 1907 and the building of the
present National Library of Wales began two years later at Penglais
on land presented by Lord Rendel. In an address that he gave to the

Honourable Society of Cymmrodorion in 1933, Sir William Llywelyn Davies, the National Librarian, acknowledged that

> the persons who met at Mold during the National Eisteddfod laid the
> foundation of structures of the importance of which they did not
> dream. I am glad to think and to be able to remind you that in a very
> large measure Wales owes its National Library and its National
> Museum to resolutions passed by a group of patriots who met together
> at a National Eisteddfod.

The Gorsedd of Bards moved in procession from the Town Hall to
the Bailey Hill on the opening day of the Mold Eisteddfod in 1873, but
it soon had to seek shelter from the rain and hold the ceremony indoors, with Yr Estyn conducting the proceedings. The weather per-
mitted the ceremonies to be held on Bailey Hill the following three
mornings during which a considerable number of persons, some of
them of doubtful worthiness, were admitted Gorsedd members.

This liberal admission was the subject of much comment and it
aroused Ceiriog to announce that he and Mynyddog, in an effort 'to
diminish the disorder and confusion of the Eisteddfodau and utilise the
great power which the national gathering possessed', proposed to put
forward a plan to establish a society of literati and musicians to be
known as *Urdd Y Ford Gron* (the Order of the Round Table). A lengthy
list of *Probatory Rules* were drafted with the aim of taking complete
charge of the organisation of Eisteddfodau and, in the absence of any
other controlling body, either for the Eisteddfod or the Gorsedd of
Bards, there seemed to be no objection to it assuming such responsibility.

The Eisteddfod held at Bangor in 1874, though described as
'national', was a local affair, and although Gurnos (Evan Jones: 1840-
1903) was 'chaired with the customary pomp', there is no evidence that
the Gorsedd of Bards took part in the ceremony. There were Gorsedd
ceremonies at Pwllheli in 1875, however, but even so, it was the Order
of the Round Table that proclaimed 'the forthcoming Great Wrexham
Eisteddfod of 1876 and the regulations under which degrees will be
granted there ... in the three orders of Ovates, Bards and Druids.'
Ovates and Bards had to pass examinations and 'Druids must be
ministers of the gospel unanimously approved by the Bards in Gorsedd.'

The Gorsedd ceremonies at Wrexham were conducted by Yr Estyn, assisted by Ceiriog and other members of the Round Table who were also members of the Gorsedd of Bards. The Chair, offered for an *awdl* to *Helen Luyddawg* (Helen of the Hosts), was awarded to one whose *nom-de-guerre* was Eurebius but its possessor, Taliesin o Eifion, the Llangollen inn sign painter, it was announced from the audience, had died. The Gorsedd officers retired from the stage, and reappeared in mourning as the band played 'The Dead March'. The chair was draped in black, and Madam Edith Wynne (Eos Cymru) sang 'Dafydd y Garreg Wen'.

At the Wrexham Eisteddfod, Clwydfardd was appointed Archdruid. He was a native of Denbigh where, like his father, he pursued his trade as a clockmaker. He was also a Wesleyan lay-preacher and frequently walked thirty miles to keep a Sunday engagement, and at the age of eighty, he succeeded in reaching the summit of Snowdon. He was awarded a silver medal for a translation of Goldsmith's 'Deserted Village' in 1827. He was the official bard of the Aberffraw Eisteddfod in 1849, and he maintained that he had been 'appointed Arch-druid ... in 1860; but it was at Wrexham Eisteddfod in the year 1876 that I was licensed as Arch-druid of the Gorsedd of Bards of the Isle of Britain.'

This would appear to be the first time for the title of Archdruid to be used to describe the chief, or presiding officer of the Gorsedd of Bards. Contrary to popular conception, Iolo Morganwg was not known by that title either at the ceremony on Primrose Hill, where he was called *Prif Fardd*, or at the Carmarthen Eisteddfod in 1819 where he was chosen to be *Y Bardd Gweinyddol* (The Executive Bard), The term had been used in the 1770's, albeit in a different connection, by certain gentlemen of Anglesey who met in Beaumaris in September 1772 to establish the Druidical Society of Anglesey. An 'Archdruid' presided over the affairs of the Society and invested new members, who were presented to him by four Regulators after a declaration had been administered to them by a Sub-Druid. In 1790 they acquired a uniform comprising a blue coat, white waistcoat and breeches and red stockings, and the officers wore medals of office. The members were drawn from the landowners, clergy and yeomen of Anglesey and included the Marquess of Anglesey and Lord Bulkeley. The Society was solely concerned with charitable work and the promotion of agriculture.

Many of the members of the Gorsedd of Bards were members also of friendly societies, and bardic processions were frequently joined by detachments of such societies, usually wearing their regalia. At the Abergavenny Eisteddfod in 1840, the procession included representatives of the Odd Fellows and the Ancient Order of Druids, and elsewhere there were Freemasons, Ivorites and members of the Ancient Order of Foresters taking part, and Gorsedd members who were also members of these societies might turn out wearing their insignia. Dr Geraint Bowen has pointed out that, at the Abergavenny Eisteddfod in 1838 there were two 'archdruids' present, but they were the chief officers of 'groves' of the Ancient Order of Druids. Cawrdaf, who presided at that Eisteddfod, wore 'a loose robe that had purple stripes on its sleeves, with a wide belt of purple, and adorned with fringes, while across his shoulder was a wide sash of blue silk from which hung a gold star and, on his head, he wore a cap of purple brocaded silk with a wide brim,' which may have been the vestments of one of the friendly societies.

The Caernarfon Eisteddfod of 1877 was duly proclaimed at a Gorsedd ceremony held in a field near Twthill the previous September, and a bond was delivered at a public meeting held that evening providing a guarantee of £10 by each of 201 inhabitants against any loss that might be incurred in staging the festival.

The Eisteddfod was opened on the morning of 21 August 1877 by Clwydfardd at a ceremony held within the bardic circle that had been erected on the green sward, close to Queen Eleanor's Gate, within the castle walls. The eisteddfod session that followed was remarkable in that no bards responded to the invitation to deliver addresses, and Sir Llewelyn Turner was able to proceed with the adjudication of the eight essays submitted on 'The Industrial Training Ship, for North Wales and the Border Counties, moored in the Menai Straits'.

Gwilym Eryri (William Roberts: 1844-95) won the Chair, for his ode on *Ieuenctid* (Youth) and he 'was chaired with all the pomp and ceremony usual on such occasions.' A special prize was offered for a poem on *Cadair Ddu Wrecsam* (The Black Chair of Wrexham) in memory of Taliesin o Eifion.

In September 1878, the Gorsedd of Bards held a proclamation ceremony at Llandrindod at which the Archdruid Clwydfardd duly proclaimed that an Eisteddfod would be held in that town the following year, but it was not found possible for it to take place. The South Wales Chair Eisteddfod was held at Cardiff, however, under the patronage of the Lords Aberdare, Tredegar and Plymouth, but there were no Gorsedd ceremonies. The Chair was awarded to Gurnos, and

Llew Llwyfo, who conducted the chairing ceremony, proclaimed him 'Chaired Bard of the Eisteddfod of South Wales'.

The Eisteddfod held at Birkenhead in 1879 was jointly organised with the Order of the Round Table, and new Gorsedd officers were created and given such titles as *Marchog yr Orsedd* and *Yswain yr Orsedd* (Knight and Squire of the Gorsedd). The 'Royal National Eisteddfod' held at Conway that year was sponsored by Gwilym Cowlyd and his Taliesin Gorsedd.

The South Wales Chair Eisteddfod Committee arranged for an Eisteddfod to be held at Swansea in 1880. It was proclaimed at a Gorsedd ceremony held outside the Royal Institution of South Wales where 'a few small rough stones had been placed in position to represent the Gorsedd, or throne, in the centre, and the signs of the Zodiac in the circle round it,' with Glanffrwd (Gwilym Thomas) presiding. No one deserved the prize for a *pryddest* on *Iolo Morganwg*, but the chair was awarded to Dewi Wyn o Essyllt for his ode to 'Sir Rowland Hill', the originator of penny postage.

1880 – 1899

THE EISTEDDFOD returned to Caernarfon sooner than one would have expected. Arrangements were made for a proclamation ceremony to be held inside the castle walls on 24 October 1879, but a downpour of rain had made the ground soggy, and so the bards met on the Castle Square, where Clwydfardd conducted a brief ceremony before the assembled company retired to the Sportsman Hotel for a luncheon at which Sir Hugh Owen proposed a toast to the success of the Eisteddfod, and Clwydfardd responded. Then they returned to the Square and formally proclaimed the next year's Eisteddfod.

The Eisteddfod was opened with a Gorsedd ceremony, held on the Castle lawn on 24 August 1880.

A paper suggesting a reform of the Eisteddfod, that had been read by Sir Hugh Owen at a meeting of the Honourable Society of Cymmrodorion at the Freemasons Tavern in London the previous April, was read again when the Society met at the Town Hall, Caernarfon, during the Eisteddfod. Sir Hugh expressed his belief that 'the present plan of devolving upon a local committee the whole of the care and responsibilities connected with the holding of a National Eisteddfod is, in many respects, unsatisfactory,' and suggested that it was 'desirable that a permanent Association be formed, and an Executive Council appointed, for the purpose – among others – of co-ordinating with the local committee and assisting in rendering the Eisteddfod arrangements in all their parts such as may still further increase the popularity and extend the usefulness of our national institution.' The proposed association would be designated 'The National Eisteddfod Association' and its Council, 'The National Eisteddfod Council'. A motion that the reform should be entrusted to the Cymmrodorion Society was defeated, lest the control should go to London and, instead, a Provisional Committee was appointed 'to consider and define the scope and functions of the Association'. The Provisional Committee comprised twenty-seven good men, of whom nineteen were members of the Gorsedd, and Thomas Marchant Williams, later stipendiary of Merthyr Tudful, was appointed its honorary secretary. It had been laid down in the resolution that it should meet at the Raven Hotel in Shrewsbury on Friday, 17 September 1880 at 10 o'clock in the forenoon, and so it did, and agreed that the objects of the Association should be:

> to raise, by means of annual subscriptions and donations, a fund which shall enable the Association to offer prizes for competition, and in other ways to promote the usefulness of the Eisteddfod;
>
> to secure the holding of only one National Eisteddfod in each year, in north and south Wales alternately, to select the place at which it shall be held, and fix the conditions attached to the selection;
>
> to assist in providing a suitable pavilion, in selecting appropriate subjects for competition, in securing men of eminence to preside at the Eisteddfod meetings, in preparing the Eisteddfod programme, and in upholding the authority of the Gorsedd;
>
> to publish a volume of the Eisteddfod transactions annually.

The first annual meeting of the Association was held at the Castle Hotel, Merthyr Tudful, when the Eisteddfod was held there in 1881, with the Archdruid Clwydfardd in the chair. Sir Watkin Williams Wynn was appointed president of the Association, and Sir Lewis Morris chairman of the Eisteddfod Council.

The Provisional Committee had lost no time in publicising the Eisteddfod that it had decided to hold at Merthyr, and in giving notice of the subjects set for the poetic competitions. Arrangements were made for examining candidates for Gorsedd degrees, but no one seems to have thought of erecting a Gorsedd circle. Sir Vincent Evans recalled that when he, and some others, arrived at the Gorsedd site on the first morning of the Eisteddfod, at the pine end of the market, they found that a Maen Llog of some sort had been provided but nothing more, and so they gathered what stones they could find, and a few bricks to make up the deficiency. The Gorsedd ceremony, over which Clwydfardd presided, wearing a broad-brimmed hat and a large badge on his chest, was opened with a blast on a borrowed trumpet, and peace was thrice declared on a sword borrowed from a passing soldier. The Chair, for an *awdl* on *Cariad* (Love) was awarded to Dyfed (Evan Rees: 1850-1923), and the Crown to Watcyn Wyn (Watkin Hezekiah Williams: 1844-1905) for his *pryddest* on *Bywyd* (Life).

A Gorsedd Circle was not considered necessary at the Denbigh Eisteddfod in 1882, and the ceremonies were held within the castle walls. Among those initiated were two American women. A gold medal, with a picture of a chair on the observe side, was offered for an *awdl* on *Dyn* (Man), but no entry was considered worthy of it.

The Cardiff Eisteddfod was opened on Monday, 6 August 1883, shortly after ten o'clock in the morning, with a Gorsedd ceremony conducted by 'the venerable bard Clwydfardd', within a stone circle that had been erected in a field adjoining the Taff Vale railway's engine shed, which had been converted for use as the Eisteddfod pavilion. The official report of the proceedings expressed the view that 'as the Gorsedd is one of the few links which bind the Eisteddfod, as we know it, to a remote and honoured past, it is much to be regretted that its meetings at Cardiff were held amid such incongruous surroundings,' and went on to complain that 'the charm of the ancient and impressive rite was destroyed by the screeching of railway locomotives on the one side and by the many hideous noises of a show-ground on the other.' The Cardiff Corporation, however, had decorated the streets of the town 'with Venetian masts, decked out with shields, and supporting festoons of banners. At the entrance to the way which, diverging from the busy streets of Cardiff, led through quiet lanes to the Eisteddfod field, was erected a magnificent and artistic triumphal arch.' Hospitality was offered each morning to those who took part in the Gorsedd processions, and the Mayor gave a banquet in the Town Hall in honour of the occasion.

The Marquess of Bute presided over the Monday morning session and gave an address on 'The Ethnology of the Welsh'. After several bardic recitals, Glanffrwd, the conductor, called for the adjudication on the main essay 'for the best History of Welsh Literature, in English or Welsh, from the year 1300 to the year 1650'. Marchant Williams stated that seven entries had been received, three of which had been written in Welsh, and that the three adjudicators had decided to award £70 of the £100 prize money to 'Llywelyn Vychan', the remainder to be paid to him after he had made certain corrections to the work. The winner was Gweirydd ap Rhys and the essay was later published as *Hanes Llenyddiaeth Gymreig 1300-1650*.

There were ten entrants for the prize of twenty guineas and a medal in the *pryddest* competition for a poem, written in English or in Welsh, on 'Llandaff'. One of the adjudicators, Elis Wyn o Wyrfai, vicar of Llangwm in Denbighshire, wanted to award the prize to one of the three entrants who had submitted a poem in English under the *nom-de-plume* 'Cyfeiliog', but his fellow-adjudicator, Glanmor, rector of Ebbw Vale, was against doing so, although he considered it to be the best poem, because the entrant had 'wandered from his simple theme, Llandaff, to dilate upon the weakness and failure of the Church in Wales'. Glanffrwd was asked to arbitrate and he decided in favour of 'Cyfeiliog', who turned out to be Anna Walter Thomas. The youngest of twenty children born to Thomas Fison and his wife, of Barningham in Suffolk, Anna was proficient in languages and had begun to take an interest in Welsh at the instigation of Dr Charles Williams, Principal of Jesus College, Oxford. In 1871 she married David Walter Thomas, vicar of Llandygai, and gave of her time to assist quarrymen to pursue their intellectual studies. She narrowly missed being appointed to the chair of modern languages at University College, Bangor in 1884. She survived her husband by fifteen years, and died in 1920 at Dyffryn Ardudwy.

No one was considered worthy of receiving the Chair, for an *awdl* to *Y Llong* (The Ship), which was the first time for it to be withheld two years running.

Thomas Henry Thomas, the Cardiff artist and naturalist, who had arranged an art exhibition at the Eisteddfod, was admitted into the Gorsedd as an Ovate under the name 'Arlunydd Penygarn'.

At the closing Gorsedd ceremony, it was announced that the petition of the people of Liverpool to have the Eisteddfod held there in 1884 had been granted, with a request that presidential speeches be curtailed to not more than twenty minutes each and that the comments of adjudicators 'should be made as short as is compatible with full and efficient adjudications'.

In the preface to the *Transactions of the Royal National Eisteddfod of Wales, Liverpool, 1884*, it is stated that nearly twelve months had elapsed, since the idea of holding the Eisteddfod at Liverpool had been conceived, before the request had been placed before 'the only tribunal which could stamp the proceedings with true Eisteddfodic authority, namely the Gorsedd of Bards, acting in conjunction with the National Eisteddfod Association, and there had been no opportunity of procuring this sanction before August 1883, when the Eisteddfod was held at Cardiff.' This was to explain why the Proclamation ceremony had not taken place until Saturday, 10 November, that year. It was held on Kensington Fields, on the banks of the river Mersey, and was opened at noon by the Archdruid, Clwydfardd. It was then adjourned, so as to take lunch, until three o'clock in the afternoon when, in the presence of a large concourse of people, the Archdruid read the Proclamation. A banquet was held after the ceremony at the Adelphi Hotel.

The opening Gorsedd ceremony of the Liverpool Eisteddfod was held on Tuesday morning, 16 September 1884, on Austin Hill, Shaw Street, before a large gathering of spectators. After Gwalchmai had intoned the Gorsedd prayer, Hwfa Môn gave an address in Welsh, and Morien spoke in English. At the closing ceremony, on the Thursday morning, there was an audience of more than five thousand people.

The Crown, for a *pryddest* on *Yr Aipht* (Egypt) was awarded to Edward Foulkes, and the best *awdl* in memory of *Gwilym Hiraethog* was submitted by Dyfed. The account of the chairing ceremony given in the *Transactions* states that 'the Archdruid, Clwydfardd, accompanied by the adjudicators Gwalchmai, Tafolog and Isaled; the Poet, Hwfa Môn; the Sword Bearer, Ceiriog; the Knight Master of Ceremonies, Gwilym Alltwen; and a trumpeter, appeared on the platform, wearing

Liverpool 1884. The Archdruid Hwfa Môn and Gorsedd members wearing sashes and Masonic-style aprons bearing the Gorsedd mystic mark.

sashes and aprons with mystic insignia. The Archdruid and his train succeeded a body of bards and literati walking in double file, some wearing green and others blue robes.' Dyfed was duly installed in the Chair, which was the gift of the Honourable Cymmrodorion Society, and, after receiving congratulatory *englynion* from a number of bards, Madame Edith Wynne sang the scena 'Far greater in his lowly state' from Gounod's *La Reine de Saba* as the chairing song.

The efforts of Arlunydd Penygarn, at the Cardiff Eisteddfod, to promote art, were supported by Major Cornwallis West, Lord Lieutenant of Denbighshire, who deplored the standards of art in Wales and urged that promising students be sent to Hubert Herkomer's school in London.

The Aberdare Eisteddfod opened with a Gorsedd ceremony held in 'a grassy enclosure close to the Eisteddfod Pavilion on Tuesday morning, 25 August 1885.' Clwydfardd, now eighty-five years of age, ascended the Logan Stone and called on the Archdeacon of Llandaff, the Venerable John Griffiths (Glan Aeron), to offer the Gorsedd prayer. The Sword was partly unsheathed three times, and the assembly responded thrice to the Archdruid's call for peace. He then 'declaimed the national watchwords' and 'declared the National Eisteddfod of 1885 to be open, *yng ngwyneb haul, llygad goleuni* (in the face of the sun, the eye of light).' Eos Dâr (Daniel Evans: 1846-1915) sang a song of welcome, and Clwydfardd, in his address, said that he 'was anxious that every Welshman should learn the English language thoroughly. They would then be one language to the fore of their Saxon friends,' having already affirmed that the Eisteddfod was 'ample proof that the Welsh language was not going to die.'

The subject set for the Chair was the Gorsedd motto *Y Gwir yn erbyn y Byd* (The Truth against the World) and Hwfa Môn and Dyfed worked their way through the crowd to bring the winner, Watcyn Wyn, to the platform to the strains of 'See the Conquering Hero comes'.

Inclement weather on the Thursday morning caused the Gorsedd ceremony to be postponed until the afternoon, when three reverend gentlemen were initiated as Druids, while the eminent poets Watcyn Wyn, Nathan Wyn (Jonathan Rees: 1841-1905) and David Onllwyn Brace were admitted to the rank of Bards.

Dr Matthew Arnold addressed the vast audience, estimated at between six and seven thousand, and said that he still retained the same interest in the Eisteddfod that he had expressed twenty years earlier to his friend Sir Hugh Owen. He declared that the immense audience exceeded anything that he had thought possible, but it also 'exceeded in bounds what it was possible for his voice to reach, and therefore having expressed his interest in the Eisteddfod, he meant to take his leave of them and sit down.'

Caernarfon town was gay with bunting to welcome the 1886 Eisteddfod as the Gorsedd of Bards paraded to the opening ceremony held within the castle walls. After the ceremony, the procession, led by the Caernarfon Town Band moved to the pavilion that had been built for the earlier festivals.

The following day, the band of the 4th Battalion Royal Welch Fusiliers led the procession to the Gorsedd Circle where the Lord Mayor of London, the Right Honourable Alderman John Staples, was admitted by the Archdruid Clwydfardd as an Ovate by the bardic name of 'Gwyddon'. As Gwyddon was the Chief Justice of Britain in Celtic times, it was considered an appropriate name for the Lord Mayor as the first magistrate in the land. He, in responding, recalled that he had been brought up in that 'unique area of druidical remains, Stonehenge.' He was present as the representative of the people of London, so many of whom were of Welsh blood, and it was his pleasure to extend a warm welcome to the National Eisteddfod to visit the metropolis the following year.

A petition signed by thirty gentlemen of London had been addressed 'to the Bards, Ovates and Druids of the Isle of Britain in Gorsedd assembled at Aberdare, and to the National Eisteddfod Association,' inviting them to hold the Eisteddfod in the city in 1887, and pledging that it 'shall be planned and carried out as a Welsh gathering; that it shall be as Welsh as possible in every particular, and that we will withstand all suggestions which may tend to give it an English character or complexion.' Despite a vociferous protest by Gwilym Cowlyd, who maintained that the Gorsedd of Bards had 'no right to take the National Eisteddfod beyond the boundaries of Wales,' it was agreed that the Eisteddfod would be held in London in 1887.

A silver crown was provided at Caernarfon for the winner of the epic poem to 'Constantine the Great', and it was placed upon the head of Cadfan who is said to have worn it on every possible Eisteddfodic occasion afterwards. The Chair was awarded to Tafolog for an *awdl* on the subject *Gobaith* (Hope).

During one of the Gorsedd ceremonies, Clwydfardd announced that it had been decided to revive the titles of the Primitive bards Plennydd, Alawn and Gwron, and that they would be assigned to himself, Gwalchmai and Hwfa Môn.

A number of candidates had presented themselves for Gorsedd degrees, and the *Transactions* noted whereas 'it was evidently considered necessary in 1862 that candidates should possess a knowledge of Welsh literature and of the rules of Welsh poetical composition, in these days, we are so advanced as to consider candidates fully qualified if they have been successful in business, even if they do not known a word of Welsh, and we pay the penalty for our enlightened action when we hear them make a joke of the Gorsedd and all its surroundings.'

Friday was declared 'the quarrymen's day', and trainloads of quarrymen and their wives and families arrived in time for the closing Gorsedd ceremony on the Friday morning. During the ceremony, it was announced that a panel of poets and literati had been set up to prepare a revised, and standard, spelling for future use in the Welsh language.

The Daily Telegraph of 10 August 1887 reported that 'last November, the Inner Temple Gardens were the scene of, as regards the locality, an unexampled observance. A Gorsedd of Bards of the Isle of Britain was held there, and Proclamation made by the Archdruid [Clwydfardd] from the Maen Llog, or Logan Stone, that "when the age of Christ is 1887, and when the period of the Bards of the Isle of Britain shall approach the Feast of the Solstice [sic] of Autumn, namely the Equinox of the Harvest of Corn, after the Notice and Summons here given to all Wales, at the sound of the trumpet from this conspicuous place in the hearing of Country and Queen, a Gorsedd and Eisteddfod will be held in the Chief City of Lud in Britain,"&c.'

'The conditions specified being considered as met yesterday, the Gorsedd and Eisteddfod were duly held: the scene of the ancient Bardic Court being a spot in Hyde Park near the Magazine, while that of the Eisteddfod was the Albert Hall.'

In case one should wonder why the Welsh should bring 'their peculiar institution out of Wales into a great centre of Anglo-Saxon and, it is to feared, unsympathetic life,' the paper adds, 'one should remember that London contains a very considerable population' of Welsh people and, 'it would appear, moreover, that our Cymric neighbours have not forgotten the time when the Isle of Britain was all theirs.'

The report refers to eisteddfodau previously held in London and, in particular, to one held in 1826 under the presidency of Lord Clive and the patronage of 'some of the finest families in the Kingdom,' at which the Duchess of Northumberland gave away the prizes. It admits that these were London-Welsh affairs, 'but yesterday the neighbourhood of the Albert Hall suggested that it had, for the time, become entirely Cumbrian' [sic].

The audience at the Albert Hall was disappointed when Henry Richard, MP, read a letter from W. E. Gladstone, the former and future Prime Minister, who had previously expressed great interest in the Eisteddfod, stating that he was unable to be present on account of a cold and loss of voice.

Lithographic illustrations in *The Graphic* and the *Illustrated London News* of a Gorsedd ceremony in Hyde Park, show the acting Archdruid, Hwfa Môn, in the absence of Clwydfardd, standing on the Maen Llog, surrounded by Gorsedd officers, while other bards stood with a foot on each of the small stones that formed the Gorsedd Circle. Most of them wore morning suits, except for a few who were dressed in breeches and leggings. None wore robes, or any distinguishing badges or medals.

The subject of the *awdl* was 'Queen Victoria', and the winner, Berwyn (R. A. Williams), was installed in a fine oak chair and presented with a gold medal and a cheque for £40. The Crown was won by Cadfan for an epic poem on 'John Penry', and a gold medal was presented to him by the Prince of Wales.

The Bards assembled at the Guildhall at Wrexham early on the morning of Tuesday, 4 September 1888, and marched in procession, led by the band of the 2nd Battalion, Royal Welch Fusiliers, through the

A Gorsedd ceremony in Hyde Park, when the Eisteddfod was held in London in 1887.

streets to an open space in Argyle Street, where a stone circle had been erected, with a blue rope placed round it to keep out members of the public. Among those who received Gorsedd honours were Sir Watkin Williams Wynn, who was given the bardic name 'Eryr Eryrod Eryri', which is also the family motto, Professor (later Sir) John Rhys (Rhys Glan Rheidol), and his wife, as 'Myfanwy Eryri', W. Llewelyn Williams (Llwydfryn), Elvet Lewis (Elfed), Anna Walter Thomas (Morfydd Eryri), and Charles Ashton, the police constable of Dinas Mawddwy who had been awarded the prize for the essay on *Gorsedd Beirdd Ynys Prydain* at that Eisteddfod. Morien was elevated to the rank of Druid and had, by now, been given an office in the Gorsedd, as *Gwyddon Tir Iarll*. Upon the death of Myfyr Morganwg earlier that year, he had assumed the mantle of archdruid of *Gorsedd Y Maen Chwŷf*.

Philip Yorke of Erddig, who had served as a Captain in the Royal Denbigh Rifles, presented his sword to the Archdruid Clwydfardd, and it was used for ceremonial purposes for the next twelve years. The Mayor of Wrexham, Councillor Edward Jones presented a silver trumpet that served as the *Corn Gwlad* until it was replaced in 1901.

The absence of a governing body to control the affairs of the Gorsedd had led to interference by other bodies, and in particular by the Eisteddfod Association, and when an offer was made by the Association to 'support the arms of the Gorsedd' it was quickly refused by the bards, who could see their affairs being managed by people with little knowledge of the bardic tradition, many of them London businessmen. It was therefore decided, during the Wrexham Eisteddfod, to establish *Cymdeithas yr Orsedd*, with its own constitution under which it appointed permanent officers for the first time. Clwydfardd was confirmed in the Archdruidship, and Eifionydd (John Thomas: 1848-1922) was appointed Recorder. Membership was confined to those who had been admitted members of the Gorsedd of Bards, and also to those who were already members of Gorsedd Taliesin and Gorsedd y Maen Chwŷf, but thereafter, only the initiates of the Gorsedd of Bards would be recognised as members. Admission to membership was by examination, the syllabus of which would be publsihed a year in advance.

The Brecon Eisteddfod was proclaimed 'with all the ancient rites from the Maen Llog of the Gorsedd by the Archdruid Clwydfardd, assisted by the Archdeacon of Llandaff, Hwfa Môn, Nathan Wyn, Dewi Wyn o Essyllt, Watcyn Wyn, Dewi Môn, Tudno, and other

Certificate of admission to the Gorsedd by examination.

Bards, on Tuesday, the 10th July 1888, at "Clos-y-Castell", within what is now the ruins of the Castle of Bernard Newmarch, at Breck-nock. The ceremony was conducted with all the pomp and grandeur of ancient days.' The procession, from the Shire Hall to the Castle, was led by the band of the 3rd Battalion, South Wales Borderers, followed by the Friendly Societies, townsmen and trades, masters and scholars of Christ College, patrons, Justices, the Police Force, and the Corpor-ation, with the Mayor and Deputy Mayor, in their robes, walking each side of the Archdruid, and then came the Gorsedd banner, followed by the Bards. The streets were thronged with onlookers, and more than two thousand people were present at the Gorsedd ceremony.

At the first Eisteddfod session, held in 'the grand pavilion erected at Cerrig Cochion' to accommodate eight thousand people, Father Ignatius, of Llanthony Abbey, 'commenced a vigorous and impas-sioned address by exclaiming at the top of his voice, in pure Welsh: '*Os anghofiaf di, Jerusalem, anghofied fy neheulaw ganu* [If I forget thee, O Jerusalem, let my right hand forget her cunning] – a sentiment which elicited hearty applause.' He urged his audience to 'study the literature and the teaching of the Druids, and the more you examine them the more you will be astonished at the great amount of truth – Christian truth – that rises pre-eminently among their pages.' He was initiated a Druid, under the bardic name 'Dewi Honddu', and so were William Abraham (Mabon), 'the miners' MP' and popular Eisteddfod con-

ductor, and Thomas Henry Thomas (Arlunydd Penygarn), who had
been admitted an Ovate at Cardiff in 1883.

The heavy drinking that had been a feature of the tavern gatherings
did not disappear with the new-style Eisteddfod. Talhaiarn, born the
son of the Harp at Llanfairtalhaearn, openly flouted the rising calls for
temperance, and often set out to shock his more puritanical fellow-
poets, while other prominent Eisteddfodwyr, like Dafydd Ddu Eryri,
Eben Fardd, Ceiriog and Llew Llwyfo, were not teetotallers. Sir
Thomas Marchant Williams, in his satirical novel, *Land of my Fathers*,
made one of his characters say that 'Poets and pothouses always run
together in my mind,' and, ten years later, the *Daily News* commented
that even 'in recent times, the bards' meetings were little better than
drunken orgies', but goes on to praise the Gorsedd which, though it
'still leaves much to be desired, nevertheless deserves the nation's
gratitude for having rescued the meetings of bards from the clutches
and the influence and the customs of the tavern.'

The Gorsedd, and the Eisteddfod, found a defender in Lord Tredegar
who, in his presidential address, on the Wednesday, stated that he
'never could understand how it was that enlightened English people
and enlightened English newspapers treated with ridicule the great
institution of the Eisteddfod,' and thought that it might be because it
bore a name which they found difficult to pronounce, and which many
of them could not understand, or it might be because 'the institution
was opened with a Gorsedd, which they described as silly and useless.'
He had had the pleasure, and the honour, of taking part in the Gorsedd
at Hyde Park, when the Eisteddfod was held in London in 1887, that
was witnessed by a large crowd, drawn from all ranks, 'from the hard-
worked Member of Parliment down to the street Arab,' and he had
not seen anybody 'look upon the proceedings with ridicule,' nor had he
heard 'one remark which indicated contempt.'

The bards met on 2 September 1890, a damp morning, for the opening ceremony of the Bangor Eisteddfod, in a circle that had been
erected at Maesylleiniau, near the railway station. The Gorsedd prayer
was read by the Right Reverend Daniel Lewis Lloyd (Llwyd o Lan
Llethi) who had recently been appointed Bishop of Bangor and, after
the ceremony, the company adjourned to the Eisteddfod Pavilion in
Ffordd y Garth, where the 1874 Eisteddfod had been held, to hear an
address by the president of the day, the Viscount Cranbrook, Lord
President of the Council.

The Queen of Romania was admitted an honorary member under

the name Carmen Sylva, the pen name under which she published her poems and other literary works. She took part in the ceremonies at which Iolo Caernarfon (John John Roberts: 1840-1914) was awarded the Crown for his poem to 'The Noble Army of Martyrs' and Tudno the Chair for his ode to 'The Labourer'. After the chairing ceremony, the bards were entertained to a feast at the Bishop's Palace.

Sir John Puleston, treasurer of the Eisteddfod Association, and G. W. Taylor, of the Colonial Institute, informed the Archdruid that new robes would be made available for himself and the Gorsedd members and, on the advice of a small panel, it was decided that the design of the robes should be a loose gown, with black biretta-like caps for the members, and a mitre of the same colour for the Archdruid, all bearing the Gorsedd emblem.

A constitution for the National Eisteddfod Association, that had been formulated during the Brecon Eisteddfod, was formally adopted at Bangor. It defined the relationship between the Association and the Gorsedd of Bards, stating that the members of the Gorsedd would also be members of the Association, and that the Gorsedd would have sole charge of all ceremonial matters relating to the Eisteddfod.

The proclamation of the Swansea Eisteddfod, in July 1890 began with a great procession, led by the Swansea Police Band and comprising, along with the Archdruid and the Gorsedd of Bards, the Freemen, Friendly Societies, the Harbour Commissioners, Members of Parliament, the Mayor, and the Mayors of the surrounding boroughs, making their way to Victoria Park, where the ceremony was enlivened by musical items rendered by the Glantawe Male Voice Choir.

At the Eisteddfod, the Crown for an epic poem on 'Oliver Cromwell' was won by Hawen (David Adams), and Pedrog (John Owen Williams: 1853-1932) was awarded the Chair for an *awdl* to *Yr Haul* (The Sun). The local committee was criticised for not having provided a suitable site for the Gorsedd ceremonies, which had to be held within the curtilage of the Town Hall during the Eisteddfod week.

A fine setting for the opening ceremony of the Rhyl Eisteddfod, on 6 September 1892, was provided by the Palace and Summer Gardens, where a Gorsedd Circle had been erected. A splendid domed pavilion of palatial proportions had been built for the purpose of housing the Eisteddfod, fit to receive the Lord Mayor of London, Sir David Treharne Evans, KCMG, who delivered an address and was afterwards invested with the honorary degree of Ovate. Both the Bishop and Dean of St Asaph were admitted to the Druid Order, and Henry

Taylor, Town Clerk of Flint, became an Ovate with the title
'Flintensis'. A Gorsedd hymn, specially composed by Cadfan, 'was
sung by persons standing at the cardinal points of the circle, and the
audience joined in the final verse.'

Iolo Caernarfon was given the Crown for his poem to *Dewi Sant*, but
only a half of the monetary prize of £20, the other half being given to
Ben Davies, Pant-teg. The adjudicators, Watcyn Wyn and Gwynedd
(Thomas Edwards: 1844-1924) could not agree which was the best of
the eight *awdlau* submitted on *Y Cenhadwr* (The Missionary), and Hwfa
Môn, who was asked to arbitrate, awarded the Chair to Gurnos.
Cynonfardd, who was to become the first Archdruid of the American
Gorsedd, was advanced to the degree of Druid.

At a meeting of the Honourable Society of Cymmrodorion held
during the Eisteddfod, H. Elvet Lewis (Elfed) revived an old argument
when he suggested offering the Chair in alternate years for the *awdl*
and the *pryddest*, and when the Chair was offered for the *pryddest*, the
winner of the *awdl* should receive the Crown, He also proposed that
the winners of the Chair and of the Crown should not be allowed to
compete for either during the five succeeding years. No action was
taken but, in 1894, it was reiterated that the two awards were of equal
status and distinction.

The Gorsedd agreed to support the endeavours of the American
Welsh to hold an International Eisteddfod at Chicago in 1893, and
Hwfa Môn travelled to the United States for that purpose.

When the Eisteddfod was held at Pontypridd in 1893, the Gorsedd
ceremonies were conducted at the Maen Chwŷf, which Clwydfardd,
at his advanced age, had some difficulty in mounting. His presence
upon it, however, was significant in that he took precedence over
Morien, the 'archdruid' of the Maen Chwŷf.

Gwilym Cowlyd caused a stir when he announced, without previous
warning, that he disagreed with his fellow adjudicators, Pedrog and
Dyfed, who wanted to award the Chair to Ceulanydd Williams for his
awdl on *Pulpud Cymru* (The Pulpit of Wales), He felt that Ben Davies
deserved the prize and wanted to explain his reasons for thinking so,
but the president, Judge Gwilym Williams, of Miskin, refused to allow
him to do so, as the purpose in having three adjudicators was to have a
majority decision in the event of a disagreement, and this had been
achieved. Cowlyd persisted, and a noisy altercation only came to an
end when the Judge, to the delight of the audience, ordered him off the
stage.

Robes were worn for the first time by members of the Gorsedd of Bards at the opening ceremony of the Caernarfon Eisteddfod held on the Castle Square, on 10 July 1894. The Druids were in white, the Bards in blue, and the Ovates in green, and they all wore black birettas, except for the Archdruid, Clwydfardd, who wore a mitre. The robes had been presented by the Marquess of Bute, Lord Mostyn, Sir Watkin Williams Wynn, and other subscribers, and it would appear that their provision was not unconnected with the visit of the Prince and Princess of Wales to the Eisteddfod.

Their Royal Highnesses, with their daughters, Princess Victoria and Princess Maud, arrived at the Pavilion to the strains of a consort of harps, and sat through the ceremony of installing Ben Davies as a crowned bard, for his poem on 'Lord Tennyson', and his investment by the Princess of Wales.

The royal party then proceeded to Castle Square, where the be-robed bards had arranged themselves within a bardic circle. The Prince of Wales was conducted to the foot of the Maen Llog, where Hwfa Môn tied a green ribbon round his right arm, and the Archdruid admitted him as an Honorary Ovate under the bardic name 'Iorwerth Dywysog'. Princess Alexandra was admitted in a similar manner, as 'Hoffedd Prydain', Princess Victoria as 'Buddug' and Princess Maud as 'Mallt'. Lord and Lady Penrhyn, Lord and Lady Mostyn, and Philip Yorke of Erddig, were also given bardic honours.

Robes were worn for the first time, at Caernarfon in 1894, with biretta-style hats, except for the Archdruid, Clwydfardd, who wears a mitre which, like the 'birettas', bears the Gorsedd symbol. Kneeling in front of the Archdruid is Eifionydd, the first Gorsedd Recorder (1888-1922). To his right and wearing a collar with medals, is Cadfan who was Archdruid, briefly, in 1923. On the left of the Mayor of Caernarfon stands Hwfa Môn, Archdruid 1895-1905.

The adjudicators again could not agree on the award of the Chair, for an ode on *Hunan-aberth* (Self-sacrifice), but Dyfed and Pedrog, with Tudno dissenting, declared Elfed worthy of the Eisteddfod's chief prize, and he was installed by the Archdruid Clwydfardd, who performed the ceremony for the last time, as he died in the following October.

The Llanelli Eisteddfod opened at a Gorsedd ceremony held in the People's Park on the morning of 30 July 1895 with an announcement of the death of Clwydfardd, who had been Archdruid for eighteen years, though he claimed to have held the office since 1860. Watcyn Wyn informed the gathering that Hwfa Môn had been appointed in his place.

Hwfa Môn was a native of Trefdraeth, in Anglesey, but he had left there with his parents at an early age to live at Rhos-tre-hwfa, near Llangefni. After being apprenticed as a carpenter, he entered the ministry and eventually had charge of Fetter Lane Congregational Church, later to become Tabernacle, King's Cross. He returned to Wales in 1881, first to Llannerch-y-medd, and then to Llangollen. He was admitted a member of the Gorsedd at Aberffraw in 1849, and won

Gorsedd ceremony on the Castle Square, Caernarfon, 1894, with the Archdruid Clwydfardd admitting as members of the Gorsedd, the Prince of Wales (later Edward VII) as 'Iorwerth Dywysog', Princess Alexandra as 'Hoffedd Prydain', and the Princesses Victoria and Maud (later Queen of Norway) as 'Buddug' and 'Mallt'.

Arlunydd Penygarn (Thos. Henry Thomas), the first Herald Bard (1895-1915).

the Chair at Caernarfon (1862), Mold (1873), and Birkenhead (1878), and the Crown at Carmarthen in 1867. He was an impressive figure on the Maen Llog, with a great presence and a voice that 'made the hills echo'.

It was announced that Arlunydd Penygarn (Thomas Henry Thomas) had been appointed Herald Bard, the first to hold the office by that name, although there is an earlier reference to Gwilym Alltwen at the Liverpool Eisteddfod in 1884, as 'Knight Master of the Ceremonies'. Thomas was the son of Thomas Thomas, principal of the Baptist College at Pontypool. He was educated at the Bristol School of Art and at the Royal Academy in London, and he went to Paris and to Rome before settling down as a painter, first in London and then in Cardiff, where he was one of the promoters of the Royal Cambrian Academy and a prominent member, and president, of the Cardiff Naturalists' Society.

When it was announced that the Chair had been awarded to Pedrog, for an *awdl* on *Dedwyddwch* (Happiness), it transpired that he was not present, and his son took his place at the chairing ceremony. Llew Llwyfo won the prize for the *pryddest* on *Ioan y Disgybl Annwyl* (John the Dear Disciple) and, this time, he was given a Crown, that he had missed being the first to receive, at Ruthin in 1868.

A contemporary account stated that 'the picturesque appearance of the platform' had been 'considerably heightened since the introduction of Gorseddic robes.'

In admitting Judge Edwards, of Scranton, Pennsylvania, Hwfa Môn said that he was 'a Judge who ruled the American people with the mere shadow of his finger'. Sir John Jones-Jenkins, MP, in a presidential speech, said he had heard that 'the Scotch Highlanders had got up an Eisteddfod at Oban, with a Campbell in the fore-front, shewing that they had not forgotten the old Celtic Institution.'

There was an art exhibition at Llanelli, 'far in advance of all previous shows,' and Professor Herkomer, the art adjudicator, called on the Eisteddfod authorities to 'make the art section as important as they had made the music.'

Happy Valley provided a pleasant background for the Gorsedd ceremony held to open the Llandudno Eisteddfod, on Tuesday, 30 June 1896. After the Archdruid, Hwfa Môn, had given his address, Sir Arthur Stepney, in the green robe of an Ovate, mounted the Maen Llog and presented him with the Gorsedd Banner, which had been designed by the Herald Bard, Arlunydd Penygarn. Miss Lena Evans, of Cardiff, who had done the embroidery work on the Banner, was admitted into the Gorsedd under the name 'Brodes Dâr'.

Professor Herkomer regretted that he had been unable to complete the new robe that he was designing for the Archdruid, but promised to have it ready by the next Eisteddfod. He had delved into history in order to find a suitable design, for the robe and for certain items of regalia, and this had taken more time than he had anticipated.

Professor (later Sir) John Morris-Jones published a series of articles in the magazine *Cymru*, in 1896, in which he cast doubt upon the authenticity of the Gorsedd of Bards which, he concluded, was the invention of the Glamorgan bards in the seventeenth century. It was only later that he realised that Iolo was its begetter.

In the same year, Gwilym Cowlyd, the 'Chief Bard Positive' of Gorsedd Taliesin, published the following Proclamation:

> Be it known to all the Loyal Bards of Wales, and all to whom it may concern: that no lawful Chair or Gorsedd of Welsh Bards will be held at Llandudno in connection with the Eisteddfod this year, and that any person or persons joining a counterfit fabrication or fraudulent imposition aping such functions will divest themselves of every Bardic privilege.

Hwfa Môn appeared in the Archdruid's new robes and marks of office designed by Herkomer at the Proclamation of the Newport,

Gwent, Eisteddfod, held at Belle Vue Park on 27 August, 1896. Herkomer had also promised to design, and have made, a Grand Sword to replace the military sword presented by Philip Yorke at Wrexham.

At the Eisteddfod the following year, the Archdruid stated that Lord Tredegar had offered to present a Hirlas Horn to the Gorsedd, and his lordship confirmed that it was being made by William Goscombe John and, as it was not yet completed, he called upon his niece, Mrs Charles Twysden-Hoare, to present a model of the Hirlas to the Archdruid.

The Archdruid Hwfa Môn wearing the new robe, crown and breastplate, designed by Herkomer, at the Proclamation of the Newport, Gwent, Eisteddfod in 1896.

Lord Tredegar was admitted into the Gorsedd as 'Ifor Hael', and others admitted included David Lloyd George (Llwyd o Wynedd), T. E. Ellis (Cynlas), Ernest Rhys (Rhys Goch o Ddyfed), Thomas Shankland (Glan Cynin), Joseph Bradney (Achyddwr Glan Troddi) and Lewis Davies Jones (Llew Tegid). Representatives of the Celtic countries admitted included Count Plunkett and Edmond Fournier d'Albe (Negesydd yr Ynys Werdd).

Gorsedd y Beirdd met, appropriately, on Bryn yr Orsedd at Blaenau Ffestiniog for the opening of the 1988 Eisteddfod, and the large gathering of spectators could not resist being amused at the sight of a billy-goat, for some unaccountable reason, being led into the circle where it remained, 'with a devotional look, among the sons of the Muse.'

Professor (later Sir) John Rhys, Fellow (and later Principal) of Jesus College, Oxford, stated, during his presidential speech, that 'the Gorsedd and the festival had never been more flourishing.'

Among those admitted into membership of the Gorsedd were Professor (later Sir) Edward Anwyl (Iorwerth Anwyl), Alfred Perceval Graves (Canwr Killarney) and John McIntosh (Capten o'r Alban). The Archdruid extended a welcome to the delegates that were present from Ireland and Scotland, and from America and South Africa and, especially, to the Welsh people from Patagonia. While greeting a Welsh missionary from darkest Africa, he called *cynghanedd* into account in stating that he had been *yn twtio'r Hotentotiaid* (Tidying up the Hottentots).

In addition to the bards, arranged on the platform in their colourful robes for the chairing of Elfyn (Robert Owen Hughes: 1858-1919) for his ode to *Awen* (Muse), there was also a royal party comprising the Duke of Cambridge and the Duke of Saxe-Reimar. The Crown was won by Gwylfa (R. Gwylfa Roberts) for a poem on 'Charles o'r Bala'. David Lloyd George, Member of Parliament for Caernarfon Boroughs, said that he appeared as a representative of Parliament seeking the help of the Gorsedd to make the world a better place to live in.

The absence of rain at Blaenau Ffestiniog caused the poet Dyfed to express his surprise by saying *Bu'r Wyl heb ambarelo* (There was not an umbrella at the festival). The threat of rain, however, made the bards to decide against wearing their robes for the closing ceremony on the Friday morning.

The Gorsedd published a list of rules and regulations, in 1898, for the better governance of its affairs and the prosperity of the festival. It was ordained:

> that no other Eisteddfod or Gorsedd lasting more than one day should be held during the months of July, August and September so as not to militate against the success of the National Eisteddfod;
>
> that no officer or member of the Gorsedd should take part in any Eisteddfod that did not undertake to observe this request;
>
> that no announcement would be made from the Maen Llog unless it had been previously approved by the Gorsedd;
>
> that no member should take part in any examination or graduation connected with any Gorsedd other than the Gorsedd of Bards;
>
> that the *Grammar* of Dewi Môn, and the system of spelling it contains, should be the standard for Gorsedd examinations;
>
> that the Chair should be offered for the *awdl*, and the Crown for the *arwrgerdd* (epic poem), and that the one would be considered equal to the other as an award and as to degree, as recommended at the Gorsedd held at the Eisteddfod in 1867;
>
> that a poet may use in his *awdl* any one or more of the Gwynedd and Morgannwg *cynghanedd* measures;
>
> that Welsh is the language of the Gorsedd.

Dewi Môn (David Rowlands: 1836-1907), a native of Rhos-y-bol, in Anglesey, was a Congregational minister who became Principal of Brecon College in 1897 and, in that year, he published a *Welsh Grammar* in which he used the revised Welsh spelling.

The Eisteddfod that was to be held at Cardiff in 1899 was proclaimed, on 4 July 1898 at a Gorsedd ceremony held in Cathays Park on a site where the City Hall now stands, and beside a massive timber pavilion that had been erected for the occasion. The Gorsedd Circle was laid out to a plan prepared by the Herald Bard, Arlunydd Penygarn, with an outer circle of upright stones, a hundred feet in diameter, and an inner circle and a Maen Llog. The circle was later removed to the Gorsedd Gardens, opposite the National Museum of Wales.

On the evening before the opening of the Eisteddfod, the Mayor, Thomas Morel, gave a reception for the Gorsedd and Eisteddfod officials, and also the representatives of the other Celtic nations who were meeting at Cardiff to finalise the arrangement for the first Pan-Celtic Congress that was to take place in Dublin the following year. They included Lord Castletown, the chairman of the Congress Committee, Edmond Fournier d'Albe (Negesydd yr Ynys Werdd), its secretary, and Count Plunket, its treasurer. Sir Hubert von Herkomer presented the Archdruid with the Grand Sword that he had promised two years earlier. While doing so, he expressed his concern about the more extreme beliefs expressed by some of the Gorsedd members, and he may well have been referring to the recently published *Guide to the Gorsedd or Round Table and the Order of the Garter* by Morien, who claimed that Christianity was 'the venerable religion of the Druids brought back to the Isles of the Gentiles from the East under a Greek name.' Lord Tredegar presented the Corn Hirlas which had not been ready for the Newport Eisteddfod and had now been completed, at a cost of £359.

Gorsedd regalia displayed during the Bangor Eisteddfod in 1902. Cochfarf holds the Grand Sword: both he and the bard behind him are still wearing the 'biretta' hats. Arlunydd Penygarn holds the Corn Gwlad *presented by Alice Needham, of Dublin. In the forefront the Hirlas rests on its dragon stand.*

*Taldir (François Jaffrennou), secretary of the Breton delegation and later Grand Druid,
speaking from the Logan Stone at the Cardiff Eisteddfod, 1899.*

The Grand Sword was proudly carried by Cochfarf (Edward Thomas: 1853-1912) in the procession from the Town Hall to the Gorsedd Circle.

The procession arrived at the Circle in two parts. In the first, Lord Tredegar, Lord Windsor, and the Archdruid Hwfa Môn, 'with a druidess sitting either side of him', came, each in his own carriage, followed by the Gorsedd members and others. Some time later came the procession of the Celtic delegates, with a Breton piper leading Lord Castletown, and the Breton deputation carrying its banner and the two half-swords borne on silk cushions embroidered, respectively, with the arms of the Duchy of Brittany and the Welsh dragon. Then came the delegates from Scotland and Ireland, bearing banners, and the Speaker of the House of Keys representing the Isle of Man.

Three Gorsedd ceremonies were held during which the Archdruid admitted into membership of the Gorsedd, among others, Lord Windsor (Ifor Bach), Sir Laurence Alma-Tadema (Tadema), Sir William Goscombe John (Gwscwm), Thomas Christopher Evans (Cadrawd), Arthur Mee (Idris) and Ifano Jones (Ifano), and representatives of the Celtic countries, among whom were Lord Castletown (Arweinydd y Celtiaid), Count Plunket (Kelleen), Alice Needham (Telyn yr Iwerddon) and Padraig Pearse (Areithiwr) from Ireland; A. S. Macbride (Cilbrede) and Alexander Ingram (Colhion) from Scotland; John Hobson Matthews (Mab Cernyw), Richard Reynolds (Gwas Piran) and his wife, 'Merch Eia', from Cornwall; the Speaker of the House of Keys, John Moore, from the Isle of Man, and François Jaffrennou (Taldir ab Hernin), Jean le Fustec (Yann ab Gwilherm) and François Vallée (Ab Hervé) from Brittany.

The ceremony of uniting the half-swords took place on the Eisteddfod platform, with the Marquis de l'Estourbeillon presenting the
Breton half to the Archdruid, who married it to the Welsh half, borne
by Cynonfardd. There followed brief addresses by representatives of
Scotland, the Isle of Man and Ireland. After Padraig Pearse had
spoken, the Archdruid expressed the hope that he would use his
influence to assist in the formation of an Irish Gorsedd, but Pearse had
become disenchanted when he saw the other Celtic delegates drink a
loyal toast.

After he had announced that no poem, on *William Ewart Gladstone*,
was considered worthy of the Chair, Watcyn Wyn, in an effort to ease
the feeling of disappointment that overwhelmed the vast audience,
called upon the Scottish delegates, who were present in their kilts, to
perform a reel. He soon realised his mistake when Mabon leapt on to
the stage to indicate his objection to the defiling influence of a dance
on the Eisteddfod platform, and later, in his speech, as President of the
South Wales Miners' Federation and Liberal Member of Parliament
for the Rhondda, he denounced the practice and held that any
celebration of a Celtic occasion with a dance surely 'signalised the
beginning of a disastrous end'. Thomas Charles Edwards, later to
become the first Principal of the University College of Wales at
Aberystwyth, told the *Daily News* reporter that 'dancing on the
platform is certainly far below the ideal of the Eisteddfod', but added
that the incident had served 'the useful purpose of emphasizing the
great difference that after all exists between the different nationalities
of the Celtic stock.'

The Archdruid announced that the Gorsedd had accepted an invitation to be represented at the Pan-Celtic Congress to be held in
Dublin, and read the Proclamation of the 1900 Eisteddfod, that was to
be held at Liverpool.

1900 – 1949

THE NEW YEAR opened, in 1900, with the recurring argument concerning the relative merits of the Chair and the Crown, and the bards now came to a resolution that for a trial period of three years, the Chair would be awarded for the *awdl* one year, and for the *pryddest* the next, but the proposal was never put into practice. They also decided to hold the Gorsedd examinations 'in various centres in the Welsh counties and in some of the main cities of England, and not during the Eisteddfod week as hitherto,' but three months in advance. No one would be admitted into membership other than by examination, except those whom the Gorsedd Committee recommended for admission *honoris causa*. Successful candidates in the examinations would be enrolled on payment of three shillings, but those who had been awarded honorary degrees would have to pay ten shillings.

The band of *HMS Indefatigable*, and the Gorsedd Banner, led the procession of bards from their robing rooms at the Alexandra Hall, Islington Square, Liverpool, to the Whitley Gardens, in Shaw Street, for the opening of the National Eisteddfod on Tuesday morning, 18 September. The Hirlas Horn was carried by four bearers on a litter and laid before the Maen Llog, and the colourful scene was enhanced by 'the presence of so many fair ovates, whose flowing robes made them exceedingly attractive figures', among them being 'The Hon. Mrs Bulkeley Owen (Gwenrhian Gwynedd), Miss Ap Caledfryn, Miss Jones (Telynores Gwalia), and Miss Parry (Telynores Lleifiad).' Mr Edmond Fournier d'Albe (Negesydd o'r Ynys Werdd) conveyed greetings from Ireland, in Welsh, and predicted for the Irish language 'a life as long as water runneth and grass groweth'. Lionel Radiguet represented the Bretons, carrying the half-sword 'which played such a prominent part in the proceedings of the Pan-Celtic gathering at Cardiff the previous year'. The Lord Mayor of Liverpool, Alderman Louis Cohen, wearing his chain of office, was received into the Gorsedd by the Archdruid, Hwfa Môn, who gave him the bardic name of 'Cohenydd' and Dr Thomas Witton-Davies, Professor of Hebrew at Bangor, received the honorary degree of Druid under the bardic title of 'Myfyr Gwent'.

The large number of English people who attended the crowning ceremony on the Wednesday afternoon may have had difficulty in appreciating the reverence in which the subject of the crown poem, *Williams Pantycelyn*, was held, and were visibly impressed when the Crown was placed on the head of the successful poet, J. T. Job, Calvinistic Methodist Minister at Bethesda in Arfon and, later, at Fishguard.

In appreciation of his services, the Archdruid was presented with a national testimonial in the form of an illuminated address and a purse containing four hundred guineas, one hundred of which came from the Treasury on the recommendation of A. J. Balfour, later Prime Minister.

At the closing session of the Gorsedd, Llyfrbryf (Isaac Foulkes: 1836-1904) stated that he had been told by a senior police officer that 'the Welsh gathering, with the possible exception of a football crowd, was the largest he had seen in Liverpool, and was remarkable for its orderliness'.

At the opening Gorsedd ceremony at Merthyr Tudful in 1901, the Hon. Mrs Bulkeley Owen (Gwenrhian Gwynedd) drew attention to 'the deplorable state of art competitions at the Eisteddfod' and suggested that 'means should be devised to raise the tone of the exhibitions, by appointing a committee, withholding the prizes, or by some other means'. She strongly objected to giving prizes for imitation art and asked: 'Why paint their native slate to imitate marble? And why grain wood to imitate oak while they had the noble tree available?' which brought loud cheers. Arlunydd Penygarn, the Herald Bard, supported her and reminded the meeting that Professor Hubert Herkomer had made an appeal at the Llanelli Eisteddfod, in 1895, for an improvement in the standard of the art exhibitions. The Association decided to offer a gold medal, designed by Sir William Goscombe John, to encourage art competition.

Gwili (John Gwili Jenkins) was crowned bard for his poem *Tywysog Tangnefedd* (The Prince of Peace), and the Chair was awarded to Dyfed for the best *awdl* on *Y Diwygiwr* (The Reformer). Ten new bards were initiated, among whom were Crwys (William Crwys Williams: 1875-1968) and Sarnicol (Thomas Jacob Thomas: 1873-1945).

Immediately following the Merthyr Eisteddfod, a bardic deputation attended the Pan-Celtic Congress at Dublin and held an extraordinary

Gorsedd ceremony on the lawn of the Mansion House, at which Alicia Needham (Telyn yr Iwerddon) presented the Archdruid with a chased silver trumpet for use as the *Corn Gwlad*. The Lord Mayor of Dublin was admitted a member of the Gorsedd.

The bards gathered at Bangor the day before the official opening of the 1902 Eisteddfod so as to be present at the unveiling of a marble obelisk erected to the memory of Llew Llwyfo, poet, author, eisteddfod conductor and 'one of the most gifted Welshmen of the nineteenth century,' at the churchyard at Llanbeblig.

They met again that evening in order to consider the situation arising from the tendency by local committees to select subjects for Eisteddfod competitions without obtaining Gorsedd approval. Beriah Gwynfe Evans (Beriah) informed the members at the annual meeting, that despite protest made at Merthyr Tudful the previous year, the Bangor committee had insisted on setting subjects, some of which had been set in earlier competitions. As the Eisteddfod could not be held without the consent of the Gorsedd, the Gorsedd therefore had control over the local committee, and it was agreed that this control be exercised in future.

The Bangor City Football Ground now stands on the site, at Maesylleiniau, where the Gorsedd held its opening ceremony on Tuesday, 9 September 1902, 'within a circle of unhewn stones ... guarded by twelve Bards placed one by each stone, and two Keepers of the Gate stationed at the entrance.' Three thousand people had gathered to witness the band of *HMS Clio* lead the procession proceeding from the Magistrates' Court, where the bards had robed, to the Gorsedd Circle, where the Archdruid Hwfa Môn was supported by Caledfryn and Cochfarf, the Sword Bearer.

The Gorsedd Prayer was offered by Myfyr Gwent, and the *Aberthged*, a sheaf of wild flowers, grasses and corn, as a token of the fruits of the earth, was presented to the Archdruid by Mrs Hunter of Plas Coch (Cerddores Menai), and the Hirlas Horn, symbolic of the wine of welcome, by Mrs Yale, on behalf of her mother, the Mayoress of Bangor.

The Marquess of Anglesey was admitted to the Gorsedd as 'Cadrawd Fardd' and Professor Hugh Johnson, a solicitor living in Egypt under the name 'Moses', which he said he had chosen out of respect for the arch-lawyer who had received the tablets of the law on Mount Sinai.

Cornwall was represented at the ceremony, and a deputation from Ireland included Alfred Perceval Graves and Lord Castletown, who thanked the Archdruid and members of the Gorsedd who had attended the Pan-Celtic Congress at Dublin.

Professor (later Sir) John Morris-Jones gave the adjudication on *Ymadawiad Arthur* (The Departure of Arthur), and announced that the winner of the Chair, for an outstanding *awdl*, was 'Tir na'n Og'. The name was called by the Archdruid, but no one responded, and it transpired later that it was the pseudonym of T. Gwynn Jones, of the *Carnarvon and Denbigh Herald*. The Bangor Committee had also upset the authorities by having a new song composed for the chairing ceremony.

A message of greeting was received from *Vereinigter Alter Orden der Druiden*, the German branch of the United Ancient Order of Druids, which had heard of the Gorsedd of Bards from Herkomer. The German Archdruid, Fricke, and the Druids, Bards and Ovates of the German Order, wanted to convey their admiration of the endeavours of the Gorsedd of Bards in keeping alive the bardic tradition, and asked to be recognised by the Gorsedd, but there is no record of a response.

The Gorsedd met in the Circle that had been prepared for it in 1895, in the People's Park, Llanelli, during the 1903 Eisteddfod. The Chair was won, for the second time, by J. T. Job for an ode to 'The Celt', and the Crown was awarded, for a *pryddest* to 'Vicar Pritchard', to John Evans Davies (Rhuddfawr). He, and Eluned Morgan from Patagonia, were among those admitted members of the Gorsedd.

In making application for the 1904 Eisteddfod to be held at Wrexham, Robert Bryan, on behalf of the promoters, stated that Eisteddfod lovers had been disturbed by the increasingly anglicised nature of the festival and promised that Wrexham would remedy this matter, but it would not be prepared to share any profit with the Eisteddfod Association, as it was felt that this should be devoted to local charities. The Association stated that such an arrangement would not be acceptable, and decided to hold the Eisteddfod at Rhyl, where the opening ceremony was held on 'the Sandhill near the Alexandra Hospital'. The ceremony was attended by a large number of delegates from the Celtic countries who had been to the second Pan-Celtic Congress held at Caernarfon, some of whom were admitted members of the Gorsedd. Lady Mostyn (Rhian y Ffynnon) was also made an honorary member, and so were Mrs Laurence Broderick (Gwendolen) and Princess Louise of Schlezwig Holstein. The ceremony of marrying the half swords was performed, with Watcyn Wyn and Taldir presenting the Welsh and Breton halves to the Archdruid. Lord Mostyn read a telegram of greetings that was signed 'Carmen Sylva' from the Queen of Romania.

Hwfa Môn, described in a promotional leaflet as 'the Archdruid of the Isle of Britain', was unable to preside over the Gorsedd ceremonies at Mountain Ash in 1905 owing to ill health, and his place was taken by Cadfan. Lord Aberdare, who was the patron of the Eisteddfod, was made an honorary member of the Gorsedd under the name 'Llew y Dyffryn'.

Hwfa Môn died on 10 November after holding the office of Archdruid for ten years. By his commanding presence and sense of dignity, he had made the Gorsedd a respected institution of which, with a few exceptions, the leading Welshmen of the day wished to become members. His successor, Dyfed, was born at Puncheston, in north Pembrokeshire, on 1 January 1850, but his parents moved to Aberdare when he was a child and, at eight years of age, he was working at the Blaen-gwawr Colliery. Fifteen years later, he removed to Cardiff and became the Calvinistic Methodist minister at Pembroke Terrace. He travelled extensively in Europe, South Africa, Asia and North America, and gained renown as a lecturer. He was awarded the Chair four times, at Merthyr Tudful (1881), Liverpool (1884), Brecon (1889) and Merthyr again in 1901 and, in 1893, he won the most valuable prize ever offered to a Welsh poet, at the International Eisteddfod held during the World Fair at Chicago. He had held the office of Bardd yr Orsedd since 1895, and he was installed Archdruid at the opening Gorsedd ceremony held in Caernarfon Castle, on 21 August 1906. He was to be the last to hold the office for life.

The Gorsedd appointed a sub-committee to produce a new code of rules and regulations for the management of its affairs. The first draft was read from the Maen Llog at the Caernarfon Eisteddfod, and amended versions at Swansea in 1907 and Llangollen in 1908, with a final reading during the London Eisteddfod in 1909, after which it was published as 'The Rules and Constitution of the Gorsedd of Bards of the Isle of Britain'.

Among those admitted at Caernarfon, as new members of the Gorsedd, *honoris causa*, were the first Principal of University College, Bangor, Sir Henry Reichel (Alawgar), Mrs David Lloyd George (Megan Ednyfed) and Thomas Matthews of Fishguard (Mathew), who acted as the liaison officer between the Welsh and the Bretons and was a close friend of Kaledvoulc'h, the Grand Bard of Brittany.

The Swansea Eisteddfod opened, on 20 August 1907, with a procession to Cwmdonkin Park. There was a strong representation from Brittany present and the 'marriage' of the split sword was performed on the Pavilion platform with the Marquis de l'Estourbeillon carrying the Breton half and Gwynedd (Thomas Edwards: 1844-1924), the Gorsedd treasurer, carrying the Welsh half. The Archdruid presented a banner bearing the arms of the Duchy of Brittany to l'Estourbeillon for the use of the Breton Gorsedd and, in the absence of David Lloyd George, the Marquis was invited to preside over the Thursday afternoon session in the pavilion.

The Gorsedd responded to an appeal by Edmond Fournier d'Albe to send a deputation to the third Pan-Celtic Congress to be held at Edinburgh the following month, and the deputation held a Gorsedd ceremony on the Esplanade, before the main gate of Edinburgh Castle.

The Proclamation of the Llangollen Eisteddfod took place on the lawn of Plas Newydd. A procession had been formed in the town, comprising a military band, contingents from the Police and the Fire Brigade, the Gorsedd, Eisteddfod officials, the Lord Lieutenant, Mayors and Magistrates, Councillors and representatives of various organisations and institutions.

At the opening Gorsedd ceremony at the Eisteddfod the following year, a deputation from Brittany was present for the purpose of extending an invitation to the Archdruid to attend a Breton Gorsedd ceremony at Brest that year. A message was read from the aged Gutyn Ebrill, who claimed to be the Archdruid of Patagonia, extending his good wishes to the Archdruid and the Gorsedd of Bards. Among those who received honorary degrees were the Viscountess St Davids (Goleuni Dyfed) and R. J. Berwyn, Patagonia.

The promoters of the 1909 Eisteddfod were most observant of the language rule. They announced that the Proclamation ceremony was to be held on Alban Hefin and that the bards would don their robes *yn Neuadd y Deml Fewnol allan o Heol y Chwernant yn Ninas Caerludd* (in the hall of the Inner Temple, off Fleet Street, in the City of London) and the ceremony took place, as it had done in 1887, in the gardens of the Inner Temple.

The Eisteddfod, when the time came, opened with a Gorsedd ceremony held in the Royal Kensington Gardens, and the competitions were conducted in the Albert Hall, which was filled to capacity throughout the week. The Prime Minister, Herbert Henry Asquith, presided over one of the sessions; the former Prime Minister, Arthur James Balfour, over another, and the Chancellor of the Exchequer,

David Lloyd George, occupied the place that was to be his for the rest of his life, as president on the Thursday afternoon.

The Chair was awarded to T. Gwynn Jones for his *Gwlad Y Bryniau* (Land of the Hills) and the Crown to W. J. Gruffydd for a poem on *Yr Arglwydd Rhys* (The Lord Rhys). Among the few admitted to the Gorsedd were Lady Eva Wyndham Quinn of Dunraven (Cerddores Gwlad Forgan) and D. R. Hughes (Myfyr Eifion).

At the Colwyn Bay Eisteddfod in 1910, the Archdruid was presented with a sceptre, designed by the Herald Bard, Arlunydd Penygarn, and made in London by Messrs Spencer of Holborn. It was the gift of Charles Edward Leigh Knight, of Swanley, and former vicar of Bexley, in Kent, who was made an honorary Ovate as 'Carwr Cymru'.

The subject of the Crown poem was *Ednyfed Fychan* and the prize was awarded to Crwys. The *awdl* competition produced one of the finest poems ever written in the Welsh language, *Yr Haf* (The Summer), for which Robert Williams Parry was awarded the Chair.

In applying for the Eisteddfod to be held at Abergavenny, Reginald McKenna, the First Lord of Admiralty, caused laughter when he said that there were still 'unlettered persons in the House of Commons who were wont to speak of Wales and Monmouthshire as if they were separate entities,' and called for the National Eisteddfod to be held at Abergavenny so as to 'prove that Gwent is in Wales', but his call went unheeded and it was decided to hold the festival at Carmarthen in 1911.

The Carmarthen Eisteddfod was described as *Eisteddfod y Brenin a'r Werin* (the Eisteddfod of the King and the Peasantry) because the subject of the chair poem was *Iorwerth y Seithfed* (Edward VII), who had recently died, and that of the *pryddest* was *Gwerin Cymru* (The Welsh Peasantry). The former was won by William Roberts (Gwilym Ceiriog), and the latter by Crwys.

The half-swords were joined together, for the first time within the Gorsedd Circle, at Carmarthen. Kaledvoulc'h, the Grand Druid, was there to carry his half, and the Welsh half was borne by the Herald Bard, Arlunydd Penygarn.

Lady St Davids, Lady Mostyn, Mrs W. Llewelyn Williams and Miss Stepney-Gulston were thanked for meeting the cost of re-furbishing the Gorsedd robes. Lady Lloyd of Bronwydd presented a silver brooch as a remembrance of the silver harp which had been at the disposal of her husband's ancestors, as lords of Cemais, like the one that was in the gift of the Mostyn family.

Sir John Morris-Jones, in an article in *Y Beirniad* (The Critic), of which he was the editor, launched an attack on the Gorsedd and charged it with being 'a recent device founded on fiction and deceit'. He accused its leaders of polluting the sources of Welsh history and, even worse, of misleading 'the poor Bretons who have been so naive as to imitate them.'

A remarkable achievement occurred at the Wrexham Eisteddfod in 1912 when T. H. Parry-Williams won both the Chair and the Crown. He had sent his entries from Germany, where he was studying at Freiberg University, but had received no word of their fate. On the morning of the crowning ceremony, which was a Wednesday that year, he arrived at the Eisteddfod after a three-hour cycle ride from his uncle's farm in the Vale of Clwyd. His pseudonym was called for the second time before he heard it, and when the Herald Bard and his retinue went to conduct him to the stage, they had to lift him over a barrier behind which he was standing, as he was too short to get over it. After he had been crowned, for his poem on 'Giraldus Cambrensis', the Archdruid, Dyfed, whispered in his ear: 'Don't go home tonight!' The following day, he was brought to the stage again, this time to be chaired for his *awdl* to *Y Mynydd* (The Mountain).

As soon as the young bard had been installed in the chair, and had had a white ribbon tied round his right arm, David Lloyd George, then Chancellor of the Exchequer, was called upon to deliver his address, but before he could speak, the stage was rushed by a group of Suffragettes who caused the proceedings to be held up for a while.

Mrs Laurence Broderick presented a pendant of Welsh gold to be worn by the Archdruid, and jewels of office were provided for the Gorsedd officers, the gift of the Reverend Charles Edward Leigh Wright and Lady Stafford Howard.

The Gorsedd Committee was informed that there was a proposal to hold another International Eisteddfod in the United States, this time at Pittsburgh, Pennsylvania, in the following year, and that there was a strong desire among American Welshmen to establish a Gorsedd in America. The proposal was welcomed, provided the Gorsedd became a 'daughter-Gorsedd' of the Gorsedd of Bards, on the same lines as the Breton Gorsedd.

The procession at the Proclamation Ceremony of the Abergavenny Eisteddfod made to outbid those of the previous century at *Eisteddfodau'r Fenni*. In addition to the societies and organisations that normally accompanied the Bards on such occasions, there were hundreds

The Archdruid Dyfed 'marrying' the two half-swords at a Gorsedd ceremony during the Abergavenny Eisteddfod in 1913, with the Breton Grand Druid, Kaledvoulc'h, beside him. The Welsh half-sword had been carried by the Mayor of Abergavenny, and the Breton half by Tangwall (Pol Diverrès). The Grand Sword lies on the Logan Stone. 'Birettas' are still worn, but Sir Vincent Evans was always bare-headed.

of children, people in Welsh costume representing rural crafts and callings, and characterizations of Gwentian historical personalities.

The Grand Druid Kaledvoulc'h was present on the Maen Llog during the Abergavenny Eisteddfod as the Archdruid Dyfed performed the marriage of the half-swords. The Welsh half was carried by the Mayor of the town, Alderman Straker, and the other by Pol Diverres (Tangwall), who was the French master at Pengam School. Wil Ifan received the Crown for a poem on *Ieuan Gwynedd*, and Sarnicol the Chair for an *awdl* on *Aelwyd y Cymro* (The Welshman's Hearth).

At the annual meeting of the Gorsedd, the Archdruid stated that he had been to Pittsburgh and had established the American Gorsedd there, and had installed Cynonfardd, who had moved to America and was the Congregational minister at Edwardsville, Pennsylvania, as its first Archdruid.

A Proclamation Ceremony was held at Bangor that year but, with war clouds looming, the festival was postponed for a year, and 1914 remains the one year in which there was no Eisteddfod, and there were no Gorsedd ceremonies. When the Eisteddfod was held there the following year, it was in a modified form.

Once more, T. H. Parry-Williams repeated his unique achievement. Again, he had not been notified of his success by the Eisteddfod authorities and he was haymaking on his uncle's farm when it was announced from the Eisteddfod platform that the Crown was his. In his absence, it was received by his father, but a telegram reached him, in the hayfield, that afternoon, charging him to be present at the Eisteddfod the next day. He later recalled his nervous feeling as he stood before the Chair in the presence of the Archdruid and the President, David Lloyd George, and the adjudicator, Sir John Morris-Jones, and the stage conductor, Llew Tegid. Sir John had been critical of the poet's 'affectation' in his reference to a 'chromatic *awdl*' and of his 'cleverness' in inventing the pseudonym *Rhuddwyn Llwyd* (Red-White-Grey) referring to the colours in his poem *Eryri* (Snowdonia), which he had written when he was a student at the Sorbonne. His experiences in Paris were featured in his Crown poem, *Y Ddinas* (The City), which shocked one of the adjudicators, Eifion Wyn, to such an extent that he could not agree with his fellow adjudicators, Gwili and Alafon (Owen Griffith Owen: 1847-1916) to award the prize. 'It was the best and the most eloquent,' he said, 'but reading it will do no good to anyone's mind or heart.'

The Aberystwyth Eisteddfod had been proclaimed in 1914, within the castle walls as it had been in 1865 but, due to the knock-on effect, it was not held until 1916. The chairman of the local Gorsedd Committee, Edward Edwards, professor of history at the University, arranged for the names of the thirteen counties of Wales to be inscribed on the stones in the bardic alphabet, *Coelbren y Beirdd*.

At the Eisteddfod, the Gorsedd mourned the passing of two men who had made major contributions in transforming the Gorsedd into a colourful piece of pageantry. They were Sir Hubert von Herkomer and the Herald Bard, Arlunydd Penygarn, who was succeeded by Dr Edward Rees (Ap Gwyddon), of Caersws.

The *pryddest* competition that year required four lyrics and the adjudicators divided the prize between Gwili and Wil Ifan. The Chair, a silver one so as to conserve timber supplies, was awarded to John Ellis Williams for an *awdl* on *Strata Florida*.

Wil Ifan was the outright winner of the Crown at the Eisteddfod held, the following year, at Birkenhead, for his poem *Pwyll, Pendefig Dyfed*, but he was not present and Llew Wynne took his place during the crowning ceremony, which took place without partly unsheathing the Sword as this part of the ceremony had been set aside for the duration of the war.

After the Prime Minister, David Lloyd George, had delivered his speech, T. Gwynn Jones gave the adjudication on the Chair poem, to *Yr Arwr* (The Hero), and stated that the *awdl* submitted by 'Fleur-de-Lis' was by far the best of the fifteen poems received. No one responded to that name, however, and the Archdruid Dyfed was informed that the successful poet had been killed at the battle of Pilkem Ridge and that his name was Private E. H. Evans (Hedd Wyn), No. 61117, C Company, 15th Battalion Royal Welch Fusiliers. The Chair was draped in a black cloth and, in place of the chairing song, Madam Laura Evans-Williams sang *I Blas Gogerddan*.

Ellis Humphrey Evans was born at Penlan, Trawsfynydd, in 1887. After little schooling, he worked on his father's farm, Yr Ysgwrn, mostly as a shepherd, and he showed an early aptitude for poetry. He won his first chair at Bala in 1907, and it was known that he had taken the second place in the competition for the Chair at Aberystwyth the previous year. On 20 August 1910, a number of bards in the locality held an *arwest* on the shores of Llyn y Morynion, above Cwm Cynfal, an occurence that is reminiscent of Gwilym Cowlyd's *arwest* at Llyn Geirionydd in 1863. The weather proved unkind, however, and the *arwest* had to be held in the Town Hall at Blaenau Ffestiniog, but a Gorsedd ceremony was conducted beside the lake, at which Bryfdir, as Bardd yr Orsedd, admitted several new bards, among them Ellis Humphrey Evans. Bryfdir is said to have suggested the bardic name 'Hedd Wyn' to him, but Alan Llwyd has pointed out that this pseudonym was used by a competitor in an *englyn* competition at a literary meeting at Trawsfynydd the previous September, and that the competitor may well have been Ellis Evans.

Hedd Wyn left his home for the RWF Training Camp at Litherland in January 1917, only a few weeks, as it happened, after Robert Graves and Siegfred Sasson had left that camp, taking his unfinished *awdl* with him. By the middle of June he was at the Infantry Base Depot at Rouen and, on 1 July, he rejoined his regiment at Fléchin, on the Franco-Belgian border, and it was here that he completed the poem.

He was killed during an advance near Iron Cross, on Pilkem Ridge, on the morning of 31 July, but his parents did not receive the official notification until 24 August. His body was later removed to the Artillery Wood War Cemetery, Boesinghe. A pilgrimage to his grave was arranged, in 1934, by Cynan and other Gorsedd members and friends of the poet. A volume of his poems was published in 1918 under the title *Cerddi'r Bugail* (The Shepherd's Songs), and a bronze statue, by L. S. Merrifield, was raised to his memory in the village of Traws-fynydd, where it was unveiled by his mother in 1923.

Despite his lack of education, Hedd Wyn was well versed in the English poets. His favourite was Shelley and it has been generally held that his inspiration for *Yr Arwr* was *Prometheus Unbound*, but Alan Llwyd, in his commemorative volume *Gwae Fi Fy Myw: Cofiant Hedd Wyn*, has shown that he was influenced even more by Shelley's longest poem, *The Revolt of Islam*.

Representatives of the Celtic countries had gathered at Birkenhead in order to plan a revival of the Celtic Congress. The Congress had last been held at Edinburgh in 1907, when it had run into financial difficul-ties, from which it had been extricated by Lord Castletown.

The band of the Welsh Guards led the procession to the Victoria Gardens for the opening of the 1918 Eisteddfod at Neath. The Celtic delegates were present again in some force, as they had met there the previous week and had succeeded in establishing the Celtic Congress, to replace the former Pan-Celtic Congress, and had appointed the Welsh industrialist and politician Edward Thomas John as its president and, as vice-presidents, Lord Ashbourne (Ireland), W. Llewelyn Williams (Wales), François Vallée (Brittany), Henry Jenner (Corn-wall) and Mona Douglas (Isle of Man), with D. Rhys Phillips (Y Beili Glas) as secretary. Henry Jenner discussed with Y Beili Glas, at these meetings, the feasibility of forming a Gorsedd in Cornwall.

The Archdruid initiated a number of persons who had been success-ful in the examinations, among them the Englishman A. S. D. Smith (Caradar), author of *Welsh Made Easy* and of *Cornish Simplified*, who had learned to speak Welsh and Cornish. Mrs Charles Coombe-Tennant (Mam o Nedd), chairman of the arts and crafts committee at the Neath Eisteddfod, was made an Honorary Ovate.

The opening Gorsedd ceremony at the Corwen Eisteddfod, on 4 August 1919, was the first to be held since the Armistice, and the Grand Sword was partly unsheathed again at the appropriate occa-sions. The ceremony was held on Penpigyn, in the rain, and the bards therefore appeared without their bardic robes.

The Pavilion in which the Corwen Chair Eisteddfod was held annu-ally during the first week of August had been extended, but it was still packed to capacity for the ceremony in which Crwys was crowned for his poem to *Morgan Llwyd o Wynedd*, and again as David Rhys Cledlyn Davies was installed, for his *awdl* to *Y Proffwyd* (The Prophet), in a Chair carved with Celtic motifs by John Kelt Edwards.

New members admitted to the Gorsedd included Lord Howard de Walden (Elis o'r Waun), Professor Miall Edwards (Dewi Derfel), Dr Lloyd Owen, Criccieth (Ap Llugwy) and T. I. Ellis (Ap Cynlas).

The dates upon which the Eisteddfod had been held each year had ranged over the summer months, with a recent tendency towards August and early September, but the success that attended the festival at Corwen caused the Eisteddfod authorities to decide on the first week in August as a permanent date, to which it has since adhered.

The Barry Eisteddfod was proclaimed at a ceremony that took place at Romilly Park, and it was there that the Gorsedd ceremonies were held during the Eisteddfod week, when Major Edgar Jones (Fychan o Fochnant) announced the syllabus of the Gorsedd examinations for the ensuing year.

During the Eisteddfod, a meeting of representatives of the Gorsedd and of the Eisteddfod met and recommended that a new governing body for the Eisteddfod be formed with representation from *Cymdeithas yr Orsedd, Cymdeithas yr Eisteddfod*, the local committee, the University of Wales and other interested institutions. Eifionydd and Sir Vincent Evans were appointed joint-secretaries.

The Caernarfon Eisteddfod produced two outstanding poems: the Chair poem *Min y Môr* (The Edge of the Sea) by Meuryn (Robert John Rowlands: 1880-1967) and the *pryddest* by Cynan (Albert Evans-Jones: 1895-1970), *Mab y Bwthyn* (The Cotter's Son), in which he gave a candid account of his experiences as a soldier in Macedonia during the 1914-18 war.

It had been the practice, hitherto, for the Aberthged and the Corn Hirlas to be presented at each of the open-air Gorsedd ceremonies, but now the Herald Bard, Ap Gwyddon, arranged for the Aberthged to be presented to the Archdruid on the Tuesday, and the Corn Hirlas at the Thursday morning ceremony. The ceremony held on the Friday morning was discontinued.

During the Gorsedd ceremony held on the Thursday morning at Caernarfon, John Edward Jones (Iorwerth Twrog), the penillion singer from Maentwrog, sang for the first time the poignant sequence of *englynion* in memory of Hedd Wyn by R. Williams Parry.

Inclement weather caused the opening ceremony at Ammanford to be curtailed, but an immense crowd had gathered on the Thursday morning, which one correspondent attributed to the publicity given to the Gorsedd by the fierce attacks made upon it by Griffith John Williams, a lecturer at the Welsh Department of the University College, Cardiff, who maintained that 'such was the pomposity and arrogance of the Gorsedd that it regarded itself as the literary court of justice in Wales.' He could not even commend it as a pageant but could see for it a future as a kind of 'academy that could produce a school of critics in Wales.'

Eifionydd who had been the Gorsedd Recorder since 1876, died in 1922, and Beriah was appointed to succeed him. In March 1923, Dyfed died, and Cadfan (John Cadfan Davies: 1846-1923) was elected in his place, despite his frailty and advanced age of seventy-six years. Y Beili Glas was appointed Examinations Organiser.

The Herald Bard, Ap Gwyddon, published a leaflet giving the order of the procession and an outline of the ceremony that was to take place on the Bailey Hill at Mold on the morning of 7 August 1923. Cadfan opened the proceedings by calling on the Bishop of St David's to read the Gorsedd Prayer, and he then handed over the conduct of the ceremony to his deputy, Elfed. Cadfan died two months later and Elfed, who was minister of Tabernacle, King's Cross, and had won the Crown at Wrexham (1888) and Brecon (1889), and the Chair at Caernarfon (1894), and was already well-known as a hymn-writer, was appointed Archdruid in his place. The appointment was now limited to a four-year term.

The Gorsedd visited, and laid wreaths on, the tombs of Richard Wilson, Daniel Owen and Alun.

Cynan won the Crown again at Mold, for his *Ynys Unig* (The Lonely Isle), and at Pontypool the following year he was awarded the Chair for his *I'r Duw Nid Adwaenir* (To the Unknown God), even though he had broken with tradition and had written the poem in a measure that was not in the classification of Dafydd ab Edmwnd.

The visit of the Prince of Wales was 'the big thing' at the Pontypool Eisteddfod in 1924, according to *Y Faner*, and it praised the Gorsedd for its arrangements for the visit. The Bards formed a circle on the Pontypool Cricket Ground to welcome the Prince, who then inspected a guard of honour of ex-servicemen before proceeding to the Pavilion where he was admitted a member of the Gorsedd under the name 'Iorwerth Dywysog', the name by which his grandfather, King Edward VII, had also been initiated.

The Prince placed the Crown upon the head of E. Prosser Rhys for his *pryddest* on *Atgof* (Remembrance), which had been sharply criticised by one of the adjudicators for its indelicacy. In his adjudication of the Chair poem, written by Cynan, Sir John Morris Jones stated that 'not everybody would agree that this was an *awdl* at all, for it is a poem written in *mesur-tri-thrawiad* (triple-beat measure) ... But the prevailing rule lies in the decision taken at the 1819 Eisteddfod that poets in the chair competition could henceforth compose in whatever measure they wished of *dosbarth Morgannwg* [the Glamorgan classification]. And the *tri-thrawiad* is in that classification.'

Wil Ifan also broke with tradition the next year, at the Eisteddfod at Pwllheli, by submitting a *pryddest*, on *Bro fy Mebyd* (My Childhood Haunts), in *vers libre*. He was awarded the Crown in the presence of Queen Marie of Romania, the second queen of that name to visit the Eisteddfod. This one was the grand-daughter of Queen Victoria and the wife of King Ferdinand, and she was made an honorary member of the Gorsedd under the name 'Mair Gwalia'.

At the Proclamation Ceremony held in Singleton Park, Swansea, on 2 July 1925, Captain Geoffrey Crawshay (Sieffre o Gyfarthfa) was installed Herald Bard in succession to Ap Gwyddon.

The Duke and Duchess of York (later King George VI and Queen Elizabeth) visited the Eisteddfod that year and were admitted honorary members of the Gorsedd under the bardic names 'Sior o Efrog' and 'Betsi o Efrog'.

The Crown awarded to the vagabond poet Dewi Emrys (David Emrys James) for his *Rhigymau'r Ffordd Fawr* (Rhymes of the Open Road) was said not to have been long in his hands before he pledged it to a Swansea pawnbroker. The chair, the gift of the Welsh community in Shanghai, was won by Gwenallt (David James Jones: 1899-1968) for his *awdl* to *Y Mynach* (The Monk), and he was chaired to the strains of a chairing song, *Henffych i'r Prifardd* written by Cynan and sung to the tune *Ymdaith Capten Morgan*. A special prize of £30, given by Tom Rees, of Chicago, was offered for the best book of the year in the opinion of the Gorsedd of Bards. The prize was awarded to Sir John Morris-Jones for his *Cerdd Dafod*, which has remained the standard work on the art of writing Welsh prosody.

The tripartite governance of the Eisteddfod, with each of the three bodies, the Eisteddfod Association, the Gorsedd Association and the local committee, striving to exercise a superiority over the others, was a cause of perpetual conflict. The local committee, as it was primarily concerned with the raising of money in its locality, objected to the Eisteddfod Association taking the profits in order to expand its own funds, and also to paying the costs and expenses incurred by the Gorsedd of Bards, despite the fact that it was the Gorsedd ceremonies that attracted the crowds and, therefore, brought in the bulk of the money. The local committee, in turn, was charged with anglicising the Eisteddfod, to which it responded that it would not be able to sponsor so large an undertaking without the patronage of the local nobility and the support of the local people whose mother-tongue was not always Welsh.

Professor Henry Lewis, in an article in *Y Llenor*, took advantage of a dispute between the local committee at Swansea and the officers of the Gorsedd concerning the selection of adjudicators and the choice of subjects set for the main poetry competitions. He charged the Gorsedd with incompetence and interference; Professor W. J. Gruffydd, editor of the journal, on the other hand, complained that the Eisteddfod was too much under the control of local committees and maintained that there was 'not enough knowledge or Welsh culture gathered in any one town in Wales to select subjects or adjudicators in a competent manner'. He claimed that 'the whole resources of the nation should be made available to the Eisteddfod' and that it should be organised each year by a standing committee comprising 'the pick of those who were proficient in literature, song and art.' He admitted that despite his 'hatred of the impudence of the Gorsedd', it was possible that it could form the nucleus of such a committee.

The attack by Henry Lewis drew a response by Cynan who dismissed all theories relating to the antiquity and druidic origins of the Gorsedd of Bards and emphasized the contribution it was making, and could make, to the Eisteddfod.

The sense of wonder of a young poet attending his first Eisteddfod to claim his reward is related by Caradog Prichard. He had arrived at Holyhead, in August 1927, after hearing a whisper that his entry in the *pryddest* competition, the set subject of which was *Y Briodas* (The Wedding), had been selected by the adjudicators as worthy of the Crown. He booked himself in at the Railway Hotel on the Monday evening and, in the foyer, found himself 'gazing in awe at some of the giants of the Eisteddfod standing around me, like Gwallter Dyfi, the Grand Sword-bearer, and Sieffre o Gyfarthfa, the Herald Bard, who rode a horse at the head of the Gorsedd procession, and many another national figure. I was listening amazed at the gaiety and the laughter and the noisy carousal around me when suddenly a voice from behind me whispered in my ear: '*Wylwch, y ffyliaid, chwerddwch!*' (Weep, ye fools, laugh!). This was a quotation from the poem he had submitted and the voice was that of R. Williams Parry, one of the adjudicators. Caradog knew that the Crown was his.

The Chair offered for a poem on *Y Derwydd* (The Druid), found no worthy poet and it was presented for use as the Judge's seat at the court at Beaumaris.

The Gorsedd Prayer was intoned for the first time at Holyhead, to music that had been specially written by the Director of Music, W. S. Gwynn Williams (Gwynn o'r Llan).

With the death of the Gorsedd Recorder, Beriah, in November 1927, his son-in-law, Gwilym Rhug (William Edward Williams) was appointed to succeed him.

Elfed was succeeded, as Archdruid, by Pedrog, minister at Kensington Congregational Church, Liverpool and chairman of the Union of Welsh Independents. He had won the Gold Medal at the Utica Eisteddfod in 1889, and the Crown at Swansea (1891), Llanelli (1895) and Liverpool (1900).

A deputation from Brittany attended the Eisteddfod at Treorchy in 1928 and appealed for closer contact with the mother-Gorsedd. Another, from Cornwall, requested the Archdruid to establish a Cornish Gorsedd at Boscawen-Un the following September.

The Archdruid and Professor Ernest Hughes were roundly criticised in *Y Faner* for pontificating on the industrial situation and were advised to confine themselves to matters relating to the Welsh language and literature rather than venture into politics which they did not understand. The Gorsedd showed impartiality, however, by bestowing honorary degrees on the industrialists David (later Lord) Davies of Llandinam and Sir D. R. Llewelyn, and upon Frank Hodges, secretary of the Miners' Federation of Great Britain, and Rhys J. Davies, MP. W. P. Thomas and the Rev. Fred Jones, president and secretary of the local committee, declined the offer of honorary membership in protest against the way in which 'unimportant people had been awarded honours'.

The Crown was won again by Caradog Prichard for his poem *Penyd* (Penance), but the Chair, for an *awdl* to *Y Sant* (The Saint) was withheld because Sir John Morris-Jones, one of the adjudicators, considered the best poem submitted, by Gwenallt, 'a heap of filth'. The poets, by now, had begun to bid defiance to the grip of Nonconformity and its accent on sexual morality. Prosser Rhys, in his *Atgof* (1924), had ventured to speak of the homosexual problems of a sensual young man, and Gwenallt had referred to the temptations of the flesh in his poem *Y Mynach*.

The custom of commemorating the names of Gorsedd members who had died during the year was begun at Treorchy. The Recorder, to the strains of *Ffarwel y Telynor* played on the harp, reads a form of remembrance composed by Wil Ifan before pronouncing the names of the departed.

Professor W. J. Gruffydd continued to make use of *Y Llenor*, to call for the establishment of a national body to govern the affairs of the Eisteddfod and warned that if this were not done, the local committee would not take long to deliver it the *coup-de-grace*. He issued an appeal again to the Gorsedd to invite 'the leaders of the nation who stood scornfully outside it', to come together in a body during the Liverpool Eisteddfod in 1929, and 'to constitute itself (I would go so far as to say) as the governing power for the benefit of the Eisteddfod'. A meeting of Gorsedd officers and other prominent Welshmen was called, but Gruffydd failed to turn up and, in protest, some of the younger poets who had not been inclined to do so, became members of the Gorsedd.

The Liverpool Eisteddfod was the last to be held outside the Principality. The Chair, for the best *awdl* on *Dafydd ap Gwilym*, was awarded to Dewi Emrys, who wrote to Trefin (Edgar Phillips) to say that he should have had the prize, as his *awdl* was nothing more than a hodge-podge of his earlier poems, 'but the fools could not see that!' Wil Ifan, one of the adjudicators, felt that Dewi's entry in the *pryddest* competition, on the subject *Y Gân Ni Chanwyd* (The Unsung Song) was also the best, but the other two awarded the prize to Caradog Prichard, who became the first man to win the Crown three times in succession.

Caradog Prichard and Prosser Rhys were among those who now sought membership of the Gorsedd, as was their right in any case as *Prifeirdd*, after the Liverpool episode. They were admitted at the same time as the Bishop of Bangor and Teifion Richards, one of the promoters of the American Gorsedd, at Llanelli in 1930.

The Crown was won at Llanelli by Gwilym Myrddin (William Jones: 1863-1946) for a *pryddest* to Ben Bowen, the young poet whose doctrinal views had got him excommunicated from Moriah Chapel, Pentre, and who died young before fulfilling his early promise. The subject of the Chair poem was *Y Galilead* (The Galilean), and when the pen-name of the successful poet, 'Llanymddyfri', was called by the Archdruid, there was no response. A rumour that it would be Dewi

Emrys was discounted when he had been seen in the Gorsedd procession and sitting among the robed bards on the Eisteddfod platform, but no one had noticed him leave the stage during the adjudication and, discarding his robe, join the multitude on the field. He did so in protest at not being informed that he had won the Chair, and he refused to take part in the chairing ceremony. He was eventually persuaded to do so in order to please the president of the day, David Lloyd George.

The Bangor Eisteddfod was opened with a Gorsedd ceremony held in the College Fields, with Elfed conducting the proceedings in the absence of Pedrog, who was indisposed. H. V. Morton was present and, in his book, *In Search of Wales*, he described it as 'one of the most interesting ceremonies' he had ever attended. 'I have seen kings crowned and I have seen them buried,' he wrote. 'I have seen nations in mourning and in times of popular rejoicing. I have seen crowds as big as this Welsh crowd whipped up into dervish frenzy about sport; but never have I seen a crowd which represents all the lights and shades of an entire nation gathered together to sing, to play musical instruments and to recite verse.'

He got up early on the Tuesday morning and went to a meadow on the slope below the University, where there was a 'druidic circle of stones' which, when he first saw them, he thought were 'as old as Stonehenge.' The Gorsedd procession arrived at the Circle and the Archdruid, wearing on his chest 'a replica of the Irish breastplate which Camden illustrated in his *Britannia*,' took his place 'at the high altar.' As the bards grouped themselves around him, 'an irreverent wind blows aside the robes to reveal trousers of serge and tweed and pin-stripe,' but one of their number had already forseen this and wore white stockings and sandals. On enquiry, Morton found that 'the sandalled one' was a bard named Cynan. 'The Reverend A. E. Jones, you know,' added his informant. That afternoon, in the Pavilion, Morton was elated to be able to recognise the poet who responded to the Archdruid's call as none other than Cynan, who was crowned for his poem *Y Dyrfa* (The Crowd). In the poem he had written of the experiences of a Welsh International rugby player who had scored the winning try at Twickenham, and had later become a missionary in China, a theme inspired by J. C. Squire's 'The Rugger Match'. The Chair was awarded to Gwenallt for his *Breuddwyd Y Bardd* (The Poet's Dream).

Gwilym Rhug was unable to continue in the office of Recorder on account of his delicate state of health and he was succeeded by Gwylfa Roberts (Gwylfa), a native of Penmaenmawr, who had been Congregational minister at Llanelli for close on forty years, and had been awarded the Crown two years running, at Blaenau Ffestiniog (1898) and Cardiff (1899). Gwili, Professor of Greek at the Baptist College, Bangor, was appointed Archdruid in succession to Pedrog.

Professor W. J. Gruffydd once more confessed, in *Y Llenor*, that he had reached an attitude of despair and had come to the conclusion that 'the National Eisteddfod is quickly drawing towards its end, and the fact that some of us have been prophesying this for some time will not ease the blow when it falls.' Cynan responded, when the festival was at Aberafan in 1932, by expressing his own fears for the future of the Eisteddfod. He felt that it was 'disintegrating through Philistinism and parochialism' and that it was high time 'to make an effort to rebuild it on a strong and proper national basis.' He was also of the opinion that the Gorsedd of Bards required some discipline.

Once again it was realised that the tripartite system of control was debilitating the Eisteddfod body. The local committees were often incompetent. The Eisteddfod Council, with less than twenty members, and its headquarters in Chancery Lane in London, was dominated by its secretary, Sir Vincent Evans, and had little contact with the governing body of the Gorsedd.

There was a choice of three subjects for the Crown competition at the Wrexham Eisteddfod in 1933, and the award went to Simon B. Jones for his *Rownd yr Horn*, while Trefin won the Chair for his *awdl* to *Harlech*. The Chair had been presented by J. R. Jones, Secretary of the International Commission in Shanghai and, later, Legal Adviser to the Hong Kong and Shanghai Banking Corporation, who travelled to the Eisteddfod each year. It was an outstanding example of Chinese art which had taken four craftsmen sixteen months to carve with symbols depicting the ancient fables of China.

The Archdruid Gwili received a deputation from Paris, led by Jacques Heugel (Telen Myrddin), seeking permission to form a *College Bardique des Gaules* for the Celts who lived in France outside Brittany. The Archdruid gave his approval and the Gorsedd was established, with Phileas Lebesgue (Ab Gwenc'hlan) as its Grand Druid. Lebesgue, Heugel and Andre Savoret (Gwalwys) were initiated members of the Gorsedd of Bards, and John Masefield, Poet Laureate, was admitted an honorary member.

The Gorsedd held its ceremonies at Neath in 1934 in the circle that had been erected in preparation for the Eisteddfod held there in 1918 and, after the initial ceremony, the Bards were entertained by the Eisteddfod president, David Evans-Bevan. Among those admitted members of the Gorsedd was the artist Evan Walters (Arlunydd Llangyfelach).

One of the *awdlau* submitted on the subject *Ogof Arthur* (Arthur's Cave) was written in *vers libre*, but with each line in *cynghanedd*, and it was ruled out of order as it was not in the traditional measures. Professor T. Gwynn Jones, one of the adjudicators, confessed that he had never been in favour of adhering strictly to the old measures, nor was he 'opposed to the thing called *vers-libre* – a similar thing to the *prosa* of Middle Latin,' but the Chair was awarded to William Morris for a traditional *awdl*.

The Professor went further at Caernarfon the following year, when the Chair was awarded to Gwyndaf Evans (Gwyndaf), a student at Aberystwyth, for his *awdl* written in *vers libre* to *Magdalen*. He pointed out that, although the poets had been given the freedom to do so in 1819, they had not strayed from the twenty-four measures of Dafydd ab Edmwnd until recently, which he welcomed. Some of the traditional measures were so restrictive that it was difficult to convey sense and, in any case, art was continually seeking new forms.

When Gwylfa, the Gorsedd Recorder, died in 1935, Cynan was appointed to his place and he, in collaboration with Sieffre o Gyfartha, the Herald Bard, introduced a discipline that had not hitherto existed among the Bards. Sir Vincent Evans, the Secretary of the Eisteddfod Council since 1881, had also died and he was succeeded by D. R. Hughes, a leader of the Welsh community in London, with whom Cynan was able to work very closely from the outset. They brought together the leading members of the Gorsedd and of the Eisteddfod Council at a meeting held at 11 Mecklenburgh Square, in London, under the chairmanship of David Lloyd George, and got them to agree that there should be one body to govern the affairs of the Eisteddfod, in which the Gorsedd and the Eisteddfod Council would be merged, and a committee representative of the two bodies was appointed to prepare a suitable constitution.

At the Proclamation of the Machynlleth Eisteddfod, in July 1936, the Floral Dance was performed for the first time. The dance, though described by the correspondent of the *Liverpool Post* as a 'quaint survival of the past', was created and choreographed by Cynan as a feature of the presentation of the Aberthged to the Archdruid. The

Aberthged and the Hirlas Horn, up to that time, had each been proffered to the Archdruid by a mature lady, often the wife of a local notable or civic leader, but with the introduction of the dance, it was decreed that the Aberthged should be presented by a young maiden. The Hirlas continued to be offered by 'one of the mothers of the neighbourhood' and she is attended by two page-boys, while the maiden has two small girls in attendance. The matron and the maiden and their attendants are chosen by the Recorder and Herald Bard from a short list of candidates prepared by the local committee.

The Eisteddfod visited Pembrokeshire for the first time in 1936, when it was at Fishguard. A Gorsedd Circle was erected on Penslade, overlooking Fishguard Bay, of stones contributed individually by the twelve neighbouring parishes, and the opening ceremony was held on Tuesday, 4 August, at a quarter past eight in the morning. At this ceremony J. J. Williams (J.J.), Congregational minister at Morriston, who had won the Chair at Caernarfon in 1906 and Llangollen in 1908, was installed Archdruid and, in view of the demise of his immediate predecessor, Gwili, the installation was carried out by the former Archdruid Elfed. The term of occupancy of the office of archdruid, which he had been for life until 1924, and for terms of four years from that date, was now determined at three years.

The Archdruid J. J. Williams after his installation by Elfed at the Fishguard Eisteddfod in 1936. The Herald Bard, Sieffre o Gyfarthfa (Captain Geoffrey Crawshay) appears in his riding outfit, and behind him is Mam o Nedd (Mrs Coombe-Tennant), Mistress of the Robes. The Grand Swordbearer is Gwallter Dyfi (J. Walter Rees) and, on his left, is Meurig Prysor (Canon Maurice Jones), the Gorsedd Treasurer.

The programme of the day gave a descriptive note of the crowning ceremony in both languages:

> The Ceremony of the Crowning of the Bard will be according to the rites of the Bards of the Isle of Britain. He will be proclaimed by the sound of a Trumpet; the Gorsedd Recorder will call the Muster of the Bards; the Adjudication will be delivered, the successful Bard will be escorted to the platform by two of the Principal Bards. The Victor will be duly invested as Crowned Bard of the National Eisteddfod of 1936. The Bards will deliver their addresses, and Madam Margaret Thomas will sing the Crowning song ... The whole of these proceedings will be under the sole control of the Gorsedd, exercised through the Recorder, and the Herald Bard as Master of the Ceremonies.

The subject set for the Crown poem, 'of not more than 500 lines in metre and rhyme', was *Yr Anialwch* (The Wilderness) and the winner, David Jones of Cilfynydd, wrote not of the Wilderness of Sin or the deserts of Arabia but of the dust disease, pneumoconiosis, the scourge of Welsh miners. The Chair was awarded to Simon B. Jones for his *awdl* to *Tŷ Ddewi* (St David's), but the adjudicators gave high praise to an entry of outstanding merit that appeared, however, to have been written in some haste and lacked the finishing touches that such a work required and it consequently could not receive the prize. It transpired that the poem was the work of Waldo Williams, and that he had composed it during a week-end stay at the home of D. J. Williams who had submitted it without the knowledge of the poet.

The Machynlleth Eisteddfod Committee received an offer from the Marquess of Londonderry of the use of his mansion, Plas Machynlleth, and its gardens, for whatever purpose they required. The committee accepted the generous offer and, in order to show their appreciation, the members invited Lord Londonderry to preside at one of the evening concerts, but they had overlooked the fact that he was the Secretary of State for Air and that Saunders Lewis, Lewis Valentine and D. J. Williams were, at the time, serving a sentence at Wormwood Scrubs for having burned down a building in protest against the siting of an aerodrome at Penyberth, on the Lleyn Peninsula. Professor W. J. Gruffydd called on the committee to withdraw its invitation but, not wishing to be discourteous, it refused to do so, and Gruffydd and some others resigned. When the time came, the Marquess wisely found a reason for being unable to be present.

A new constitution was agreed at Machynlleth, bringing together the Eisteddfod Council and the Gorsedd Board in equal partnership under the Eisteddfod Court, which is the corporate body comprising all the members of the Eisteddfod and of the Gorsedd of Bards, The constitution also established, for all time, that Welsh is the language of the Eisteddfod.

Whereas it had been the custom for the succesful bard to be taken out of the Pavilion to a retiring room by the Herald Bard and his retinue, to be dressed in a purple gown, at Machynlleth a new gown was provided, suitable for the bard to don *in situ* so that he could be led straight on to the platform. J. M. Edwards, who won the Crown for his *pryddest* to *Y Pentref* (The Village), was so led, and he was also the first to be honoured with a *cywydd* specially written for the crowned bard by the Archdruid J.J., and sung to the air *Cainc y Datgeiniad*. The Chair was awarded to T. Rowland Hughes for an *awdl* to *Y Ffin* (The Boundary). The bard, in each case, was led to the stage to the strains of *Ymdaith Capten Llwyd*, instead of 'See, the Conquering Hero Comes'.

A Gold Medal for Literature was presented by Sir Howell Williams as the chief prize for prose writing, and it was awarded to J. O. Williams, Bethesda, for his *Tua'r Gorllewin ac Ysgrifau Eraill* (Towards the West and Other Essays). The Medal is worn on a blue ribbon by the recipient, who is offered membership of the Gorsedd with the same status as the winners of the Crown and the Chair.

The implementation of an all-Welsh rule was not easy, and doubts were expressed as to the effect of such a constraint on the festival and upon its finances. Professor W. J. Gruffydd, as chairman of its literary committee, informed the promoters of the Cardiff Eisteddfod, in 1938, however, that 'we are going to make Cardiff the most Welsh Eisteddfod held for many years as far as the literary committee is concerned.' When David Lloyd George was unable to preside over the Thursday session and Gruffydd was asked to occupy his place, he took full advantage of the occasion to advocate the exclusive use of Welsh at the Eisteddfod.

For reasons of location, the Gorsedd Circle that had been removed to the Gorsedd Gardens after the 1899 Eisteddfod could not be used in 1938 and another was erected within the grounds of Cardiff Castle, by permission of the Marquess of Bute who had also offered to provide it, but when the Proclamation Day arrived, the bards found that, instead of natural or quarried stones, the Gorsedd Circle consisted of concrete pillars, which the Marquess had ordered so as to save expense.

The poets were given a choice of subjects both for the Crown and Chair poems. The former was won by Edgar Thomas for a *pryddest* to *Peniel*, and the latter by Gwilym R. Jones for an *awdl* on the hymn line *'Rwy'n edrych dros y bryniau pell* (I look beyond the distant hills). Dr Iorwerth Peate had arranged for the Chair to be made by craftsmen at the Brynmawr Settlement, and it was said to be the first chair in which one could sit with any degree of comfort.

The progressive increase in the size of the Eisteddfod, and the extent of its anglicisation, were matters that caused considerable concern during the 1930s. Professor Gruffydd expressed the view of many Eisteddfodwyr when he urged that the festival should curtail its activities, and have its costs controlled, lest it should lose its traditional values and have to confine itself to the conurbations. Dr Iorwerth Peate considered that 'the Eisteddfod must decide whether it goes to a city or large town ... or to small country towns', and called for 'a small permanent body of erudite Welshmen' to run the festival each year, in view of the agreement reached between the Eisteddfod Council and the Gorsedd Board under the new constitution. He could not resist the temptation to stir the waters, however, by giving vent to his animosity toward the Gorsedd by intimating that 'the kindest thing one could say about it is that it should be buried quietly without a tear being shed on its grave.'

Despite the inevitability of war, the Eisteddfod was held at Denbigh in August 1939, and it was historic in that it was the first to be conducted under the provisions of the new constitution agreed at Machynlleth. The festival was now the responsibility of *Llys yr Eisteddfod* (The Eisteddfod Court), with its day-to-day affairs administered by the Council, and *Bwrdd yr Orsedd* (The Gorsedd Board) being responsible for the ceremonial and all matters relating to the Gorsedd of Bards. The festival that year was significantly described as *Yr Eisteddfod Genedlaethol yn Ninbych* (The National Eisteddfod in Denbigh) in preference to previous descriptions, such as *Eisteddfod Genedlaethol Caerdydd* (The National Eisteddfod of Cardiff). It received a poor start, however, as it was the first Eisteddfod at which both the Chair and the Crown had to be withheld, as no poet was worthy of either.

Crwys was appointed Archdruid in succession to J.J. at the Proclamation ceremony held at Bridgend in 1939. He was the first to be appointed for a limited term of three years but, owing to the war, he held the office until 1947. The Eisteddfod could not be held there, however, as this industrial area, contributing substantially to the war effort, was declared by the Government to be liable to aerial attack, and so advantage was taken of a pavilion, seating five thousand people, at Mountain Ash, and a Proclamation ceremony was held at Parc-ydyffryn, in that town, in May 1940. The rule requiring the Proclamation to be made a year and a day in advance, was waived that year and for the duration of the war. Following the fall of France, the Government again intervened, stating that the Cynon Valley had now been listed as subject to enemy attack and the Eisteddfod could not be held at Mountain Ash. The Council then appointed an emergency committee, which approached the Welsh department of the BBC at Bangor for its advice and co-operation and, as a result, a 'Radio Eisteddfod', or 'Eisteddfod of the Air', was held.

Every effort was made to restore the Eisteddfod to its traditional form in 1941, but the result was a three-day affair held in the local church hall at Old Colwyn. It was a literary festival in its entirety and, in that respect, it fulfilled the long expressed desire of Professor W. J. Gruffydd for such a festival, but after the Old Colwyn experience, he was the first to call for the return of music and song.

It was not possible to hold the usual Gorsedd ceremonies, but those who had graduated were received by the Archdruid in the Church Hall, and informed that they would be initiated in the Gorsedd Circle as soon as possible after the war was over.

Despite disagreement among the adjudicators, the prize for the best *awdl* was awarded to Roland Jones (Rolant o Fôn) for a poem on *Hydref* (Autumn), and J. M. Edwards won the award for the *pryddest* on *Peiriannau* (Machines). The prizes consisted of medals, designed by Sir William Goscombe John, for the duration of the war in order to comply with the restriction on the use of timber and of metals.

Music competitions were restored at the truncated festival held at Cardigan in 1942. No poet submitted an *awdl* worthy of the Chair, even though the subject was *Rhyfel* (War), but the prize for the *pryddest* was awarded to Herman Jones, for a poem to *Ebargofiant* (Oblivion).

It had been planned to hold the Eisteddfod at Llangefni in 1943 but, at the request of the Ministry of Transport, in an endeavour to reduce travel, it was held at the County Theatre at Bangor. Dewi Emrys, who received the Medal for his *awdl* to *Cymylau Amser* (The Clouds of Time) had already won both the Chair and the Crown, and a Medal in place of the Crown was awarded to Dafydd Owen, a student at Bala-Bangor Theological College who had learnt much of his poetic art by following Dewi Emrys's weekly poetry column in *Y Cymro*.

The Archdruid Crwys received as representatives of the subjugated nations of Europe, on the Eisteddfod platform, the Deputy Premier of Yugoslavia, the Minister of the Interior of Czechoslovakia, and the Belgian Under-Secretary of Education, together with an observer from the Soviet Embassy. In presenting them, the Recorder Cynan said that at no time since the time of Owain Glyndŵr had four European nations sent their 'ambassadors' to Wales.

The people of Llandybie co-operated with the Eisteddfod authorities in 1944 in order to make the Eisteddfod a week-long festival again. More than five thousand people gathered round the stone circle to witness the opening Gorsedd ceremony, and the marquee erected beside the village hall was not large enough to hold the crowds that wished to be present at the Crowning and Chairing ceremonies. An international concert, at which performances were given by a Polish Army choir and members of the Norwegian, French, Belgian and American forces stationed in Britain, is considered to have provided the inspiration for an idea that developed as the International Musical Eisteddfod held each year, since 1947, at Llangollen.

The Archdruid Crwys was about to close the proceedings, following the chairing of David Lloyd Jenkins for his *awdl* to *Ofn* (Fear), when the chairman of the Eisteddfod Council, D. Owen Evans, Member of Parliament for Cardiganshire, asked leave to present, 'as at Bangor the previous year, representatives of other nations, some of them from countries that had been overrun by the enemy,' to the Archdruid. Crwys received graciously a representative each from the United States of America, Belgium, Czechoslovakia, Free France, Luxembourg, Holland, Norway, Poland, the USSR and China, and each gave a message in his own language, of which Cynan, the Recorder, gave a prepared translation. As he finished translating the message of Chen Wi Yuan, a black man appeared from the audience and marched up to the platform unannounced. He was allowed to convey his greeting, in a strange tongue, following which the audience called for a translation by Cynan. Crwys, with a mischievous glance at Cynan, held up his hand and said 'Don't expect too much of the Recorder. I understood the young man perfectly. He said that he was from the Gold Coast, that it was warmer there than it is at Llandybie, and that he had heard that your ancestors had gone to his country digging for gold!' No one ever got to know who the man was, nor which language he spoke, but the incident enabled the next day's morning newspaper to have as its headline: 'No colour bar at the Eisteddfod'.

The Rhosllannerchrugog Eisteddfod opened with the news of the dropping of an atomic bomb on Hiroshima and a solemn realisation that a new era in the history of man had dawned.

The Gorsedd of Bards conducted its ritual in the drizzling rain on the Tuesday morning, but on the Thursday the scene was enlivened by bright sunshine that gave a colourful innocence to the Floral Dance. At the end of the ceremony, the news came that a second atomic bomb had been dropped, on Nagasaki.

That evening, during a concert held in the Pavilion, an official welcome was given to those who had served in the Forces during the war. Several hundred soldiers, sailors, airmen and nurses were assembled on the Eisteddfod platform, together with the band of the Welsh Guards, to be greeted by the Archdruid Crwys, the Bishop of St Asaph and the Chairman of the Eisteddfod Council, Alderman Emyr Williams. Captain Edward Jones, commodore of the Atlantic Fleet, and the author, were chosen to respond to the welcome, and David Lloyd, himself a Welsh Guardsman, and Tudor Evans, sang to the accompaniment of the Welsh Guards Band.

The Eisteddfod proceedings were interrupted the following morning, during the choral-speaking competition, for the audience to be informed that the Japanese had sought terms of surrender. The former Archdruid Elfed, now blind, was led to a microphone and, with one hand raised, he bid 'Gweddiwn!' (Let us pray), and thanked God that the war was over. The silence that followed his 'Amen' was broken only when he announced 'Cyfamod hedd, cyfamod cadarn Duw' (Covenant of peace, firm covenant of God), and that hymn was sung as it had never been sung before.

The Eisteddfod that should have been held at Mountain Ash in 1940 came there without Proclamation, in 1946, and the people of the neighbourhood were well pleased with the postponement when they found that Princess Elizabeth was attending the festival. At a ceremony that took place in a bosky glade in Dyffryn Park, on the morning of 6 August, the Princess was admitted into the Gorsedd of Bards wearing the green robe of the novitiate, the material for which she had provided, as cloth was still on ration. She placed her hands in those of the Archdruid Crwys, who received her as an Honorary Ovate under the bardic name 'Elisabeth o Windsor'.

The Princess then opened the Eisteddfod with a few words of Welsh, and was present at the Pavilion in the afternoon for the crowning ceremony, when she greeted Rhydwen Williams as he received the award for his *pryddest* to *Yr Arloeswr* (The Pioneer). The winner of the chair

Her Majesty the Queen, as Princess Elizabeth, being admitted a member of the Gorsedd by the Archdruid Crwys at the Mountain Ash Eisteddfod as 'Elisabeth o Windsor'.

poem, *Moliant i'r Amaethwr* (In Praise of the Farmer), was Dr Geraint Bowen (Geraint).

The Gorsedd Board, in its meetings after the war, had to deal with a number of contentious matters, not the least of which was an appearance by the Archdruid Crwys and the Herald Bard, Sieffre o Gyfarthfa, at the Wessex Festival in their robes of office. They had been persuaded by two members of the Gorsedd who lived in England to attend this event which they found, only after arrival at a country house in Dorset, to be weird and heretical, and a photograph which had appeared in the papers showed the Archdruid as though he were about to sacrifice a calf. Their explanation for their action was accepted by the Board, which then resolved that none of the robes or regalia should be removed from its storage without the consent of the Recorder and the Herald Bard.

An invitation to join the Ancient Order of Druid Hermetists was left on the table, and a request from the New York Welsh Society to establish a branch of the Gorsedd of Bards in that city was deferred until further information was available as to the present state of the American Gorsedd, that had been founded during the International Eisteddfod at Pittsburgh in 1913.

Welsh Members of Parliament were asked to intercede on behalf of Taldir, the Grand Druid of Brittany, who had been incarcerated as a *collaborateur* of the Vichy Government, and a letter was sent to him, in Quimper Gaol, to inform him of the action taken.

The Board had previously agreed that graduates in Welsh, of the University of Wales, should be admitted to the Ovate Order without having to take the Gorsedd examinations, but an attempt to include those who had graduated at St David's College, Lampeter, failed. Bachelors of Music and Fellows of the Royal College of Organists were now admitted provided they were fluent in the Welsh language.

A deputation that included the President of the Eisteddfod Council, the Archdruid and the Gorsedd Recorder, visited Brittany at the invitation of the French Government to assess the status of the Breton language in education and community life and, on its return, it published its report in Welsh, Breton, English and French.

The Mistress of the Robes, Mam o Nedd, presented a new Proclamation Scroll, the work of the Artist Meirion o Feirion (Meirion Roberts), to the Archdruid at the Mountain Ash Eisteddfod. The Scroll, on vellum, is decorated with the coats of arms of the thirteen Welsh shires, and the Proclamation, literally translated reads:

> When the age of Christ is [*blank*] and the time of the Bards of the Isle of Britain being in Alban Hefin, following this summons and invitation to the whole of Wales at the sound of the *Corn Gwlad*, and under notice of a period of a year and a day, in the sight of hearing of country and sovereign and in the face of the sun, the eye of light, be it known that a Gorsedd and a National Eisteddfod will be held in the town of [*blank*], with protection for all who might seek privilege and graduation and licence in Poetry and Music to repair to that town, where there will not be a naked weapon against them. And there will be present the Archdruid and the Officers of the Gorsedd, and other Bards and Graduates by the privilege and custom of the Bards of the

Isle of Britain; and there will be considered the judgement of the Chair and Gorsedd upon Poetry and Bardism, and concerning poetic gift, conduct and knowledge of those who seek the graduation of the Royal National Eisteddfod of Wales under the privilege and custom of the Gorsedd of Bards of the Isle of Britain.

Crwys, who had been appointed Archdruid for a period of three years in 1939, remained in that office throughout the war, and his ready wit and ease of manner provided a much appreciated relief from the prevailing gloom of those years. He was succeeded by Wil Ifan who was installed in 1947, during the Proclamation of the Bridgend Eisteddfod, which was most fitting as he was a Congregational minister in that town. He had won the Crown at Abergavenny (1913), Birkenhead (1917) and Pwllheli (1925).

The office of Archdruid was confined to *Prifeirdd*, who had won either the Chair or the Crown, but repeated attempts to alter that rule were made by Meurig Prysor (Canon Maurice Jones), who wanted to be appointed to the office even though he had won neither. He was Principal of St David's College, Lampeter, and had served as Gorsedd treasurer from 1925 until 1938, when he was made *Bardd yr Orsedd*. Not satisfied with that, a new office was specially created for him in 1947, that of *Derwydd Gweinyddol* (Attendant Druid), with no specific duty except to preside in the absence of the Archdruid and all former Archdruids.

Captain Geoffrey Crawshay (Sieffre o Gyfarthfa) resigned from the office of Herald Bard in 1947, owing to ill health, and his place was taken by Captain R. W. Jones (Erfyl Fychan), historian and one of the founders of *Cymdeithas Cerdd Dant*.

There had never been any limitation on the number of times that either the Chair or the Crown could be won. The Chair had been awarded to Dyfed on four occasions, at Merthyr Tudful (1881), Liverpool (1884), Brecon (1889), and Merthyr again in 1901 and J. T. Job, who had won it three times, at Newport (1897), Llanelli (1903) and Neath (1918) and he had also been awarded the Crown at Liverpool in 1900, a feat that had been equalled only by Dewi Emrys. Cynan and Caradog Prichard had both received the Crown three times, and had also won the Chair. Pedrog had been awarded the Chair three times, and the Crown had been won three times by Ben Davies, J. M. Edwards, Wil Ifan and Crwys. T. H. Parry Williams had been awarded the Chair and the Crown at the same Eisteddfod, at Wrexham (1912) and again at Bangor in 1915.

Dewi Emrys' turbulent character had become public knowledge at Pontypool in 1924, after he had been denied the prize for the Crown poem on *Atgof* (Rememberance). The winning *pryddest*, by E. Prosser Rhys, had been criticised for its salaciousness and Dewi maintained that his entry was more apposite, free from obscenity and a better poem anyway. Two of the adjudicators, Gwili and Crwys, had placed his poem second, but the other, Professor W. J. Gruffydd, had given it third place in the competition. A contentious press correspondence ensued during which a long-standing enmity, that had its origins, according to rumour, in rivalry for the hand of a fair lady, was aired as professor and poet hurled abuse at each other.

The Crown had been offered at Swansea in 1926, for a collection of poems. Dewi Emrys, by that time, had left the ministry and led the life of a tramp, sleeping in barns and hayricks, most of the time in north Pembrokeshire. He used to recall an occasion when he had been denied shelter, by a Nonconformist minister on a dark and rainy night, and had had to sleep in a hay barn. 'The organ notes of the rain beating on the tin roof gave me a song,' he wrote later. 'I decided there and then to compete for the National Crown.' At Swansea, he submitted a selection of poems which he called, appropriately, *Rhigymau'r Ffordd Fawr* (Rhymes of the Open Road) and it was the unanimous choice of the three adjudicators, Elfed, Professor T. Gwynn Jones and Professor W. J. Gruffydd, out of thirty-two entries, to receive the Crown. Dewi's *nom-de-guerre* was *Crythor Crwydrad* (Wandering Minstrel) and contemporary press reports were quick to compare him with W. H. Davies, the tramp poet. He celebrated his success by entertaining his friends at the Mackworth Hotel, after pawning his Crown, which was later redeemed by a man from New Quay for £3 and given pride of place in his home, that was only a stone's throw from the house in which Dewi had been born.

Dewi was awarded the Chair at the Liverpool Eisteddfod in 1929, and he was also the runner-up for the Crown. He won the Chair again the following year, at Llanelli, for his *Y Galilead* (The Galilean), and his was the best *awdl* at Bangor in 1943, where he had to be content with a silver medal, instead of a chair, on account of the exigencies of the war.

The Chair awarded at the Bridgend Eisteddfod in 1948 for an *awdl* on *Yr Alltud* (The Exile), was again his, and he thus became the first person to win the Chair competition four times, as well as winning the

Crown. His submission of a poem at Bridgend was an act of defiance that could be seen in his face as he assumed the Chair in the manner of a man who wished to cock a snook at his critics and at authority in general.

It was decided that, henceforth, no one could be awarded either the Chair or the Crown on more than two occasions, but the rule did not prevent Caradog Prichard from winning the Chair in 1962 for, although he had won the Crown three times, he had not captured the Chair.

In 1949 the Gorsedd published the first issue of its journal *Y Corn Gwlad*, so named after the fanfare sounded at its ceremonies. It contained articles, stories, poems and music, along with the syllabus of the Gorsedd examinations. Its editor, John Eilian, was awarded the Crown at the Eisteddfod held that year at Dolgellau, to add to the Chair he had won two years previously at Colwyn Bay. *Y Corn Gwlad* was hailed as 'a dignified, attractive and lively journal that would be a permanent link between an enlightened people and its national festival.' Sad to say, it ceased after the first issue.

In order to provide a closer relationship between the Celtic nations, the Gorsedd decided to arrange regular exchange visits with the daughter-Gorseddau in Brittany and Cornwall, and with the *Oireachtas* in Ireland and the *Mod* in Scotland. In the following year, a strong deputation from the Gorsedd attended a joint-Gorsedd of Welsh, Breton and Cornish Bards at Tregastel, in Brittany, which was considered to have been beneficial to the Breton cause.

At the Proclamation of the Llanrwst Eisteddfod, in June 1950, Cynan was installed Archdruid in succession to Wil Ifan, and his duties as Recorder were carried out by the Herald Bard, Erfyl Fychan. At the ceremony, two trumpeters from the Welsh Guards sounded the fanfares of the Corn Gwlad and this arrangement continued until 1954 when their place was taken by members of the Llanrug and Deiniolen Band.

1950 – 1992

LTHOUGH THE promoters of the Eisteddfod at Dolgellau could claim to have held the festival almost entirely in Welsh, and had even provided a Welsh translation for every musical work, it was at Caerffili, in 1950, that 'the all-Welsh rule' was fully implemented. The competitions and the adjudications and the general proceedings were conducted in Welsh throughout the festival. The rule was broken only by the Lord Mayor of Cardiff, inadvertently, while he welcomed overseas visitors, and by Ness Edwards, the local Member of Parliament, deliberately, in a speech attacking the Eisteddfod's language policy.

A Gorsedd delegation visiting the Breton Gorsedd at Trehorenteuc, on the edge of the Forêt de Paimpont, in 1951, found the Bretons learning Welsh from *Cymraeg Hep Poen* (Welsh Without Pain), a Breton translation of Caradar's *Welsh Made Easy* by Pierre Loisel (Eostig Sarzhau), the Grand Druid of Brittany.

The Eisteddfod held at Llanrwst in 1951 was featured as a part of the Festival of Britain that was held that year. The little town was overjoyed when it saw the Crown being awarded to one of its own sons, T. Glynne Davies, for his *Adfeilion* (Ruins). The Chair was won by Brinli (Brinley Richards) for an *awdl* on *Y Dyffryn* (The Valley).

The constitution embodying the agreement made at Machynlleth, owing to the intervention of the war, was not completed until 1952 when it was presented at the annual meeting of the Eisteddfod Court, during the Eisteddfod held at Aberystwyth, by Sir David Hughes Parry, one of the Eisteddfod's legal advisers, who apologised for the delay of fifteen years in its finalisation. It provided that the National Eisteddfod would be governed by an Eisteddfod Court, comprising all the subscribing members, with its administration being undertaken by the Eisteddfod Council, and the affairs of the Gorsedd of Bards being governed by the Gorsedd Board, the two bodies having equal status.

Although Cynan's term of office as Archdruid had come to an end in

1953, it was extended by one year, so that he was still in office at the time of the Coronation of Her Majesty the Queen (Elisabeth o Windsor). The Queen, during her Coronation tour, visited Llangollen International Eisteddfod and called at the pavilion that was being prepared for the Eisteddfod to be held at Rhyl.

The year of the Queen's Coronation was also the year in which the Crown was awarded to a woman for the first time. Cynan and Ernest Roberts, the joint secretaries of the Eisteddfod, wishing to keep the matter a secret, conspired to mislead by inventing a rumour to the effect that the Crown had been won by someone who had already won it twice before and was, therefore, ineligible to receive it. The story was spread through an unsuspecting accomplice at Morris's Bookshop in Caernarfon and, as a result, the vast audience in the Pavilion at Rhyl was taken completely by surprise when Dilys Cadwaladr was led to the Eisteddfod platform to have the Crown placed on her head for her *pryddest* to *Y Llen* (The Veil). The Chair was awarded to Erni Llwyd Williams for an *awdl* to *Y Ffordd* (The Way).

The Eisteddfod held at Ystradgynlais in 1954 is remembered, above all, for the rain that fell without respite throughout the week. As it had not been possible to hold any of the Gorsedd ceremonies out of doors, and so as not to disappoint the children, it was decided that the Floral Dance should take place on the Pavilion stage during the chairing ceremony. This proved to be so popular a move that it was henceforth incorporated in both the crowning and chairing ceremonies as a tribute to the successful bard.

At Ystradgynlais, too, began the custom of greeting the delegates from the Celtic countries on the Eisteddfod platform during the crowning ceremony, when one of the delegates from each of the five countries was invited to address the audience in a few words in his, or her, own tongue.

Captain Geoffrey Crawshay (Sieffre o Gyfarthfa), who had been Herald Bard from 1926 to 1947, died in 1954 and the Gorsedd was represented at his memorial service at the Royal Military Chapel, Wellington Barracks. He had played a significant role, with Cynan and Mam o Nedd, in reforming the Gorsedd ceremonies and, in his memory, two silver trumpets, that had sounded the fanfare at the Coronation of Her Majesty the Queen at Westminster Abbey, were presented to the Gorsedd for use by its trumpeters.

Dyfnallt (Dyfnallt Owen), who had won the Chair at Swansea in 1907, and was now over eighty years of age, was installed Archdruid in succession to Cynan at the Proclamation Ceremony at Pwllheli in 1954.

The Mistress of the Robes, Mrs W. M. Coombe-Tennant (Mam o Nedd) resigned that year after holding the office for thirty years, and she was succeeded by Mrs Maude Thomas (Telynores Rhondda). Mrs Coombe-Tennant died two years later, and left the Gorsedd a legacy of £5,000 towards the maintenance of the Gorsedd regalia.

The following year the correspondent of the *Manchester Guardian* recalled 'the semi-amphibious Gorsedd ceremony' at Ystradgynlais, when one wondered 'which is the most desolate sight – a white-robed Druid under an umbrella, or a white-robed Druid looking as if he wished he had one,' and went on to assure his readers that there would have been no need of an umbrella at the Eisteddfod at Pwllheli. There, when 'the oblates, bards and druids filed into the circle of stones set on a patch of ground between the tall grey lodging-houses and the pale grass of the sandhills, the sun, "the eye of light"... was already hot'. He was of the opinion that, for the satirist, 'the hocus-pocus which Iolo Morganwg had invented for the bardic system is an over-easy target. The truth is that after some 160 years, Iolo Morganwg is himself historic.'

The office of *Cymrawd* (Fellow) was created as a mark of honour that could be bestowed upon a person who had rendered outstanding service to the Eisteddfod over a long period of time. Not more than one person could receive the honour in any one year, and not more than five may hold it at the same time. It was the intention that its first recipient should be D. R. Hughes who, apart from his work among the Welsh community in London and his care for the welfare of Welsh service men and women serving overseas during the war, had served as joint-secretary, with Cynan, of the Eisteddfod Council from 1935 to 1947. He died, however, before the honour could be bestowed upon him, and the distinction then fell on Meurig Prysor. The office of *Derwydd Gweinyddol* that had been specially created for him was perpetuated by the appointment to it, in 1956, of Caerwyn (Owen Ellis Roberts), who was best known as an Eisteddfod conductor.

The Crown was offered for a play in verse, instead of the traditional *pryddest*, at the Aberdare Eisteddfod in 1956, but none of the entries was considered worthy of the prize.

The Gorsedd Board published a handbook for the guidance of local committees, indicating the procedure to follow in making preparations for Gorsedd ceremonies.

William Morris, who had won the Chair at Neath in 1934, was installed Archdruid in succession to Dyfnallt at the Proclamaion of the Ebbw Vale Eisteddfod in 1957.

The Crown was again offered for a verse-play at Llangefni in 1957 and, this time, an entry worthy of the award was found in Dyfnallt Morgan's *Rhwng Dau* (Between Two).

The shortage of materials still made it difficult to be able to provide new robes but, in August 1957, the Herald Bard, Erfyl Fychan, was able to report that, at long last, he had obtained a quotation from Messrs Caldwell of Stockport for the production of bardic robes at a cost of 35 shillings (£1.75) each.

The Eisteddfod returned to the county of Monmouth in 1958 after an absence of thirty-four years. Earlier invitations from Ebbw Vale had been tactfully declined in view of the anglicised nature of the locality, but the festival held there in 1958 was a resounding success. A commentator who asked afterwards 'What's left apart form the Gorsedd pillars?' also gave the answer by pointing out that there remained a new understanding of, and for, things Welsh, together with the realisation among the ordinary folk of Gwent that they, too, were the inheritors of a great Welsh patrimony.

At its annual meeting, at Ebbw Vale, the Eisteddfod Court decided to send a loyal message to the Queen expressing its pleasure that Her Majesty had ordered 'Letters Patent to be passed under the Great Seal for creating His Royal Highness Prince Charles Philip Arthur George, Duke of Cornwall and Rothesay, Earl of Carrick, Baron of Renfrew, Lord of the Isles and Great Steward of Scotland, Prince of Wales and Earl of Chester'. The Gorsedd Board sent its greetings to the Prince, with a specially bound copy of *Hanes yr Eisteddfod* (The Story of the Eisteddfod), and commissioned its Recorder, Cynan, to prepare a revised version of *Tywysog Gwlad y Bryniau*, that had been translated as 'God Bless the Prince of Wales', so that it could be sung at the close of the chairing ceremony.

The Gorsedd Board had taken the lead in objecting to an augmented version of the Dragon Badge of Wales issued by the Welsh Office in 1953, in which the dragon was charged upon a shield encircled with a riband, ensigned with the Royal Crown and bearing the motto *Y Ddraig Goch Ddyry Cychwyn* (The Red Dragon gives the lead) which, the bards recollected, was a line taken from a *cywydd* by Deio ab Ieuan Ddu (*fl.* 1450) requesting the gift of a bull and a heifer. This badge was widely held to be unacceptable as it usurped the dragon passant of

Cadwaladr, which Henry Tudor had carried at Bosworth Field and which had been described as the Welsh national emblem as early as the eighth century. The Board made representations to the Secretary of State for Wales, Henry Brooke, and invited Welsh institutions and public bodies throughout Wales to give their support, to which more than two hundred local authorities and organisations responded. The Constable of Caernarfon Castle had failed to give an undertaking that the traditional flag would be flown from the Eagle Tower during the Proclamation Ceremony to be held at Caernarfon but, as a result of the approach to the Secretary of State, such an assurance was given. The Secretary of State also made a statement in Parliament conveying the Queen's wish that the traditional flag alone should fly from Government buildings henceforth and should be regarded as the official banner of Wales.

The Proclamation Ceremony held within the walls of Caernarfon Castle in June 1958 was enlivened by the aerobatic display, and high-pitched calls, of a sociable chough that wanted to perch on the harp and on the Archdruid's crown.

A proposal to hold the Eisteddfod in London in 1959, to mark the

Presentation of the Aberthged *to the Archdruid Wiliam Morris at a Gorsedd ceremony in Caernarfon Castle, 1959.*

fiftieth anniversary of the festival held at the Albert Hall in 1909, was discussed at a meeting of leading members of the London Welsh community but, as there was no unanimity, the invitation was not extended and the Eisteddfod was held, for the seventh time, at Caernarfon.

A woman's-eye view of the Gorsedd was given, during the Caernarfon Eisteddfod, by the *Western Mail* correspondent Jane Pugh, who wondered who was 'responsible for making the Archdruid look like a cross between a Pharaoh and a Roman Senator', and divined that 'the inspiration must have come from the painting of Dante's meeting with Beatrice on the Bridge'.

She returned, two days later, to remind her readers of the time when Professor Timothy Lewis, although he was the son-in-law of one Gorsedd Recorder, Beriah, and brother-in-law of another, Gwilym Rhug, had delivered a withering comment on the untidiness of the Gorsedd bards, and had maintained that Cynan had been appointed Recorder in 1933 (*recté* 1935) with a mandate to spruce up the bards, and that the Herald Bard had been mounted on horse-back so that he could keep better control of the Gorsedd procession. Before then, she claimed, 'the Bards were all wearing dark lounge suits and black shoes with their robes and, as far as my memory serves me, the Archdruid alone wore laurel leaves. After 1933 the Gorsedd dress started to get fancier and fancier. Bits of gold lamé and lashings of laurel leaves arrived, and white shoes peeping out coyly from beneath the robes like friendly little white mice.'

The degree to which secrecy concerning the identity of the winner of the Chair or Crown is observed was related by Brinley Richards, (Brinli). He, and T. Llew Jones who had been awarded the Chair at Ebbw Vale the previous year, were invited to address congratulatory verses to the successful chaired bard at Caernarfon. They had met frequently on the Eisteddfod field during the early part of the week, and had even discussed their joint assignment. Brinli was taken aback, therefore, when, in response to the Archdruid's call, the winner of the chair, for his poem *Y Dringwr* (The Climber), got to his feet and turned out to be none other than T. Llew Jones.

At the Proclamation of the Dyffryn Maelor Eisteddfod at Rhosllannerchrugog on 22 June 1960, Trefin (Edgar Phillips: 1889-1962) was installed Archdruid in succession to William Morris. He had been the Grand Sword-bearer since 1945 and he was succeeded in that office by the author.

Trefin (Edgar Phillips), Grand Swordbearer (1947-60) and Archdruid (1960-62).

The Gorsedd Banner had become frayed and faded, after long use, and a new one, of the same design as the old, was made by Miss Iles of Brynsiecyn. Its cost, amounting to £100, was met by Señor Hywel Hughes of Bogota. Telynores Rhondda resigned that year and her place, as Mistress of the Robes, was taken by Mrs Anne Weeks (Cerddores Moelfre).

The opening Gorsedd ceremony at the Cardiff Eisteddfod was held in the grounds of Cardiff Castle, in a circle of stone pillars brought from Craig-yr-hesg Quarries, near Pontypridd, and Trefin appeared resplendent in a new robe, presented by the London Welsh Association at a cost of £100. The weather had changed by the Thursday morning, however, and the Bards had to meet indoors, in the Reardon Smith Lecture Theatre.

Although the contestants for the Chair had been given a choice of subjects, *Morgannwg* (Glamorgan) or *Dydd Barn a Diwedd Byd* (Day of Judgement and World's End), none was sufficiently inspired to write an *awdl* worthy of the prize. The Herald Bard and the Grand Sword-bearer therefore, in accordance with custom, laid the Grand Sword across the Chair, that had been carved of oak from the Llanover estate, to indicate that the Chair of the Eisteddfod held at Cardiff in 1960 had found no deserving poet. The gloom that descends on *eisteddfodwyr* on such occasions was relieved the next day when the Queen visited the festival and was invited to occupy the chair while she received an address of welcome, delivered in Welsh, by the President of the Eisteddfod, Sir Thomas Herbert Parry-Williams. The address recalled that Her Majesty, as Princess Elizabeth had been 'graciously pleased to visit the National Eisteddfod in the year 1946 at Mountain Ash,' and on that occasion had been 'invested as an Honorary Ovate of the Gorsedd of Bards with the title *Elisabeth o Windsor*,' and humbly thanked her 'for continuing the tradition of Royal patronage for the National Eisteddfod of Wales'. It rejoiced in the thought that her presence would 'enhance the dignity of this national institution, whose main objects are the fostering of the language and the promotion of the arts of Wales, the land whose name, we are proud to recall, is borne by Your Majesty's eldest son'.

The Duke of Edinburgh was initiated a member of the Gorsedd of Bards by the Archdruid Trefin, under the bardic name *Philip Meirionydd*, in reference to his title as Earl of Merioneth.

The Queen was so impressed with the performace of the young singers competing for the Osborne Roberts Medal that she and the Duke returned the following morning and brought with them, for his first public appearance in the Principality, the newly created Prince of Wales, together with the Princess Anne, Princess Alexandra and Prince Michael of Kent.

The royal visit attracted record crowds, but it brought discord too. Seven of the leading members of the local committee had resigned on the pretext that the all-Welsh rule would be infringed, but as the Queen did not speak, the rule remained unbroken.

The introduction of nylon robes for members of the Gorsedd provided a timely subject for the *Western Mail* cartoonist, Geoffrey Evans, who portrayed a couple of robed bards walking in the rain, with one saying to the other: 'Fortunately, my tailor used drip-dry material!'

The Eisteddfod returned to Rhosllannerchrugog in 1961, but this time it was known as Eisteddfod Dyffryn Maelor. Another *Western Mail* correspondent, John Lloyd, now came forward to express his views on the Eisteddfod in an article under the heading 'The Annual Market Place for Welsh Cutlure'. The Eisteddfod, he considered, was 'the most confused institution in a confused nation. Half circus and half concert, it has garnishings from chapel vestry, brains trust, school prize day, literary luncheon, sale of work and cocktail bar without cocktails ... Apart from the House of Commons, no national assembly can ever have had so many critics and still flourish like a sprouting tree.' He pointed out that 'much of the criticism and animosity comes, understandably, from those unable to speak Welsh who accuse the Eisteddfod of locking the doors against them. But there remains a general ignorance of its aims, purpose and character'. The editor quietly observed that 'in a country worried by Berlin, H-bombs, the space race and the common market, it is a striking thing that some people can still centre their main passions and anxieties in the preservation of the all-Welsh rule.'

The rift in the Breton Gorsedd continued to cause concern and, after weighing the claims of the contending parties, the Gorsedd of Bards recognised the leadership claim of Eostig Sarzhau and he was duly installed Grand Druid of Brittany by the Archdruid Trefin at a ceremony held at St Malo in 1961.

The Proclamation of the Llanelli Eisteddfod was held, by chance, on the summer solstice, and was witnessed by a crowd of thirty thousand people. The writer and broadcaster Robert Robinson was present at the Eisteddfod the following year and gave his impressions in an article headed 'Bardolatry' in the *Sunday Times*. Of the Pavilion, he declared that 'the object of the building was to put a roof over as much space as possible, and from the inside the walls seemed to be standing at the horizon.' The bards, he said, 'looked like super-surgeons in sterile robes on their way to a Gothic operation. The Archdruid was in gold and a tall man with a moustache, who looked like one of nature's Flight-Lieutenants, carried an enormous sword.' Caradog Prichard, 'a journalist and popular with all,' was installed in the Chair for his *Llef Un yn Llefain* (The Cry of One Crying) and, at the end of the ceremony, the bards departed, 'leaving behind them an impression of spontaneous, familial, perhaps slightly claustrophobic expression of togetherness, flawed by a ritual which looked religious and was nothing of the sort'.

Llywelyn Fadog (Trefor H. Hughes) was appointed to the new office of *Pensaer* (Architect) in 1962.

The health of the Archdruid Trefin was visibly failing during the Llanelli Eisteddfod. He died at the end of August and his ashes were interred in the soil of his native Pembrokeshire. He was succeeded by Cynan, who thus became the first person to serve a second term as Archdruid. Ab Eos (T. W. Thomas), the Gorsedd Treasurer was temporarily appointed Recorder in his place.

At the Llandudno Eisteddfod in 1963, Sir Thomas Parry-Williams and the Deputy Archdruid Williams Morris, two of the adjudicators, did not consider any of the eleven *awdlau* submitted, on the subject *Genesis*, worthy of the Chair, but Thomas Parry, the other, was of the view that one of the entries, inspired by John Piper's window in Coventry Cathedral, deserved the prize, although he confessed that he found its meaning abstruse. After the Grand Sword had been laid across the Chair, the Archdruid Cynan strongly refuted allegations made by 'some people, either through ignorance or possibly from irresponsible malice, that officials had tried to persuade the adjudicators to change their minds rather than that the cermony should be lost.' The Gorsedd, he said, was simply concerned that the highest standards should be maintained.

Alan Villiers, who had sailed *Mayflower II* across the Atlantic in 1959, visited the Eisteddfod at Llandudno and, afterwards, gave his impressions in the *National Geographic Magazine* under the heading 'Wales, Land of the Bards', in which he stated that 'a spontaneous roar of the most intensely felt emotion, ... a moaning roar of heartfelt disappointment, with overtones almost of despair' arose from the audience when it was announced that 'the ritual Chairing of the Bard would not take place. And as 'the three Orders of the Gorsedd filed slowly from the stage and up the long aisle, the archdruid and sword-bearer leading them ... and passed out into the gray day, the 8,000 still sat there in the huge pavilion, as if they had been stunned. Where else, I thought, would a people feel so intensely about poetry?'

Once again, the Queen came to dispel the air of gloom by paying a visit to the Eisteddfod, with her husband, the Duke of Edinburgh, who had been admitted into the Gorsedd three years previously as Philip Meirionydd. As Her Majesty had, the previous day, appointed Major Francis Jones (Breudeth) to the new office of Wales Herald of Arms

Extraordinary, a title that had not been in use since the end of the fourteenth century, there was an expectation, that proved unfounded, that she would announce the date of the Investiture of the Prince of Wales.

A new lapel badge, designed by the artist Douglas Williams, and depicting the Gorsedd symbol of the three shafts of light, was prepared in time for the Llandudno Eisteddfod.

The Gorsedd ceremonies at Llandudno were held, as in 1896, in a leafy glade in the attractive surroundings of Happy Valley.

Having, apparently, mended the rift in the Breton Gorsedd, it now transpired that its members had consorted with other, unrecognised, Druid Orders and the Gorsedd of Bards withdrew its recognition and refused to visit Brittany in 1964.

The Eisteddfod was held that year at Swansea, in Singleton Park, which was convenient for Gorsedd cricket-lovers, among whom none was more fervent than the former Archdruid Crwys. They were able to visit St Helen's between ceremonies, where Glamorgan was playing the Australians.

The needs of those who were unable to speak or understand Welsh were met by Television Wales and the West who provided a closed circuit service giving instant translation into English of all the stage events as they occurred, both on screen in a small marquee and on hand receivers that were supplied free of charge for use in the Pavilion, or on the Eisteddfod field.

For a number of years, the prose writers had expressed their dissatisfaction with the chief prize, the Prose Medal, and with the ceremony at which it was presented. Some of them felt that the two most colourful ceremonies of the Eisteddfod were being 'wasted on compiling poetry which the majority of the Welsh people do not understand,' and others wanted to have the Crown offered for the best prose, leaving the Chair for poetry. In an effort to solve the discontentment, a panel of leading poets and prose writers was appointed in 1965 to consider the relationship between poetry and prose competitions and to endeavour to establish an equal status for all creative writing. It recommended, however, that the Crown should remain the award for a *pryddest*, or sequence of poems, and made suggestions for the improvement of the ceremony at which the Prose Medal was presented, and that the ceremony should be known as *Seremoni'r Prif Lenor Rhyddiaith* (The Chief Prose-writer's Cermony). These recommendations were adopted by the Eisteddfod Court at its annual meeting held during the Eisteddfod at Newtown in 1965 and implemented the following year at Aberafan.

The subject of the *awdl* competition at Swansea was *Patagonia* and the Chair was awarded, most fittingly, to Bryn Williams (Bryn) who had been brought up in Patagonia and had lived there until he was twenty years of age. The centenary of the foundation of the Welsh settlement there was celebrated with a pageant during the Eisteddfod at Newtown, and the Patagonian delegation, always assured of a warm welcome, were given an especially cordial reception at the Eisteddfod that year.

The Gorsedd Board heard with some concern that the minutes of its earlier meetings had been sold to Harvard University by one J. R. Morris, and the National Library of Wales was asked to obtain photostat copies.

The Eisteddfod had obtained royal patronage for many years but it was necessary for an application to be addressed to Buckingham Palace each year. In 1965, it was decided to submit a petition for a Royal Charter but, in the meantime a communication was received from the Home Secretary stating that the Queen had given her consent for the Eisteddfod to be known permanently as *Eisteddfod Genedlaethol Frenhinol Cymru* (The Royal National Eisteddfod of Wales).

The Chair was awarded, at Aberafan, to Dic Jones for his poem *Y Cynhaeaf* (The Harvest), described by one of the adjudicators as 'one of the best *awdlau* ever to emerge from an Eisteddfod competition ... truly a masterpiece,' and compared, for excellence, with R. Williams Parry's poem *Yr Haf* (The Summer), which had won the Chair at Colwyn Bay in 1910. The Crown, awarded to Dafydd Jones, of Ffair Rhos, was made, not of the customary silver but of steel, to symbolize the industry that had made Port Talbot world famous.

Cynan was succeeded as Archdruid, at the Proclamation ceremony at Bala in 1966, by Gwyndaf, who had won the Chair at Caernarfon in 1935 for his *vers libre* poem *Magdalen*.

Erfyl Fychan retired from the office of Herald Bard, which he had held for twenty years, and he was succeeded by the author, to whose place as Grand Sword-bearer, T. Gwynn Jones (Gwynn Tregarth) was elected. Erfyl Fychan became Director of Examinations in succession to Brynallt (G. Brynallt Williams) who had held that office, and also acted as Treasurer and Membership Secretary. When Erfyl died in 1967, Huw Davies (Huw Tegai) became the Director of Examinations.

Eluned Phillips (Luned Teifi), in winning the Crown for her poem

Corlannau (Pinfolds) at the Bala Eisteddfod in 1967, became only the second woman to have done so, following Dilys Cadwaladr (1953), and it was revealed that she had also written the *pryddest* that was considered the next best.

Sir Thomas Parry-Williams retired from the presidency of the Eisteddfod Court that year and Cynan, the Gorsedd Recorder and Joint-Secretary of the Eisteddfod Court and twice Archdruid, was elected in his place.

The ceremonial duties of the Gorsedd of Bards are confined to the National Eisteddfod but, in 1968, the Gorsedd took part in a festival at Caerwys held to commemorate the four-hundredth anniversary of the Eisteddfod held there by commission of Queen Elizabeth I. Among those present were several descendants of the gentlemen named in the royal commission.

One of the Presidents of the Day at the Barry Eisteddfod, in 1968, was Sir Cennydd Traherne, Lord Lieutenant of Glamorgan, who had learned to speak Welsh. He reminded his audience that the Eisteddfod was the biggest cultural festival in Europe, as well as being the most powerful bastion of the Welsh language. Sir Cennydd, a member of the Gorsedd, was appointed a Knight of the Most Noble Order of the Garter, and may have been the first Welshman in Wales to receive that dignity since it was bestowed on Sir Rhys ap Thomas in 1507.

In January 1968 the Archdruid Gwyndaf and Cynan, the Recorder, were invited to attend a meeting of the Earl Marshal's Committee to make preliminary arrangements for the Investiture of the Prince of Wales. They were informed that the Gorsedd and the Eisteddfod had been allotted places for a deputation of sixteen members to attend the Investiture of the Prince of Wales in 1911, but they succeeded in increasing this number to thirty representatives. It was decided that the deputation should comprise seven Eisteddfod Council officials, eleven Gorsedd officers and twelve Gorsedd members drawn equally from the three Orders of the Gorsedd.

One the day of the Investiture, the first of July 1969, the Gorsedd procession entered the Water Gate at Caernarfon Castle and emerged from the Eagle Tower on to the greensward, escorted by a Green Staff Officer of the Royal Household, Sir Jeremy Mostyn, Bart., a descendent of William Mostyn who was present at Caerwys. It was led by the Herald Bard who was followed by four Ovates, in green robes, four Bards in blue, four Druids in white, the Gorsedd officers, the Archdruid Tilsli, who had succeeded Gwyndaf in the interim, and the seven officers of the Eisteddfod Court in purple robes, all of which

The Prince of Wales, after his Investiture at Caernarfon Castle in 1969, visited the National Eisteddfod at Flint, where he was greeted by the author, as Herald Bard.

added greatly to the colourful pageantry within the castle walls and provided a contrast to the uniforms of the Yeomen of the Guard, the Gentlemen-at-Arms, the Heralds and Kings of Arms.

Following the Investiture, Cynan received the honour of Knighthood, and his fellow officers arranged a dinner in his honour at The Queen Hotel at Chester.

The Prince of Wales paid a visit to the Eisteddfod held at Flint where he was given an ecstatic welcome by the people in the packed Pavilion and on the Eisteddfod field.

The Chair was awarded to James Nicholas for his *awdl* to *Yr Alwad* (The Call), and the Crown, offered for a sequence of poems, was won by Dafydd Rowlands for his *I Gwestiynnau Fy Mab* (To my Son's Questions), consisting of ten poems written in *vers libre*. The high standard of the work, and the appeal of the genre, caused the innovation to be adopted as an alternative form to the *pryddest* in successive years.

The Gorsedd felt devastated in 1970 by the death of its most influential figure, Cynan, who had been its Recorder for half a life span and had shared the secretaryship of the Eisteddfod Council, first with D. R. Hughes and then with Ernest Roberts, for almost as long. He was the only person ever to be twice Archdruid, and was President of the Eisteddfod Court when he died. He had attracted attention as a soldier-poet in the First World War, with his poem *Nico*, in which he sent a goldfinch as a love-messenger to his sweetheart, Megan, in Anglesey and, from the time that he won the Crown for his contro-

Cynan (Sir Cynan Evans-Jones), Gorsedd Recorder (1935-70) and twice Archdruid (1950-54 and 1963-66).

versial poem *Mab Y Bwthyn* at the Caernarfon Eisteddfod in 1921, he had been an outstanding Eisteddfod figure. He gave the Gorsedd a new dimension in the structure of the National Eisteddfod and he, with Captain Geoffrey Crawshay, the Herald Bard, brought order and discipline to its colourful pageantry.

Gwyndaf the former Archdruid, was appointed Recorder to succeed Cynan.

Apart from honorary members, the Gorsedd admitted only candidiates who had gained proficiency in its examinations in poetry, literature or music, that were conducted at convenient centres throughout Wales during the month of April each year. In 1970 the Board agreed to admit without further examination, any person who had obtained a University degree in Welsh or Welsh Literature, or in Music and was Welsh-speaking, into the Order of the Blue Robe.

The Chair was won, at the Ammanford Eisteddfod, in 1970 by Tomi Evans for his *awdl* in *vers libre* to the legendary wild boar *Y Twrch*

Trwyth, and Bryan Martin Davies received the Crown for a sequence of poems, *Darluniau ar Gynfas* (Portraits on Canvas). Honorary members admitted to the Gorsedd that year included Wynford Vaughan-Thomas, the BBC commentator Alun Williams, and the popular singer Mary Hopkin.

The Eisteddfod was held at Bangor, in 1971 in the grounds of Penrhyn Castle which had been built by the second Lord Penrhyn in 1827-47 as a manifestation of his status as owner of the Bethesda slate quarries, at a cost of half a million pounds. Guto'r Glyn and Rhys Goch Eryri had been here to sing the praises of the lords of an earlier time. The subject of the Chair poem, not inappropriately, was *Y Chwarelwr* (The Quarryman) and the President of the Day, Ernest Roberts, who had retired that year as joint-secretary of the Eisteddfod Court and was himself the son of a quarryman, pointed out that the three adjudicators, William Morris, Gwilym R. Jones and Dr (later Sir) Thomas Parry, were also the sons of quarrymen.

D. Hugh Thomas (Huw Tomos) was appointed Membership Secretary in succession to Alun Ogwen who had died suddenly during the Eisteddfod at Ammanford the previous year.

The singer Mary Hopkin admitted at Ammanford in 1970, with the Recorder Gwyndaf, Mistress of the Robes Cerddores Moelfre, the Herald Bard and the Archdruid Tilsli.

Proposals were laid before the Gorsedd Board by Euros (Euros Bowen) to modify the Gorsedd ceremonies 'so as to relate them more closely with the aims of the Eisteddfod, namely the fostering of the Welsh language and the promotion of culture and of the arts in Wales.' The word *Aberthged* he found to be offensive as, in its literal meaning, it could be taken to denote a sacrificial offering, whereas, in fact, it had by long usage referred simply to a sheaf of corn and flowers of the field that was presented to the Archdruid at Gorsedd ceremonies. In its place was substituted *Blodeuged*, a word invented to mean 'a gift of flowers', and the sheaf was replaced by a reticular tray of wild flowers.

In an attempt to settle the differences that had existed between the Gorsedd of Bards and the Breton Gorsedd over the previous eighteen years, and to establish the relationship between the Gorsedd and its daughter-Gorseddau in Brittany and Cornwall, the three Gorsedd leaders met at Carlyon Bay in Cornwall and signed the following agreement:

> We, Tilsli, Archdruid of Wales, Eostig Sarzhau, Grand Druid of Brittany and Trevanyon, Grand Bard of Cornwall, together with Gwyndaf, Recorder of the Gorsedd of Bards and former Archdruid of Wales, in convocation on this the third day of September 1971 at Carlyon Bay, hereby reaffirm our personal allegiance and that of our respective Gorseddau to the Celtic Heritage that has brought us together.
>
> We acknowledge:
> 1. The supreme authority of the Archdruid of the Gorsedd of Bards of the Isle of Britain in all matters of Gorseddau constitution and practice.
> 2. The absolute necessity of guarding our respective gatherings against intrusion by alien and non-Celtic elements and personnel.
> 3. The complete autonomy of the Gorseddau of Wales, Brittany and Cornwall in their own domestic affairs.

The Dyffryn Clwyd Eisteddfod was proclaimed amid roses and peacocks in the grounds of Ruthin Castle. Brinley Richards (Brinli), who had won the Chair at Llanrwst in 1951, was installed Archdruid, in succession to Tilsli. He claimed that, as a solicitor, in Maesteg, and a legal adviser to the Eisteddfod Court, it was appropriate that he should be the first of his profession to hold the high office.

The Eisteddfod ventured into 'Little England beyond Wales, for the first time when it visited Haverfordwest in 1972. The Gorsedd ceremonies were held in a Circle erected in the Bridge Meadow, adjoining the cattle mart and the soccer ground, on the banks of the river Cleddau. The procession at the Proclamation ceremony was one of the most impressive ever witnessed, largely because of the unusually large number of schoolchildren that took part, for it was, in fact, Eisteddfod Sir Benfro, drawing upon a wide hinterland.

The entries for the chair poem, on *Preselau*, were generally disappointing and the prize was awarded to the *awdl* submitted by Dafydd Owen, who had dedicated it to the memory of Waldo Williams. The winner of the Crown, for his *Dadeni* (Rebirth), Dafydd Rowlands, performed the unique feat of also winning the Prose Medal for twelve creative essays entitled *Ysgrifau yr Hanner Bardd* (The Essays of the Half-Poet).

Through the good offices of Sir Alun Talfan Davies, new staves of office, for use by the Gorsedd Marshals, were presented to the Gorsedd by the Alcoa Aluminium Company, Waunarlwydd. The staves, coloured white, blue, green and purple, had hand-tooled heads bearing the Gorsedd symbol, designed by the Herald Bard.

On account of its location, much of the preparatory work for the Eisteddfod had to be carried out in English and A. J. Davies, the Surveyor of the Haverfordwest Rural District Council, when asked by the chairman of the local Gorsedd Committee to assist in building the stone circle, produced a plan upon which he marked the stones in Welsh, English and Latin: *Maen Porth*/Gate Stone/*Lapis accessus; Maen y Cyfamod*/Covenant Stone/*Lapis pactionis; Maen Llog* was *Adytum,* and the harpist's seat *Sedes citharistarum.*

The Gorsedd regalia, which had hitherto been stored and displayed at the National Museum of Wales, had to be removed to the Welsh Folk Museum, at St Fagan's, owing to shortage of space at the National Museum.

Sixty years had gone by since the Chair and the Crown had first been won at the same Eisteddfod, and although T. H. Parry-Williams had repeated the feat two years later, no one else had succeeded in doing so. At Ruthin, however, Alan Llwyd (Alan Lloyd Roberts) captured the Crown for his poem on *Y Dref* (The Town), and the Chair for his ode, *Llef dros y Lleiafrifoedd* (Cry for the Minorities).

In an effort to improve the financial position of the Eisteddfod, the Recorder Gwyndaf launched his *Mil o Filoedd* appeal to raise a million pounds, the interest on which was to be used to prime local funds each year.

When the Eisteddfod was held at Carmarthen in 1974, it was felt that something should be done to commemorate the event that had taken place at the Ivy Bush Inn, now the Royal Ivy Bush Hotel, in 1819. Following a suggestion made by the Herald Bard to the proprietor, Ken Kaminski, that a suitable memorial be set in a window overlooking the garden where the first Gorsedd ceremony in Wales was held, a colourful stained glass window was desinged by the artist John Petts, and a Circle of small boulders was placed in the garden. The window drew comment from Trevor Fishlock, *The Times* representative in Wales, in a light-hearted view of the Gorsedd that he gave in his book *Talking of Wales*:

> Iolo's truimph of invention was the *Gorsedd Beirdd Ynys Prydain*, or Assembly of the Bards of the Island of Britain. It is now an established part of the *eisteddfod* and it was Iolo the Fib who grafted it on. The *gorsedd* is a sort of guild of literati and it provides at 'the national' the ceremonial aspect, the incantations, the robes of white, blue and green, the dancing elves, the sword of peace, the horn of plenty, the sheaf of corn. All the tribes of the world like ritual, badges, medals, strange hats, parades and archaic nomenclature and language. If you were to apply hard logic and harder accountancy to many of the other ceremonies and other frills that decorate human existence they could not be justified. But people want them. Englishmen, and Welshmen too, titter to see the bardic rituals, yet see nothing wrong with people dressing in feathers and black stockings for Garter ceremonies. Indeed, Englishmen strip off readily to dress up like court cards, and town councillors everywhere have an ambition to be a mayor, a preening panjandrum in a tricorn hat. No, Wales likes its own pageantry and peacockry ...
>
> In 1974, when the national *eisteddfod* was held at Carmarthen, Iolo was half-canonized. A stained-glass window to his memory, and to his *eisteddfod* of 1819, was unveiled in the lounge bar of the Ivy Bush Hotel. Who but the Welsh would erect, in a bar, a stained-glass window in memory of a loveable faker and poet?

The silver crown awarded to W. R. P. George (Ap Llysor) was so heavy that a replica of light alloy had to be made for the crowning ceremony. The Chair was won by Moses Glyn Jones of Mynytho for an *awdl* on *Y Dewin* (The Sorcerer), and he was escorted to the platform by Lord Justice Edmund-Davies and Sir Cennydd Traherne, KG.

The membership of the Gorsedd continued to increase and now exceeded one thousand for the first time.

The Proclamation of the Cardigan Eisteddfod was conducted in a Circle of Preselau 'bluestones' that had been brought from Carn Meini, the source of the stones taken to Stonehenge, and erected on the lawn of a house on the Aberystwyth road. During the ceremony, Richard Bryn Williams (Bryn), who was the chaired bard at Swansea (1964) and Barry (1968), was installed Archdruid.

At the Criccieth Eisteddfod that year, a deputation from Patagonia received a special greeting from the new Archdruid as he, though born at Blaenau Ffestiniog, had been taken as a child by his parents to Trelew, in the Chubut Valley, and had written extensively about life and conditions in the Welsh settlement in the Argentine.

The death of Sir Thomas Parry-Williams was marked by the institution of a commemorative medal that was to be awarded each year to a person who had rendered outstanding voluntary work in promoting Welsh culture among young people, and the Gorsedd agreed to invite its holder to be admitted a member.

The Eisteddfod held at Cardigan in 1976 quietly celebrated the eight hundredth anniversary of the 'the special feast', the first recorded eisteddfod, held at Cardigan Castle, under the patronage of the Lord Rhys, in 1176. In remembering the eighth centenary, the Gorsedd forgot to observe the hundred-and-fiftieth anniversary of the death of its founder, Iolo Morganwg. He would have been content, however, to know that the professors of Welsh at the four University Colleges of Wales were admitted honorary members of the Gorsedd at Cardigan, along with the Bishop of Swansea and Brecon, a Roman Catholic priest from Ireland, and the Welsh rugby player, Gareth Edwards.

The Crown offered at Cardigan for a sequence of poems on *Troeon Bywyd* (The Twists of Fate), was awarded to Alan Llwyd, who had won the Chair and the Crown at Ruthin, and there was much speculation as to whether he could repeat the performance. It became known, however, that the Chair was to be awarded to Dic Jones, who had won at Aberafan in 1966, but it was realised, at a late moment, that he was a member of the Eisteddfod's local literary committee and, as such, was not eligible to enter the competition. The adjudicators had stated in their adjudication that there was another outstanding poem, among the twenty-five submitted, that thoroughly deserved the Chair. Its author, it transpired, was Alan Llwyd, but he now felt that he had been placed in an embarrassing situation and could not accept the

Chair. He was eventually persuaded to do so, however, and thus became the first poet to equal the feat of Sir Thomas Parry-Williams.

When the preparations for the Proclamation of the Cardiff Eisteddfod were being made, on the Magnolia Lawn in the grounds of Cardiff Castle, the stones that had been quarried at Craig-yr-hesg for the Gorsedd Circle in 1960 and had been removed to a place of storage for use on any future occasion, were nowhere to be found. It appeared that they had been used to shore up the banks of the river Taf against flooding, and a new circle had to be provided.

At the Wrexham Eisteddfod, in 1977, Donald Evans, of Banc Sion Cwilt, hit 'double top' by winning both the Crown and the Chair, and he did so again at the Dyffryn Lliw Eisteddfod at Gowerton, in 1980, and thus matched the achievement of Parry-Williams and Alan Llwyd.

Trevor Fishlock came to the defence of the Gorsedd once more in an article in *The Times*. 'All societies,' he wrote, 'need their pageantry, and all pageantry comes within an ace of being silly. The Archdruid looks no more foolish than a judge, who wears a silver wig and a red dressing gown; the Herald Bard no more an ass than a Garter Knight. Wales needs its ceremonial as it needs the Eisteddfod.'

Geraint Bowen (Geraint), who had won the Chair at Mountain Ash in 1946 and who was author and editor of several volumes of literary criticism, was installed Archdruid at the Proclamation ceremony held at Caernarfon in 1978.

The Eisteddfod visited Cardiff for the seventh time when it came there in 1978. On three of the former occasions, in 1883, 1899 and 1960, the adjudicators had refused to award the Chair, and it was withheld again in 1978. The subject set was *Y Ddinas* (The City) and Euros, one of the adjudicators, considered that one of the nine entrants, who had taken the city of Cardiff as his subject, was worthy of the prize. The other two, Brinli and Derec Llwyd Morgan, preferred another poem but felt that the poet had strayed from his subject in choosing to write about Dinas Meulig, an Iron Age settlement. The Archdruid Geraint regretted that the decision had been leaked, firstly by one of the adjudicators, who had had the misfortune of being overheard at a dinner party, and then by publication in the *Western Mail*. He emphasized, however, that the action of the adjudicators in withholding the Chair was in keeping with the Gorsedd of Bards' insistence on maintaining the highest standards. The Herald Bard and the Grand Sword-bearer then laid the Grand Sword across the empty chair in the traditional manner, a ceremony which the vast audience observed in complete silence. The gloom was relieved when Sir Geraint Evans stepped forward and sang the chairing song, in the absence of a Bard, in honour of the Muse. The reception was such that he had to sing again and, in the intense heat he flung off his head-dress and gave full voice to the old favourite *Y Marchog*.

Cerddores Moelfre resigned as Mistress of the Robes and Menna (Lady Cynan Evans-Jones) was appointed to succeed her.

The Manx cultural festival, *Yn Chruinnaght*, which had been revived in 1978, requested to be represented at Gorsedd ceremonies and a warm welcome was extended to its first representative, Mona Douglas, who had been admitted a member of the Gorsedd at Birkenhead in 1917.

In an attempt to resolve the recurring controversy relating to the relative merits of the Chair and the Crown, a panel of *Prifeirdd* was set up by the Gorsedd to prepare a report on the matter. The panel affirmed that the Chair should be awarded for a poem, not exceeding three hundred lines, written completely in *cynghanedd*, and the Crown for a poem, or sequence of poems, not exceeding three hundred lines, other than in *cynghanedd*. This was endorsed by the Gorsedd at its annual meeting held at Cardiff and was enunciated by the Archdruid Geraint from the Maen Llog at the Proclamation of the Dyffryn Lliw Eisteddfod at Gowerton, in 1979, in the following terms:

> The Gorsedd of Bards of the Isle of Britain informs bards and adjudicators that it will continue to chair the author of a poem written in full *cynghanedd* that is deemed to be the best piece of work by the majority of the adjudicators in the competition for the Chair at the National Eisteddfod, whether it is in rhyme or not, in accordance with their custom. As those who know are aware, the *Awdl* has changed from age to age. It never had a stable form and the Gorsedd does not wish to deny it this traditional freedom to change and develop as a verse form.

The Gorsedd Circle prepared for the Eisteddfod at Caernarfon in 1979 had the unenviable distinction of not being used for any of the ceremonies. It rained at the time of the Proclamation, and it rained on both the Tuesday and Thursday mornings of the Eisteddfod week. The Crown was awarded to Meirion Evans for a sequence of poems, but the Chair was again withheld. This time, Delme Bryn Jones sang to comfort the downcast audience, in which sat Sir Geraint Evans.

Gwyndaf resigned from the Recordership and James Nicholas, who had won the Chair at Flint, was appointed in his place.

In January 1980 the Gorsedd Board resolved to write to the Home Secretary, William Whitelaw, requesting the Government to allocate the Fourth Channel for the production of programmes in the Welsh language. At the same time, it asked the Eisteddfod Council to appoint a deputation, comprising the Archbishop of Wales, Lord Cledwyn and Sir Goronwy Daniel, to wait upon the Home Secretary in support of the request.

The Gorsedd accepted an invitation to be represented at a Celtic festival held at Salzburg by the Archdruid in his insignia of office, and overcame the rule that the regalia and robes shall only be worn at Gorsedd ceremonies by holding such a ceremony in the Austrian city.

Menna, who had been appointed Mistress of the Robes in 1978, had to relinquish the post for domestic reasons in May 1980 and Cerddores Moelfre again took up the office pending the appointment of a successor.

Charles Gunston (Siarl o Ardudwy), an Englishman who had learnt Welsh in his latter years, performed the remarkable achievement of passing, with honours, both the poetry and literature examinations, which entitled him to be admitted, on two counts, to the order of Bards, wearing the blue robe. The Gorsedd Board showed its appreciation of his efforts by raising him to the Order of the Druids, in the white robe.

The Gorsedd Recorder, James Nicholas, was installed Archdruid during the Proclamation ceremony at Swansea in 1981, in succession to Geraint, and Alun Tegryn was appointed to act as Recorder. Ifan Eryri (Ifan Lloyd Williams) was appointed Gorsedd Architect in the room of the late Llywelyn Fadog.

The weather plays an exacting part in the Gorsedd ceremonies as they lose a great deal of their pageantry and impact if they cannot be held out of doors, in the Gorsedd Circle. The first week in August, for the last decade or two, has vied with April for showers of rain that are even more unpredictable than in the opening month, and the Herald Bard, has to decide, only too frequently, whether he can take a chance, at the risk of having up to three hundred robes, let alone the valuable vestments of the Archdruid, wet and unuseable for the Crowning or Chairing ceremony in the afternoon. When such a chance was taken at Machynlleth, in response to the usual, understandable, pressure to have a ceremony in the open, and in this case on top of the Norman motte, it came to rain as the bards assembled at the foot of the site and they had to make for their coaches and return to the Bro Dyfi School hall for the ceremony.

At Swansea Eisteddfod, in 1982, the Crown was awarded to Eirwyn George for a sequence of poems, *Y Rhod* (The Wheel) and the Chair to Gerallt Lloyd Owen for an *awdl* commemorating the seven hundredth anniversary of the death of Llywelyn the Last at Cilmeri, near Builth Wells. The Gorsedd held an extraordinary meeting on the site later in the year.

Gwenc'hlan, the Grand Druid of Brittany, attended a meeting of the Gorsedd Board during the Swansea Eisteddfod at which he stated that the Breton Gorsedd was anxious to re-establish a relationship with the Gorsedd of Bards, and a joint meeting was arranged, through the good offices of Geraint and Zonia Bowen, in August 1983.

Eluned Phillips (Luned Teifi), who had won the Crown at Bala in 1967, became the first woman to win it the second time, at Llangefni in 1983, with a poem, *Clymau* (Knots), based on the Falklands campaign.

The Gorsedd was represented at the unveiling of a memorial to the former Archdruid Dyfed at his birthplace, in Puncheston, in north Pembrokeshire.

Elerydd (W. J. Gruffydd), who had won the Crown at Pwllheli (1955) and at Cardiff (1960), and who was the author of several novels and collections of short stories, was installed Archdruid at the Proclamation ceremony held at Rhyl in June 1984.

Cerddores Moelfre resigned finally as Mistress of the Robes and her place was taken by Sian Aman (Jean Huw Jones).

At the Lampeter Eisteddfod, in 1984, Gwyndaf eloquently delivered the adjudication on the Crown poem without consulting a note, a feat that drew the immediate admiration of the audience. The Crown was awarded to John Roderick Rees, for his poem to *Llygaid* (Eyes), and the chaired bard, for an *awdl* on *Y Pethau Bychain* (The Little Things), was Dr Aled Rhys Wiliam, who was escorted to the platform by his father, Professor Stephen J. Williams.

The former Archdruid Brinli, who was also the Legal Adviser to the Gorsedd, died in 1981 and he was succeeded in the latter office by Robyn Lewis (Robyn Llŷn). Gwynn Tregarth became Director of Music in place of the late Peleg Williams, and Delme Evans (Delme Bro Myrddin) was appointed Grand Sword Bearer to succeed him.

John Roderick Rees was awarded the Crown again, at Rhyl, in 1985, for a poem the subject of which was *Glannau* (Shores). One of the entrants had hopefuly submitted a *pryddest* which he had unsuccessfully offered at the 1972 Eisteddfod at Haverfordwest when the subject was the Preselau Hills. The Chair, for an *awdl* on *Cynefin* (Habitat), was awarded to Robat Powel, who was a Welsh learner.

The Eisteddfod returned to Fishguard in 1986. The Gorsedd Circle that had been erected fifty years earlier, on Penslade, could no longer be used as it stood on the edge of a steep slope and the site was too limited for the larger numbers expected to attend the ceremonies. A new Circle was provided, in Lota Park, where the pavilion was situate on the former occasion, and the stone pillars, that were brought from Pencaer were lifted into place by the single cylinder Marshall steam traction engine that had served that purpose in 1936.

The chairing ceremony lost its element of surprise by the disclosure beforehand that the recipient of the chief award would be Gwyn ap Gwilym, and even the correspondent of the *Sunday Times* was moved to report that 'the centrepiece of the week, the chairing of the Bard, was overshadowed by a massive row which had almost everyone going purple in the face.' He explained that, after the adjudication had been given, the Archdruid announced the *nom-de-guerre* of the successful poet. 'The announcement is always a top secret until that great moment when the nation's eyes moist over and the throat thickens and the new king is asked to stand; except that this year some rat reporter from the *Western Mail* had printed the name the day before and spoiled the surprise.'

The Gorsedd heard with regret of the death of Gwyndaf, who was Archdruid from 1966 to 1969 and Gorsedd Recorder from 1970 to 1979. A native of Llanfachreth, he was celebrated as a *penillion* singer before he won the chair at the Inter-College Eisteddfod in 1934 with an *awdl* written in free verse to *Deirdre'r Gofidiau* (Deirdre of the Sorrows). The following year he was awarded the Chair at the Caernarfon National Eisteddfod for an *awdl*, in the same controversial style, to *Magdalen*, and, at the same time, he narrowly missed winning the Crown.

At the Portmadoc Eisteddfod, Mrs Margaret Miles, of New York, presented to the Archdruid the silver crown that had been awarded, at the first crowning ceremony, to her ancestor, R. Mawddwy Jones, at the Holywell Crown Eisteddfod in 1869.

Emyr Wyn Feddyg resigned from the office of Attendant Druid, which he had held for twenty years, and was succeeded by W. Rhys Nicholas.

Emrys Deudraeth (Emrys Roberts), chaired bard at Bala (1967) and Bangor (1971), became Archdruid in succession to Elerydd at the Proclamation ceremony held at Newport in June 1987. He had published five volumes of verse and three collections of stories for children, and was editor of the poetry column, *Byd y Beirdd*, in the weekly newspaper *Y Cymro*.

The inclement weather during the Eisteddfod week at Newport in 1988, prevented the Gorsedd from holding its ceremonies in the Gorsedd Circle that had been erected in the beautiful setting of Tredegar Park, and the Hirlas Horn that Lord Tredegar had presented ninety years earlier had to be proffered to the Archdruid in the assembly hall of St Joseph's Roman Catholic School.

The Pavilion that had been transported back and forth, north and south, since it was first used at Wrexham in 1977, was abandoned at Portmadoc and a marquee, that was immediately christened, from its striped canvas, 'the circus tent', was erected in its place, in Tredegar Park. Its lack of depth seriously detracted from the theatrical effect of the Gorsedd procession's progress down the centre aisle towards the platform and, in an effort to minimise this visual loss, it was arranged, the following year at Llanrwst, for the procession to be divided into three columns approaching the platform from different directions.

New robes for the officers of the Eisteddfod Court were presented to the Gorsedd by the Welsh Development Agency, together with a purple robe for the successful Bard which was made to a design prepared, after competition among the students, at the Dyfed College of Art.

The Gorsedd Board decided to revive its journal *Y Corn Gwlad* in 1989, under the joint editorship of Eirwyn George (Brychan), who had suggested the revival, and W. Rhys Nicholas. The response of the Gorsedd members was no better than it had been when the previous attempt at publication had been made forty years earlier, and, once again, it was not possible to publish a second issue.

The artist Meirion Roberts (Meirion o Feirion) presented the Gorsedd, at the Llanrwst Eisteddfod in 1989, with a new Proclamation Scroll, inscribed on vellum and decorated in the same manner as the one he had previously made in 1946.

The Proclamation of the Mold Eisteddfod was held on the Bailey

Hill, where it had been held in 1923, even though the space was rather confined to accommodate the enhanced numbers attending the ceremony. At the ceremony, W. R. P. George (Ap Llysor), who had won the Crown at Carmarthen in 1974 and who had published volumes of verse, and biographies of his uncle, David Lloyd George, was installed Archdruid.

The Gorsedd Circle was erected, for the Rhymney Valley Eisteddfod, at Bargoed Park, and the robing rooms were at Bargoed, while the Pavilion was situated on Bryn Bach, some twelve miles distant. This separation, together with the traffic congestion, caused problems that had to be overcome, but it was possible to hold the ceremonies out of doors and to arrive on the Eisteddfod field in time for the crowning and the chairing.

The 1992 Eisteddfod was proclaimed at a ceremony held within the ruined walls of Aberystwyth Castle, in the Circle of inscribed stones that had been erected for the Proclamation ceremony in 1914, and used again for the same purpose in 1951.

The Chair, at the Bro Delyn Eisteddfod, held at Mold, was offered for a poem of praise to a person and it was awarded to Robin Llwyd ab Owain, for his *Awdl Foliant i Ferch ein Hamserau*, 'an ode to a lady of our time', to wit, his wife. The Crown was won by Einir Jones for a sequence of poems on *Pelydrau* (Rays) which she interpreted as 'a prism of the imagination'. She became the third woman to win the Crown, but the Chair continued to elude the fair sex.

An attempt to have the Grand Sword removed from the Gorsedd ceremonies, on the specious premise that Iolo Morganwg had cast aside the sword at the ceremony held on Primrose Hill in 1792, found little support.

Preparatory to the celebration of the bicentenary of the Gorsedd in 1992, a commemorative plate was designed by Meirion o Feirion, together with a porcelain mug bearing the same design, and produced by the Dolwyddelan Pottery.

An authoritative volume, *Hanes Gorsedd y Beirdd* (The History of the Gorsedd of Bards), by Geraint and Zonia Bowen, was published during the Eisteddfod at Mold. An exhibition of prints and photographs was held at the National Library of Wales and a selection of these appeared in another volume, *Golwg ar Orsedd y Beirdd* (A View of the Gorsedd of Bards) by Geraint.

By 1992 the membership of the Gorsedd approached 1,500, and continued to constitute more than two-thirds of the total membership of the Eisteddfod Court.

The discontentment felt by the prose writers on account of the prestige given to poetry at the Eisteddfod continued to rankle. Suggestions were made that the Crown should be awarded, not for verse but for a novel or play or collection of stories, and there was an awareness that the ceremony at which the Prose Medal was awarded, despite a number of efforts to embellish it, did not compare with the Crowning and Chairing ceremonies. The Gorsedd agreed to assume responsibility for the ceremony with effect from 1992 and to recognise the winner of the Medal as *Y Prif Lenor* (The Chief Prose Writer), with the same status as a *Prifardd*, eligible to be admitted in the same grade as a member of the Gorsedd and, therefore, open to election to the office of Archdruid, which had hitherto been confined to *Prifeirdd*.

GORSEDD ROBES AND REGALIA

THOSE WHO WERE admitted into the Gorsedd of Bards at the ceremony held on Primrose Hill in 1792 had a ribbon of green, blue or white, to indicate the Order into which they had been admitted, tied round the right arm. This continued to be the practice and there is no evidence that any vestments were officially worn until the end of the following century, although it is possible, if not likely, that Gorseddogion may have donned the insignia of other bodies to which they belonged, while taking part in Gorsedd processions. From the late eighteenth century onward, men were encouraged to belong to a friendly society, such as the Ancient Order of Foresters, the Independent Order of Odd Fellows, the Ivorites, or the Ancient Order of Druids, so as to provide financial support in time of sickness or in the event of death. Most of these societies would parade, and join other parades, including Gorsedd processions, wearing their sashes or aprons or other marks of distinction. Gorsedd members who were also members of a friendly society would enter the Gorsedd Circle wearing the insignia of that society.

Ab Ithel referred to the fact that these societies wore 'distinguishing livery' and saw no reason why 'the oldest brotherhood in the world', as he described the Gorsedd, 'should be different in this respect, especially as it had a right to neat and symbolic vestments. An attempt to restore them had been successful, in part. The main inhibition was the lack of accordant knowledge as to the design of the vestments, – and those who could not afford them.' He pleaded that as they were 'forming the Bards, Ovates and Druids into a brotherhood, similar to the Odd Fellows and Ivorites, it is necessary to obtain special vestments to distinguish the various members.'

Ab Ithel put this into practice at the Llangollen Eisteddfod in 1858 where he wore 'his white robe as a Druid-Bard' on the Maen Llog, while 'the Ovates, Bards and Druids grouped around him – their respective dresses of green, blue and white, typefying the progress of knowledge, the truth of poesy and the purity of religion.' Four young women who were admitted as Ovates, wore dresses 'of an ancient Welsh style and, on their heads, chaplets of mistletoe, oak leaves, ears of corn and leeks.' Myfyr Morganwg, the 'archdruid of *Y Maen Chwŷf*', appeared in his white robe 'with the mystic egg on a string round his neck', and other eccentrics were attired in whimsical garb. One Pym ab Ednyfed wore clothes of rainbow colours, and Dr William Price, Llantrisant, was dressed in a 'hunting suit with an enormous foxskin cap' and carried a sword, while his daughter, also with a head dress of fox skin, wore a long scarlet robe. The reaction to this masquerade was sufficient for it not to be repeated.

A photograph of Gorsedd members, presumably officers, at the Liverpool Eisteddfod in 1884, shows them wearing pale blue sashes and aprons, similar to those worn by Freemasons except that they bore the Gorsedd symbol, along with the medals they had won in previous competitions. These vestments had been provided by Gwilym Alltwen but, despite an appeal by Morien, they were not worn at Aberdare the following year.

The Gorsedd was informed at the Bangor Eisteddfod in 1890 that Sir John Puleston, MP, the Eisteddfod treasurer, and G. W. Taylor, of the Colonial Institute, were prepared to meet the cost of providing robes for its members, and a small panel, comprising Hwfa Môn, Gwynedd (Thomas Edwards) and Eifionydd, was appointed to select a design. They chose a loose gown, in colours to match the Orders, with a black biretta-style cap. The Archdruid was to have a black mitre with gold edging with the Gorsedd emblem on its front. They did not appear, however, until the Caernarfon Eisteddfod, in 1894, when it was announced that they were the gift of the Marquess of Bute, Lord Mostyn and Sir Watkin Williams Wynn. They had been designed by Professor Hubert Herkomer.

Herkomer was born at Raal, near Landsberg, in Bavaria in 1849, the son of Lorenz Herkomer, a woodcarver. The family emigrated to the United States of America in 1851, but came to this country six years later and settled at Southampton, where Hubert studied at the Southampton Art School before proceeding to the Munich Academy in 1865. He returned two years later and was engaged by the editor of *The Graphic*, a weekly illustrated magazine that first appeared in 1869, to provide engravings of mid-Victorian life.

From 1870 onward, his paintings were accepted for Royal Academy exhibitions and he became a popular portrait painter among whose subjects were Ruskin and Wagner. Always motivated by a desire to improve art education he opened a free school at Bushey in 1883 at which his students included Lucy Kemp-Welch, Algernon Talmadge and William Nicholson. He was Slade Professor of Fine Art at Oxford from 1885 to 1894, and was elected a Royal Academician in 1890. He was appointed Companion of the Victorian Order in 1900, and knighted in 1907. On being invested with the Maximilian Order for Merit in 1899, he assumed the prefix 'von'.

Beside being a painter, Herkomer was also an engraver, wood carver, ironsmith, architect, journalist, playwright, composer, singer and actor, and an enthusiast for 'colour music' in which different colours, instead of sounds, were produced by a keyboard.

In 1874 he married Anna Weise of Berlin and, after her death in 1883, he took as his wife Lulu Griffiths, of Stanley House, Ruthin. Such was his devotion to her that he called his extravagant Hollywood-style mansion at Bushey 'Lululand', and when she died, in 1885, he wanted to marry her sister, Edith. As such a liaison was illegal in this country, the wedding ceremony had to take place in Landsberg.

Herkomer became friendly with the Mansel Lewis family of Stradey Castle, Llanelli, where he was a frequent visitor. He died at Budleigh Salterton in 1914, leaving a son, Lorenzo. The contents of his studio, which had remained untouched until the death of his widow in 1988, came under the hammer at Bonham's in 1990.

After the Caernarfon Eisteddfod, Arlunydd Penygarn wrote to the Archdruid stating that there was no historical precedence for the mitre, or for the biretta-like hats, and suggested that members should wear hoods of the same colour as the robe, and that the Archdruid should wear 'a wreath of oak leaves'. It would appear that Herkomer was asked to produce designs on these lines, and that he and Arlunydd Penygarn got together and conceived ideas for other items of Gorsedd regalia.

Herkomer based his design for the Archdruid's robe on early engravings. The title page of *De Dis Germanis* by Elias Schedius, printed in Amsterdam in 1648, shows a dignified, bearded figure wearing a wreath of oak leaves on his head, and a long robe girded with a sash. In his right hand is a sacrificial knife and in his left, a cup which, presumably, held the blood of the several decapitated human corpses that lie strewn over the ground in a grove in the background. An engraving of a Druid in Aylett Sammes' *Britannia Antiqua Illustrata* (1676) was adapted for Henry Rowlands' *Mona Antiqua Deserta* (1723) and captioned 'The

'*An Archdruid in his Judicial Habit*', *from* The Costume of the Original Inhabitants of
the British Isles *(1815) by Samuel Rush Meyrick and Charles Hamilton Smith.*

Chief Druid'. The exemplar appears to have been the coloured aquatint entitled 'An Archdruid in his Judicial Habit' in *The Costume of the Original Inhabitants of the British Islands* (1815) by Samuel Rush Meyrick and Charles Hamilton Smith, who wears a voluminous white robe, with an ornate belt, and on his head a diadem, which is an inverted lunula, and a gorget of gold round his neck. He stands beside a stone altar at the foot of which a serpent feeds from a saucer, and his left hand rests on a *peithynen*.

Herkomer had hoped to have the robe, as well as the crown and breastplate, ready to present to the Archdruid at the Llanelli Eisteddfod in 1895, but he wrote to the Herald Bard, Arlunydd Penygarn, apologising for his inability to do so, stating:

> I am working upon the costume for the Arch Druid, making the whole of the ornament, Breast Plate ... & Tiara with oak leaves – all with the exception of the oak leaves, of pure solid gold. W. Mansel Lewis & I present it to the Gorsedd, bearing all expence together.

They were not ready again for the Llandudno Eisteddfod held at the beginning of July 1896, for Herkomer, presiding over the opening session of that Eisteddfod, admitted in his speech that he had not been able to complete the task as his researches had taken him to the distant past for a design for the breastplate.

Morton Nance (Mordon), the Grand Bard of Cornwall, writing in *The Cornish Review* in 1951, stated that he had been a student under Herkomer at Bushey and recalled that when he was making the crown, Herkomer copied the bronze leaves and acorns from a branch of oak which he had beside him, and that he had based the breastplate on a Late Bronze Age breastplate, similar to one discovered at Glensheen and now at the National Museum of Ireland. Dr Kate Bosse-Griffiths has drawn attention to the resemblance between this design and the one on a stone found at Bagnolo, Valcamonica, in northern Italy, and points to its similarity to the gold breastplate of Tutankhamun, and she advances the view that it could be an indication of the spread of sun-worship from Egypt through Asia Minor to Italy and, eventually, to Ireland.

The robe, the crown and the breastplate, were first worn by the Archdruid, Hwfa Môn, at the Proclamation ceremony held at Belle Vue Park, Newport, Monmouthshire, on 27 August 1896.

After cleaning and renovation at the Victoria and Albert Museum in

The Archdruid's crown, sceptre and breastplate.

1923, the robe lasted until 1960 when a new one, with an embroidered stole bearing the Gorsedd symbol, a red dragon and a sprig of mistletoe at each end, was made, at a cost of £100 and presented by the London Welsh Association. It required renewal again in 1981.

Having received a generous offer from Towyn Roberts (Towyn) to meet the cost of a new robe, that finally exceeded £1,000, the Herald Bard experienced great difficulty in obtaining a suitable material for its making. The search entailed enquiries at upwards of a hundred establishments extending from Lancashire mills to Laura Ashley and David Benjamin, from Savile Row to Soho stall-holders, from royal couturiers to canonical clothiers, from Brussels to Zurich, over a period lasting four years. When all sources appeared to have been exhausted, the material was found, by chance, at a shop in Haverford-west, not a hundred yards from the enquirer's home. It was the last bolt of heavy satin, of the exact requirement, and the Mistress of the Robes was able to have it made into a splendid new robe.

The Archdruid wears a jewel of office and carries a sceptre which was designed by Arlunydd Penygarn and was made by Messrs Spencer & Co., Great Queen Street, London. It has a large crystal, representing an acorn, sitting in a gold cup decorated with oak leaves and an inscription states that it was presented to the Gorsedd of Bards at Colwyn Bay on 13 September 1910 by the Reverend Charles Edward Leigh Wright, of Swanley, and former vicar of Bexley, in Kent. He was made an honorary Ovate, under the name 'Carwr Cymru' and was later given the honorific title of Keeper of the Sceptre. The jewel, made of Welsh gold, was the gift of the Hon. Mrs Laurence Brodrick of Coed Coch, Abergele, who presented it to the Archdruid at the Wrexham Eisteddfod in 1912. At the same time, jewels indicating the office of the other Gorsedd officers were given to the Gorsedd by the Reverend Charles Wright and Lady Stafford Howard, who later adopted the additional name of Stepney.

In designing the robe for the Gorsedd members Herkomer is said to have followed Iolo's injunction that the garment should envelope the body so that there would be no visible difference between person and person, and should be of a uniform and symbolic colour:

> green for the Ovate, to signify the novitiate's growth and increase in learning;
>
> blue of the sky in a serene summer for the Order of the Bards, Musi-

cians and Literati, as an indication of peace and tranquillity, and that all things visible are seen best in that heavenly light;

white for the Order of Druids in token of that uncomprising and unsullied truth which should claim their full allegiance in all their work, whether in art or in science, in accordance with their motto *Y gwir yn erbyn y byd.*

By 1899 most of the Gorsedd members wore a head-dress similar to that worn today, and a drawing by Arlunydd Penygarn, the Herald Bard, in 1901, showing the layout of the Gorsedd Circle and the disposition of the members could almost be that of a Gorsedd in session at the present time. There is evidence, however, that some members clung to the black cap for several years to come.

According to a report by Mrs Charles Coombe-Tennant, who was later to become Mistress of the Robes, the bards did not present a prepossessing sight at the Proclamation ceremony held at Neath in 1917. Winifred Coombe-Tennant was the daughter of George Edward Pearce-Serocold of Cherryhinton in Cambridgeshire and she had married Charles Coombe-Tennant of Cadoxton Lodge, Glyn Neath,

A plan prepared by the Herald Bard, Arlunydd Penygarn, dated 1901, showing an outer and an inner circle of stones garlanded with oak leaves and indicating the positions of the Gorsedd officers.

in 1895. She had been appointed chairman of the arts and crafts committee of the Neath Eisteddfod, and admitted an honorary Ovate under the name of 'Mam o Nedd'. She maintained that the robes worn by the bards at the Proclamation were dirty and torn, some knee-brief and others kept from trailing by the use of safety-pins. Some members carried umbrellas and some smoked their pipes in the procession, and some broke ranks to greet acquaintances in the crowded streets. There was hubbub and disorder even within the Gorsedd Circle until the Archdruid Dyfed ascended the Maen Llog and began to pronounce the Gorsedd Prayer.

Mam o Nedd consulted prominent Gorsedd members in the Swansea area and discussed with them ways and means of improving the image of the Gorsedd, a consequence of which was the setting up of a Gorsedd Robes Committee in 1921, comprising Lady Mostyn, Lady Hughes-Hunter, Lady Howard-Stepney and Angela Stepney-Gulston, with Mam o Nedd as chairman and Y Beili Glas as convenor. Mair Taliesin, who had looked after the robes, a task in which she was assisted by Awen Mona (Mrs L. J. Williams), was co-opted to the committee. The committee purchased three dozen new robes, and published an instructional booklet for the benefit of local committees making arrangements for Gorsedd ceremonies. A Gorsedd Commission, under the chairmanship of Pedrog, was set up in 1925, by which time Mam o Nedd had been appointed Mistress of the Robes and Sieffre o Gyfarthfa (Captain Geoffrey Crawshay) had been appointed Herald Bard in succession to Ap Gwyddon (Edward Rees). The commission met at Cadoxton Lodge in February 1926 and continued to function until 1932.

The Grand Sword

The Grand Sword was presented to the Gorsedd during the Cardiff Eisteddfod in 1899 by Herkomer who explained its symbolism in a letter he sent to Owen Morgan (Morien):

> The natural crystal in the hilt stands for mystery. Within it are drilled the three sacred lines supposed to be the first attempt to write 'Jehovah', the dragon guarding both. The hand-guard is of wrought steel, the dragon and handle of copper gilt. The scabbard being of wood symbolizes peace. On the five bands that encircle the scabbard will be found embossed the words 'Y Gwir yn erbyn y byd, Duw a

The Grand Sword, the Half-sword and the Herald Bard's Staff.

phob daioni, Calon wrth Galon, A laddo a leddir, Iesu na ad gam-
waith.'

The inscriptions are the mottos of the Gorsedd, 'The Truth against the
World', and of the four 'chairs': Cadair Morgannwg a Gwent, 'God
and all Goodness'; Cadair Dyfed, 'Heart to Heart'; Cadair Powys, 'He
who kills shall die', and Cadair Gwynedd, 'Jesus, let there be no
injustice'.

The Grand Sword is borne by the Grand Sword-bearer before the
Archdruid in procession. It is never unsheathed, except partly during
certain ceremonies.

The Split-Sword

The Split-Sword comprises two halves with oak handles, resembling
bayonets, that were made to give effect to an idea arising from a poem
by Lamartine which was inspired by the refusal of Welsh and Breton
troops to fight against each other at the battle of St Cast and in which
they united the two halves of a split sword in a symbolic manner. The
halves were made at the instigation of Jean le Fustec who led the
Breton delegation from the Union Régionaliste Breton to the Cardiff
Eisteddfod in 1899. The Welsh half-sword bears the stamp of J. J.
Williams, Castle Arcade, Cardiff. It has a silver shield bearing the
Welsh dragon on its hilt, and its blade is chased with leeks, while the
Breton half has the ermine banner of Brittany inscribed upon it. The
ceremony of uniting the two halves was devised by the Herald Bard,
Arlunydd Penygarn, and it first took place at the Cardiff Eisteddfod
that year, when the Welsh half was carried by Thomas Edwards
(Cynonfardd) and the Breton half by the Marquis Regis de
l'Estourbeillon, and they were presented to the Archdruid, who united
them as 'a symbol of the spiritual unity of King Arthur's Sword
between the Welsh and Breton nations.' The ceremony takes place
when there are joint meetings of the Gorsedd of Bards and the Breton
Gorsedd.

The Hirlas Horn

Sir William Goscombe John, RA, a native of Cardiff, is credited
with the design of the Hirlas Horn although he stated that the idea had
come from the Herald Bard, Arlunydd Penygarn. It was said to have
been the horn of an ox that had been harnessed to a waggon conveying
Afrikaners during the Great Trek from the Cape Province to the

Transvaal in 1838, but Sir William maintained that it had belonged to a Cape Buffalo. The Hirlas is silver mounted and, when not in use, it has a silver cover with dragons curled round precious stones within a ring of castellated towers and surmounted by a druid holding a harp. It rests on a huge silver dragon the claws of which grasp a large crystal ball. On a silver shield fixed to the side of the Horn are the arms of Lord Tredegar: *or*, a gryphon segreant *sable*, for Morgan, and *or*, on a chevron, between three roses *azure*, as many thistles, slipped, of the field, for Gould. Lord Tredegar had commissioned the work for the Eisteddfod held at Newport in 1897 but, as it was not ready by then, his niece handed a replica to the Archdruid. The Horn was completed by 1899, at a cost of £359, and it was presented to the Archdruid Hwfa Môn by Lord Tredegar during the Cardiff Eisteddfod.

The *hirlas* (literally, 'the long, blue') was a drinking horn.

The scarlet Celtic mantles worn by the Matron, who presents the Hirlas to the Archruid, and by the Maiden who presents the Blodeuged, were designed by Arlunydd Penygarn for the Cardiff Cymmrodorion Society and presented to the Gorsedd in 1923. Gold lace head-dresses were presented by Oswyn Afan and, in 1985, Mrs Anna Roose of Rhyl made, and gave, new robes and head-dresses.

Y Corn Gwlad

At the Wrexham Eisteddfod in 1888 a trumpet was presented to the Gorsedd by Edward Jones, Mayor of Pwllheli, and this instrument was used as *Y Corn Gwlad* at Gorsedd ceremonies until 1901. During the Pan-Celtic Congress held that year at Dublin, the Irish composer Alice Needham (Telynores Iwerddon), who had been admitted an honorary member of the Gorsedd at Cardiff in 1899, presented a silver trumpet, with a pendent banner, to the Archdruid Hwfa Môn, in place of 'the Cornet which was used at Cardiff'. Dr Haydn Morris (Haydn Bencerdd) composed a set of seven fanfares to be sounded on appropriate occasions.

In 1954, a pair of silver trumpets that had been used at the coronation of Her Majesty the Queen were presented in memory of the former Herald Bard, Sieffre o Gyfarthfa, and pendent banners, embroidered by Miss Iles, of Brynsiencyn, were the gift of the Misses Margaret and Gwendolen Davies of Gregynog.

Caps and gowns were provided for the trumpeters, and for the bearers of the Banner and of the Hirlas when carried on its stand, at the Mold Eisteddfod in 1923, to a design prepared by Isaac Williams of the National Museum of Wales.

The Banner

The Gorsedd Banner was presented by Sir Arthur Stepney at the Llandudno Eisteddfod in 1896. It was designed by the Herald Bard, Arlunydd Penygarn, and embroidered by Miss Lena Evans (Brodes Dâr), of Cardiff. Upon a background of azure blue, to represent the firmament, there are golden garlands of oak and mistletoe and, overall, the mottoes *Yn wyneb haul llygad goleuni* and *Y gwir yn erbyn y byd*. In the upper half, a dragon rampant stands on a radiant sun, three rays of which form the mystic sign, while in the lower part a ring of crystals symbolises the Gorsedd Circle in which is embroidered the word *Heddwch* and around it are oak leaves, a leek, a daffodil and mistletoe.

Herald Bard's Staff

The Herald Bard's Staff was presented by the retiring Herald Bard, Sieffre o Gyfarthfa (Captain Geoffrey Crawshay) in 1947. It is made of a select piece of oak provided by the Star Shipbuilding Company, Cardiff Docks. Its decoration with bronze and silver oak leaves and mistletoe was by Frank Roper of the Cardiff College of Art.

The custom of leading the Gorsedd procession mounted on horseback, introduced by Sieffre o Gyfarthfa, was discontinued by his successor but was revived, at the request of the Gorsedd Board, when the author was appointed to the office in 1966, and a special outfit was designed by Cynan and made by Mrs E. Stanley of Colwyn Bay. The custom was again abandoned after the death of Cynan and the Herald Bard appeared on horseback for the last time at the Proclamation of the Ammanford Eisteddfod in 1969.

Marshals' Staves

The staves carried by the Gorsedd Marshals, and by the Eisteddfod Court Officers, were made by the Alcoa Manufacturing Company, Waunarlwydd, and obtained through the good offices of Sir Alun Talfan Davies. They are made of aluminium, with hand-tooled heads bearing the Gorsedd symbol, designed by the Herald Bard, and they were presented to the Archdruid Brinli at the Eisteddfod held at Haverfordwest in 1972.

THE BRETON GORSEDD

THE ORIGIN of the Breton Gorsedd is to be traced to the town of Abergavenny and, at least in part, to the meeting of two men from that vicinity. The one was Thomas Price (Carnhuanawc), vicar of Llanfihangel Cwm Du, who had learned Breton and was largely responsible for making the Bretons and the Welsh aware of their ancient kinship. He had visited Brittany in 1829 and had sponsored Gonidec's translation of the Bible into Breton. He had suggested the formation of a Cambro-Breton Literary Society, and had urged his contemporaries in Wales, without success, to arrange for an eisteddfod to be held in Brittany. Through his efforts, the Welsh Literary Society was established at Brecon in 1823, and he was the first on the list of members of the Cymreigyddion Society of Abergavenny that came into being ten years later. The other man was Alexis François Rio, a Breton gentleman of Morbihan, who had recently married Appolonia, youngest daughter of John Jones of Llanarth Court, near Raglan, and was an active member of the Abergavenny Society. The Society sponsored a series of eisteddfodau, *Eisteddfodau y Fenni*, that flourished, from 1834, for a period of ten years.

It was through the influence of either, or both, of these gentlemen that a party of Breton scholars, sent by the French department of education to Wales to study Welsh manuscripts, came to the Eisteddfod held at Abergavenny in 1838. The party was led by Le Vicomte Theodore Hersart de la Villemarqué, and he was received into the Gorsedd by the presiding bard, Cawrdaf, and given the bardic name 'Bard Nizon' after his birthplace near Pont-Aven.

Villemarqué, on his return to Brittany, published his collection of Breton ballads, *Barzaz Breiz*, which created a new interest in Breton literature and, in 1855, he brought together the Breton bards in a society called *Breuriez Breiz* (the Breton Brotherhood), the members of which wrote in the vernacular and used bardic names. He came again to Wales in 1857 when the *Cambrian Journal*, referring to his visit, commented that the Celtic languages formed 'the great literary point towards which the eyes of continental scholars especially converge.'

Evidence of efforts being made to hold an eisteddfod in Brittany is to be found in Mathew Arnold's book, *On the Study of Celtic Literature*, where the author recalls that:

> 'last year [1866] there was a project of holding a Breton Eisteddfod at Quimper in Brittany, and the French Home Secretary, whether wishing to protect the magnificent unity of France from in-roads of Bretonism, or fearing lest the design should be used in furtherance of Legitimist intrigues, or from whatever motive, issued an order which prohibited the meeting. If Mr Walpole had issued an order prohibiting the Chester Eisteddfod, all the Englishmen from Cornwall to John o' Groat's House would have rushed to the rescue; and our strong sense and sturdy morality would never have stopped gnashing their teeth and rending their garments till the prohibition was rescinded.'

In 1867 a Welsh delegation attended the Celtic Congress organised by *le Societe d'Emulation des Cotes-du-Nord* at St Brieuc at which Villemarqué unsuccessfully tried to form *Association Celto-Bretonne*. In 1869 a meeting was held at Morlaix at which *Breuriez Breiz-Izel* (the Brotherhood of Lower Brittany) was formed, but Villemarqué had kept away, having taken offence at being accused of irregularities in publishing his ballads.

At another meeting at Morlaix, in 1898, the *Union Regionaliste Bretonne* (URB) was established, with a number of departments or sections covering various aspects of Breton life. One of these was devoted to the Breton language and literature of which Françoise Vallée (Ab Hervé) was president and François Jaffrennou (Taldir) was secretary. Edmond Fournier d'Albe, secretary of the Pan-Celtic Congress, who had been admitted into the Gorsedd at Newport in 1897 under the bardic title 'Negesydd yr Ynys Werdd,' wrote to Taldir inviting the URB to represent Brittany on the General Committee of the Congress.

Fournier d'Albe also suggested to the local committee of the Cardiff National Eisteddfod that a deputation from Brittany should be invited to attend the Eisteddfod, and an invitation was extended to twenty Bretons, most of them members of the URB, including the president, Anatol le Braz, Ab Hervé, Taldir, Jean le Fustec, secretary of the Fine Arts section of URB, and Le Marquis Régis de l'Estourbeillon (Hoel Broerek).

The ceremony of uniting the half-swords of Wales and Brittany, inspired by Villemarqué's reference to the battle of St Cast during his visit to the Abergavenny Eisteddfod in 1838, was performed for the first time on the Eisteddfod platform at Cardiff in 1899. Le Fustec had arranged for a sword to be split during a previous visit to Cardiff and, in a ceremony devised by the Herald Bard, Arlunydd Penygarn, the Breton half was borne by the Marquis, and the Welsh half by Thomas Edwards (Cynonfardd), and presented to the Archdruid Hwfa Môn who united them as 'a symbol of the spiritual unity of King Arthur's sword between the Welsh and Breton nations.' The Bretons were then admitted as Bards of the Gorsedd of Bards of the Isle of Britain.

The ceremony was performed for the first time in Brittany at the Vannes festival, at the end of August, during an interval in the performance of a Breton play, at which a Welsh delegation, led by Cochfarf, was present to attend the URB annual conference.

When the conference was held at Guingamp the following year, a group of poets led by Le Fustec met at the widow Faucher's hotel and decided to form *Goursez Barzhed Gourenez Breizh-Vihan* (the Gorsedd of Bards of the Peninsula of Little Britain). Le Fustec was appointed Grand Druid and Taldir was made Herald Bard.

The Gorsedd of Bards gave recognition to the Breton Goursez, on condition that it obeyed the rules and regulations, and regarded it as a daughter-Gorsedd of the Gorsedd of Bards of the Isle of Britain. It was to have the same three Orders, of Druid, Bard and Ovate, and its ceremonies were similar except that the Bretons distributed sprigs of mistletoe, that had been gathered in a large white sheet so that it would not have touched the ground. The Grand Druid wears a wrought silver circlet of mistletoe surrounding a black pillbox cap.

The formation of the Goursez was kept a secret, however, in case the French Government should regard it as a manifestation of Breton nationalism, or that it would be denounced by the Catholic Church as a revival of Druidism. It was at a Gorsedd ceremony, over which the Archdruid Hwfa Môn presided, on the lawn of the Mansion House in Dublin during the Pan-Celtic Congress in 1901, that Taldir publicly revealed the existence of the Breton Gorsedd, but the news was not released in Brittany or France until May 1902, when the French President visited Brest and Taldir addressed a poem of loyalty to the Republic.

In September that year, during the URB conference held at Auray, Goursez members met in secret at Carnac and, wearing their robes for the first time, held a ceremony among the megaliths, over which Yves Berthou (Kaledvoulc'h) presided in the absence of le Fustec.

The first ceremony to be held in public took place at Ker-roch, near Brignogan, in September 1903, while the URB was meeting at Lesneven. The Grand Druid le Fustec presided, assisted by the Herald Bard Taldir, and new members were admitted and had ribbons tied round their arms. The event drew adverse publicity, however, and the Goursez was accused of political motives and of conducting esoteric practices.

Members of the Breton deputation attending the Pan-Celtic Congress at Caernarfon in 1904 came on to the Eisteddfod at Rhyl and a sword-uniting ceremony was held on the Pavilion stage with Taldir carrying the Breton half and Watcyn Wyn the Welsh one. The ceremony was performed again the following month, during the URB conference at Gourin when the Welsh half was carried by the Mayor of Caernarfon and the Breton part by the Marquis de l'Estourbeillon.

In 1905 a Goursez was held on the Pointe de Perhardy, near Roscoff, and the following year the Archdruid Dyfed led a deputation from Wales to St Brieuc, where he and the Grand Druid Kaledvoulc'h jointly presided. The half-sword ceremony, which had hitherto been performed indoors took place within a stone circle at St Brieuc, but the two halves were joined together on the Eisteddfod platform at the

The first Breton Gorsedd to be held in public view, at the Ker-roch dolmen, near Brignogan on 10 September 1903. The centre figure on the dolmen is the Grand Druid Yann ab Gwilherm (Jean le Fustec).

Swansea Eisteddfod in 1907. During that Eisteddfod, the Breton Gorsedd was presented with a banner bearing the arms of the Duchy of Brittany, designed by the Herald Bard, Arlunydd Penygarn.

The Gorsedd of Bards, having reiterated, in 1908, that it was non-political and non-sectarian, announced that it did not recognise the URB, which it regarded as a political body even though it had been the promoter of the Breton Gorsedd. It expressed the view that the half-sword was the property of the Goursez and called upon the Marquis de l'Estourbeillon, who was the president of the URB, to hand it over to the Grand Druid. The Marquis refused, stating that the Breton Gorsedd was not yet in existence when the half-sword was acquired.

The Goursez was formally registered in 1908 and it produced a constitution under the terms of which the Grand Druid was to hold office for life.

The ceremony held during the Nantes Festival in 1910 was witnessed by some twenty thousand people, and was attended by the Archdruid Dyfed, accompanied by over fifty members of the Gorsedd of Bards. The Bretons took advantage of their presence to address a letter to David Lloyd George congratulating him on his appointment as Chancellor of the Exchequer and asking him to use his influence with the French Government to allow the teaching of Breton in Breton schools.

The half-swords were united for the first time within the Gorsedd circle at a ceremony held during the Carmarthen Eisteddfod in 1911, and Taldir's translation of the Welsh national anthem into Breton was first sung at the ceremony. The growing disagreement between the Goursez members and the URB came to a head that year with the formation of the *Federation Regionaliste Bretonne* (FRB), which was comprised almost entirely of Goursez members. From now on, Goursez ceremonies took place during the annual meetings of that body, rather than during the URB conference.

The onset of the 1914 war prevented the holding of any Goursez ceremonies, and the increasing dissension between members of differing political and religious persuasions impeded any attempt to revive its activities until 1927 when a ceremony was arranged, under the patronage of le Vicomte Jean de Saisy, to take place at Riec-sur-Belon. A postcard of the ceremony given to the author by Mme Hervé of the Hotel de l'Europe, Quimperlé, who was present, shows Cynan sharing the Maen Llog with Taldir, who was deputising for Kaledvoulc'h, and Gwallter Dyfi (J. Walter Rees), the Grand Swordbearer, and several Gorseddogion from Wales together with a number of ladies in Welsh

Breton Gorsedd ceremony at Riec-sur-Belon, 1927. Beside Taldir, deputising for Kaledvoulc'h, stands Cynan, and, on his right, wearing a sash, is the Breton Swordbearer. The Grand Swordbearer, Gwallter Dyfi, stands below Cynan and, next to him is the bearer of the Breton half-sword. To his left, talking to ladies in Welsh costume, is Y Beili Glas (D. Rhys Phillips).

costume. The Welsh delegates had forgotten to bring the Welsh half-sword and the ceremony was carried out with the aid of a French soldier's bayonet.

By 1929 the FRB ceased to exist and a new body, called *Armorica*, was established with responsibility for arranging the Goursez ceremonies.

Representatives of parts of France, other than Brittany, were present at the Goursez held at Pontivy in 1932. Among those admitted as new members was Jacques Heugel (Telen Myrddin), who then announced that he proposed to set up a French, or Gallic, Gorsedd, provided he could obtain the consent of the Archdruid Gwili, The new Gorsedd was established, with Phileas Lebesgue (Ab Gwenc'hlan), from Picardy, as Grand Druid, and it sent a delegation to the Eisteddfod at Wrexham that year, where Lebesgue and Heugel were admitted members of the Gorsedd of Bards, and the Archdruid gave his blessing on the Gorsedd of Gaul.

Kaledvoulc'h died in 1933 and Taldir was appointed to succeed him at the Goursez held at Plestin that year. In 1934 the Goursez met at Roscoff to coincide with a festival arranged to commemorate the landing of the six-year-old Mary, Queen of Scots, there in 1548 on her way to marry the Dauphin, later King Francis II, and of Charles the

Young Pretender after his defeat at Culloden in 1746, which brought a number of Scots, among them Seton Gordon, representing *An Commun Gaedhelach*, who was made a member of the Goursez. At the same ceremony the Marquis de l'Estourbeillon was elevated to the Druidic Order.

At Quimperlé in 1935 a divided sword ceremony was held at a joint meeting of the Goursez and the Gallic Gorsedd, and a special half-sword was made for the purpose. There was also present a delegation from the *College Bardique de Wallonie*.

A revised constitution was agreed in 1937, during the Goursez held at Perros-Guirec, in which it was laid down that the Grand Druid would henceforth be elected by ballot by the twelve members forming the executive committee, all of whom would have to be able to speak Breton. A ceremony was held at Chateaulin in 1938.

Gorsedd representatives from Wales, Cornwall and Gaul were present at a Goursez ceremony held during the Vannes festival in 1939. The archdruid Crwys was accompanied by Y Beili Glas (D. Rhys Phillips), Gwynn o'r Llan (W. S. Gwynn Williams) and the Recorder, Cynan, who had devised a new ceremony for 'the marriage of the swords'. The Gallic Gorsedd ceased that year, and it was replaced by the *College Druidique des Gaules* which consorted with the Stonehenge Druids and was not recognised by the Gorsedd of Bards.

The occupation of France during the last war caused even further divisions among the Breton Gorsedd members, some of whom, including Taldir, supported Marshal Petain and the Vichy Government and were regarded as *collaborateurs*. The Gorsedd of Bards felt, however, that Taldir, and others like him, had been unjustly imprisoned and it made representations to the Welsh Members of Parliament, the French Embassy and the French Minister of Justice, and the Eisteddfod Council was also in contact with the French Ambassador. An invitation was received from the French Government to send a deputation of eight to Paris and Brittany to inquire into the status of the Breton language in education and community life, and with powers to interview the Breton leaders that were known in Wales. The deputation included Professor W. J. Gruffydd, President of the Eisteddfod Council, the Archdruid Crwys, the Recorder Cynan, Dyfnallt, Meurig Prysor, Emyr Cyfeiliog, Morgan Watcyn and D. R. Hughes. In its report, the deputation expressed the opinion that some of the Bretons who had been imprisoned had no political motives and should be given an amnesty, and it recommended that the Breton Gorsedd should be revived.

Taldir was released in December 1946 on condition that he no longer resided in Brittany. He resigned as Grand Druid and Pierre Loisel (Eostig Sarzhau) was installed in his place by the Archdruid Cynan at the first post-war Goursez, that was held at Tregastel in April 1950. Loisel told the author that he had chosen the name Eostig because he liked to sing like a little *eos* (nightingale), and Sarzhau because he had been held prisoner in that place during the war.

Eostig was made an honorary Druid at the Aberystwyth Eisteddfod in 1952, in recognition of his work in reviving the Breton Gorsedd, but the continuing dissension among the Goursez members was such that he resigned the following year. François Ters (Stivellig an Dour Don) was appointed Grand Druid, but more than half the members wanted Eostig to continue in office, to which he had been elected for life. In an effort to reconcile the differences, the Gorsedd of Bards invited Eostig and Ters to appear before the Gorsedd Board during the Ystradgynlais Eisteddfod in 1954, but neither appeared. Eostig, however, accepted an invitation by his friend, Dr Leigh Henry, who was a member of the Gorsedd of Bards and of other unrecognised Druidic Orders, to attend the ceremony of one of these Orders held on the Isle of Mull.

No Goursez ceremony was held during 1954 but Eostig was persuaded to conduct one at Carnac in the following year. The Ters faction had taken possession of the robes and regalia and Eostig had to obtain replacements in order to hold the ceremony. The Gorsedd of Bards declined an invitation to be present, and no invitation was extended to the Bretons to attend the Eisteddfod at Pwllheli that year.

In 1956 Eostig was confirmed as the Grand Druid of his group and he conducted a Goursez at St Brieuc at which Leigh Henry presented him with a new Corn Gwlad. At Le Faouet, the following year, Dr George MacGregor Reid, Chief Druid of the Church of the Universal Bond, was present, as well as Leigh Henry and, at the summer solstice in 1958, Eostig and also representatives of the Cornish Gorsedd, were present at the Universal Bond ceremony at Stonehenge.

The Gorsedd of Bards again invited the two Grand Druids to appear at the Ebbw Vale Eisteddfod, but there was no response. By now, it had come to the knowledge of the Gorsedd that Eostig was promoting branches of his Goursez in Paris, in New Caledonia and in Morocco. He eventually appeared before the Gorsedd Board at Rhosllannerchrugog on 22 June 1960 and was recognised by the Board as the true Grand Druid. Ters accepted the ruling and most of his followers joined him in supporting Eostig. The Archdruid Trefin attended the Goursez held at St Malo that year.

The Gorsedd of Bards, however, could not ignore the association of the Goursez with the *College Druidique des Gaules* and with other Druidic Orders. Cynan, when he became Archdruid again in 1963, demanded that the Goursez should cease to have any relationship with anybody other than *Gorsedd Y Beirdd* and *Gorseth Kernow*, as it had been agreed, but Eostig replied that the Gorsedd Board had no right to interfere in the internal affairs of the Goursez, and maintained that the restriction of membership to professed Christians, as Cynan had requested, would cause a further schism. The Gorsedd of Bards then broke off its connection with the Breton Gorsedd and did not resume a relationship until the Archdruid Tilsli, the Grand Druid Eostig Sarzhau, and the Grand Bard Trevanyon, signed the Carlyon Bay agreement in 1971.

The Goursez ceremony at Gourin in 1972 was attended by the Archdruid Brinli, and he went to Nantes in 1974 only to find that there had been more internal strife and no arrangements had been made for a ceremony to be held. At the Goursez held at Guingamp in August 1976, Eostig, whose health was visibly failing, agreed to hand over the office of Grand Druid to Ters, and he presided, for the last time, over a ceremony held in a circle in the grounds of the Chateau de Salle. The author, who was present as Herald Bard, was taken aback when he noticed that the stones moved at the touch, and found that they were deceptively realistic plastic pillars. Following the ceremony, a tablet was unveiled on the wall of the house of the widow Faucher, in Rue des Salles, to commemorate the meeting at which a decision had been made to form *Goursez Barzhed Gourenez Breizh* seventy-six years earlier.

Ters officiated at the ceremonies held at Le Faouet in 1977 and at Mur-de-Bretagne in 1978, but he did not wish to continue in office and Gwenc'hlan ar Skouezek (Gwenc'hlan) was appointed, and was installed Grand Druid by the Archdruid Geraint at a ceremony held at Porz-an-Breton, near Quimperlé, in September 1979.

Gwenc'hlan attended the Gorsedd ceremonies during the Machynlleth Eisteddfod in 1981, and he was also present at the Cornish Gorsedd held at Camborne that year. In August 1982 he appeared before the Gorsedd Board meeting at the Bishop Gore School during the Swansea Eisteddfod, and agreed to a suggestion that a joint Gorsedd be held at Rennes the next year.

At the Goursez ceremony held at Combourg in 1982 some of the members appeared dressed in white suits, with sashes of the colour of their Order, as a protest against wearing robes which they considered outdated and a hindrance to increasing the membership. Their leader, Ab Louzaouer, was dismissed for such behaviour and he, together with Kadvan, thereupon formed *Kelc'h Maksen Wledic* (the Magnus Max-imus Circle) with a view to reforming the Goursez, but its influence was critical rather than constructive.

In August 1983 a deputation comprising more than a hundred mem-bers of the Gorsedd, led by the Archdruid James Nicholas, gathered at Rennes and, after being entertained at a mayoral reception, they assembled outside the Old Breton Parliament to hear addresses given by the Archdruid and by Gwenc'hlan, who reminded them that it was the sixteen hundredth anniversary of the legendary arrival of Macsen Wledig, the Roman emperor Magnus Maximus, in Armorica, with an army of Welsh soldiers who had settled and become the forebears of the Breton people.

There followed a visit to the Museé de Bretagne where Professor Léon Fleuriot of the Sorbonne, gave an address in Welsh, and in the evening there was a Celtic concert at Quimper. The next morning, a joint Gorsedd ceremony was conducted beside the lake at Paimpont, in the Forêt de Broceliande, at which the Welsh bardic representation far outnumbered the Breton.

The election of Gwenc'hlan appeared, at first, to bring order to the affairs of the Breton Gorsedd, but differences on a number of issues soon arose and, in 1984, he announced that there would be no Goursez ceremony held that year. In the following year, however, a successful ceremony was held in a glade in the oakwoods at Kerantorec, near Moëlan-sur-Mer.

In 1986, Ters was appointed Honorary Grand Druid of the *College des Druides des Gaules* and Gwenc'hlan threatened to expel any member consorting with that, or any other similar, body in France. A cere-mony was held that year at Porz-an-Breton.

By 1987 a permanent site for the Goursez had been chosen at St Kadvan, below Montagne St Michel, north of Brasparts, and near the headquarters it had established in that town, where its records were kept and its regalia stored. The ceremony coincides, each year, with a festival and exhibition connected with esoteric druidism held at Brasparts.

Opposition to the admission of non-Celts to the Goursez was raised by a group calling itself *Traditionalistes*, whom Gwenc'hlan accused of being racist, and he, in turn, was charged with using the Goursez as a platform for political leftism, and was further castigated for omitting the name of God from the Goursez prayer. He then expelled his critics on the grounds that they had conducted unauthorised meetings to discuss Goursez affairs, and they formed themselves into a new body which they registered as *Le Groupe de Druides et Bardes du Gorsedd Traditionel*, with the veteran Paul-Yves Burel (Diblizer Kernev) as its president. Despite this rift, there was a goodly number of Breton bards present at the ceremony held at St Kadvan in 1990.

Zonia Bowen, in the conclusion of her researches into the history and development of the Breton Gorsedd, directs attention to the fact that it has never had a *raison d'etre* to compare with the bardic tradition in Wales, nor contact with a body such as the National Eisteddfod to uphold that tradition, and this, in part, explains its tempestuous history. She also points out that, while most of the societies that burgeoned in Brittany during the present century have perished, the Breton Gorsedd has survived.

THE CORNISH GORSEDD

GORSEDD BYRTH KERNOW, or the Cornish College of Bards, was established in 1928, at a ceremony held within the stone circle at Boscawen-Un, near Land's End.

Although Dolly Pentreath, who died in 1777, is now known not to have been the last native Cornish speaker, the language did not long survive her, and a century and more was to pass before any concerted efforts were made to resuscitate it with the formation of the Celtic-Cornish Society in 1901. The Society was set up with the twin objects of reviving spoken Cornish, and 'the re-establishment [*sic*] of a Cornish Gorsedd', and it had among its members, Sir Arthur Quiller-Couch and Henry Jenner, with Duncombe Jewell as its secretary.

Among delegates of the various Celtic countries that were present at the Cardiff Eisteddfod in 1899 there were three Cornish representatives, namely, John Hobson Matthews (Mab Cernyw), the Cardiff architect, Richard Reynolds (Gwas Piran) and his wife (Merch Eia), and they were made members of the Gorsedd of Bards. In 1903, Henry Jenner attended the Breton Gorsedd at Brignogan and became a member of that Gorsedd under the bardic name 'Gwaz Mikael', which he later Cornicised as 'Gwas Myghal'. In the following year he succeeded in getting the Pan-Celtic Congress, meeting at Caernarfon, to recognise Cornwall as one of the six Celtic nations.

Jenner, a native of St Columb Major, where his father was curate, became Keeper of Manuscripts at the British Museum, and while he was working there he found a fragment of an early fifteenth century Cornish play written on the back of a charter of 1340, which added considerably to the meagre knowledge of the language. Jenner travelled Cornwall collecting remembered words and songs and phrases and, in 1904, he published his *Handbook of the Cornish Language*, which proved to be a turning point in the revival of interest in the language. In that year, Mrs Jenner, the Cornish novelist Kitty Lee (Morvoren), and Duncombe Jewell (Bardd Glas), were admitted members of the Gorsedd of Bards at the Rhyl Eisteddfod.

At the Neath Eisteddfod in 1917, Jenner met D. Rhys Phillips (Y Beili Glas) who was enthusiastic to promote the formation of a Cornish Gorsedd, but Jenner was busily involved, with Robert Morton Nance, in finding a replacement for the Celtic-Cornish Society, that had foundered during the 1914-18 war. In 1920 they formed the Old Cornwall Society at St Ives, the first of over thirty such societies that were set up in the Duchy and, in 1924, the Federation of Old Cornwall Societies was established, with Jenner as its president. In June 1927 the Federation made a pilgrimage to Boscawen-Un, where Jenner stood in 'the most noteworthy stone circle in Cornwall', as he described it, wearing his Breton bardic robes, and suggested that there should be a Cornish Gorsedd, along with the Welsh and Breton Gorseddau, 'and then the concert of the three Brythonic nations would be complete.'

In the meantime, Y Beili Glas had nurtured the idea among his own people, and had begun a correspondence on the matter with Robert Morton Nance (Mordon), who had been born in Cardiff, of Cornish parents, and had studied art at Bushey under Sir Hubert von Herkomer. They then met at Riec-sur-Belon, at the first post-war Breton Gorsedd, in 1927, following which Y Beili Glas, wrote to Mordon stating that he could arrange for 'the reception of 3 or 4 Cornish scholars' at the Treorchy Eisteddfod, in August 1928, and suggested that the Duchy should then, in mid-September, invite 'a group of Chief Gorsedd officials, who would emblazon the history of Cornwall by carrying out a Gorsedd celebration such as never was on land or sea.' Following a further suggestion by Y Beili Glas, the Federation of Old Cornwall Societies sent a formal petition to the Gorsedd of Bards requesting it to hold a Gorsedd at Boscawen-Un during the month of September and, 'if it so please you, then and there to inaugurate a Cornish Gorsedd and to confer on it such sanction and powers as are necessary for its validity.' It was signed by Jenner, Nance and Hamilton Jenkin (Lef Stenoryon), as President, Recorder and Honorary Secretary, respectively, of the Federation.

The petition also gave the names of ten Cornish people to be made members of *Gorsedd y Beirdd* at Treorchy, but when asked which of them should be admitted to the various degrees, Nance had to say that it was not possible to distinguish their merits, and it was agreed that they should all be installed Bards. There was some discussion, too, as to the style of dress, and whether they should wear a robe similar to the Welsh one, or of the design of a mayoral robe, and it was agreed that all members of the Cornish Gorsedd should wear a blue robe, differenced from the Welsh robe only by a black and yellow headband, representing the colours in the arms of the Duchy of Cornwall, *sable* fifteen bezants. The Cornish Banner is also of these colours, and bears the *awen*, the Cornish word for the *nod cyfrin*, and a border of bezants. As there was only one Order, that of Bards, their leader was styled Grand Bard, rather than Grand Druid as in Brittany, and he wears a crown of oak leaves, and a breastplate, or plastron, both, fittingly, made of copper.

The Bards admitted at Treorchy, which included Mordon, left for Cardiff after the ceremony, and adjourned to Cox's Cafe that morning where they constituted themselves the Council of *Gorseth Kernow* and recommended that Gwas Myghal should be Grand Bard, with Mordon as his Deputy; confirmed that there should be only one degree, that of Bard, 'until the Council shall determine otherwise', and discussed 'the appropriate qualifications for bardship', which particularly required that the candidate should exhibit a manifestation of the Celtic spirit.

On the morning of 21 September 1928 which, by accident or design was Alban Elfed, the Archdruid Pedrog, accompanied by the Deputy Archdruid Elfed and ten other members of the Gorsedd of Bards, made 'an excursion' to the grave of Dolly Pentreath in the churchyard in the village of Paul, and visited the *Dans Maen*, or Merry Maidens, stone circle, and had lunch at St Buryan, and robed there before proceeding to Boscawen-Un farm, where a procession was formed and moved along the grass grown lane led by the Penzance Silver Band. It comprised a dozen bare-headed Cornish initiates, members of the Gorsedd of Bards and the Archdruid, the Cornish bards initiated at Treorchy, Gwas Myghel, members of Old Cornwall Societies, and the mayors of seven Cornish boroughs. After arrival at the circle, the *Corn Gwlas* called to the four corners of Cornwall, and the Gorsedd Prayer was offered in Cornish and in Welsh. The Archdruid then performed the opening ceremony, and received 'the Fruits of the Earth' from the Lady of Cornwall who, on this occasion, was the wife of the Mayor of Penzance. He then 'proclaimed the Cornish Gorsedd and gave his benison to it'. Gwas Myghel was led forward between two members of the Gorsedd of Bards and the Archdruid installed him *Bardd Mur* (Grand Bard) of *Gorseth Byrth Kernow* (Gorsedd of the Bards of Cornwall), and then initiated the first twelve members, which included Sir Arthur Quiller-Couch (Marghak Cough). The Welsh song, *Toriad y Dydd* was sung to Cornish and English words, and a number of speeches were made before the proceedings closed with the singing of *Hen Wlad fy Nhadau* in Welsh, Cornish and Breton, the last achieved with the assistance of M Séité, a Breton onion-seller, and his son.

*The first Cornish Gorsedd, held at Boscawen-Un in 1928. The Archdruid Pedrog
is about to receive the* Aberthged *from the Lady of Cornwall, before installing
Gwas Myghal (Henry Jenner) as the Grand Bard of Cornwall.*

The ceremony of the Sword of Arthur was later introduced, during
which the Bards swear fealty to Cornwall, and sing *Arta Ef a Dhe* (He
will come again), which betokens a belief in the return of Arthur to
restore the nationhood of Cornwall.

The Breton Gorsedd was well represented at the ceremony held on
Carn Brea the following year, and there were Breton girls in their
national costume, and a team of Breton wrestlers to meet their Cornish
counterparts.

The 1930 Gorsedd was held at Truro, where it coincided with the
International Congress of Arthurians. In addition to initiating new
Bards, the Gorsedd began, that year, to admit as Honorary Members
persons who had made a conspicuous contribution to Cornish life and
letters. These, in years to come, were to include Douglas Hyde, President of the Irish Free State, C. A. Ralegh Radford, George Thalben-
Ball, Malcolm Arnold, Dame Barbara Hepworth, and A. L. Rowse.

The ceremony was conducted indoors, on account of the inclement
weather, at Penzance in 1931, instead of in the Merry Maidens stone
circle, but it was held there the following year. This Gorsedd was the
first to admit Language Bards, that is, those who had learnt the

language, and among those admitted was A. S. D. Smith (Caradar), the author of *Welsh Made Easy* and *Cornish Simplified*. Later on, learners were 'accepted' as Disciples after they had reached a certain level of proficiency in the language, and were allowed to wear a blue sash.

Gwas Myghel died in 1934, in his eighty-fifth year, and Mordon succeeded him.

The Gorseth ceremony, and also the Celtic Congress, that had been arranged to take place at Truro in September 1939, had to be cancelled on account of the war, and no further ceremonies were held until 1946. Efforts were then made to enliven, and popularise, the ceremonies by limiting the number, and length, of speeches, and by arranging a concert in the evening.

When Mordon died in 1958, he was only the second person to have held the office of Grand Bard in thirty years, as he and Gwas Myghel had been appointed for life. It was decided that, in future, the term of office should be three years, with a right to re-elect for one further period of three years only. E. G. Retallack Hooper (Talek) was the first to be appointed under the new regime. During his reign he maintained close links with the Gorseddau of Wales and Brittany, and saw the introduction of the Floral Dance as a colourful addition to the Cornish Gorsedd.

Talek was succeeded by Gunwyn (G. Pawley White) in 1964 and he, at the outset, reminded his colleagues that *Gorseth Kernow* was 'a College of Bards that should have influence in every cultural activity in Cornwall' and that it 'should unite all the people of Cornwall in the service of Cornwall.'

The continuing disregard of the rules by the Breton Gorsedd was beginning to affect the conduct of affairs in the Cornish Gorsedd, and it was therefore considered necessary to make some effort to establish the relationship between the three bodies. The Archdruid Tilsli, accompanied by the Recorder, Gwyndaf, met the Grand Druid of Brittany, Eostig Sarzhau, and the Grand Bard of Cornwall, Trevanyon, at Carlyon Bay on 3 September 1971 and came to an agreement on the status and duty of each.

Trevanyon (Denis Trevanion) had succeeded Gunwyn in 1970 and, during his period of office, he did much to establish contact with Cornishmen overseas. He later visited Cornish communities in the United States, Australia and New Zealand, and in Australia he endeavoured to establish an assembly of Cornish Bards.

Gorseth Kernow's fiftieth anniversary was celebrated with two ceremonies, over which Map Dyvroedd (Richard Jenkin) presided as Grand Bard. One was held at the circle of the Merry Maidens, and another, at Boscawen-Un, where the first Gorsedd had been held. A history of the Cornish Gorsedd, written by Den Toll (Hugh Miners), was published that year under the title *Gorseth Kernow: The First Fifty Years*.

Den Toll was installed Grand Bard at a ceremony held at Plen-an-Gwary in 1982 and he was succeeded, in 1985, by his predecessor, Map Dyvroeth.

In March, 1987, in conjunction with the Cornish County Music Festival, *Gorseth Kernow* held its first Eisteddfod, at which the Bards appeared, in their robes, to proclaim the Gorsedd ceremony that was to take place the following September at Torpoint.

Gwas Costentyn (Dr John Chesterfield) was installed Grand Bard in 1988, when the Gorsedd celebrated its sixtieth anniversary, at Poldhu, near Mullion. Five Australian Cornishmen were admitted as Bards and the Grand Bard spoke, by cellular radio-telephone, with his Deputy, Map Kenwyn (Major Cecil Beer), who was in Melbourne, from the place where the first radio signals were sent across the Atlantic to Guglielmo Marconi in St John, Newfoundland, and from where also the first signals had been transmitted to Sydney, in 1901.

Caradok (George Ansell) succeeded Gwas Costentyn in 1991 and was installed at a ceremony held in the shadow of the hundred-foot high schorl outcrop, surmounted by St Michael's Chapel and hermit cell, at Roche.

THE AMERICAN GORSEDD

URING THE Chicago International Eisteddfod of 1893, it is claimed, a number of Welsh Americans were admitted into membership of the Gorsedd of Bards of the Isle of Britain. This 'Gorsedd conclave' was present at the International Eisteddfod held at Pittsburgh in 1913, by which time some of the leading American Welshmen were campaigning for the establishment of an American Gorsedd. Robert H. Davies (Gomerian), Secretary of the Pittsburgh Eisteddfod Association, had been to Wales the previous year to meet the Archdruid Dyfed and Gorsedd officers at the Wrexham Eisteddfod, with a request that such a Gorsedd be formed, and it was agreed that the Archdruid, accompanied by a deputation of the Gorsedd of Bards, should travel to Pittsburgh for that purpose.

Dyfed conducted a Gorsedd ceremony which took place within a circle of twelve stones erected on a site adjoining the Fort Pitt Block-house, near the Exposition Hall at which the Eisteddfod was held. The American journal *The Druid* reported that 'when Archdruid Dyfed, on Wednesday morning, July 2, stepped upon the Logan stone of the bardic circle formed on a historical spot within a stone's throw of the confluence of the Allegheny and Monongahela rivers, the initial ceremony culminated in the realisation of the fond hopes of ardent Welsh-American bards and literati in the formation of an auxiliary branch of the ancient Order of the Bards of Great Britain'. The Archdruid had opened the ceremony, according to the *Pittsburgh Post*, with 'the rite of the sword', which he held high while the bards who sat on the stone pillars got up and 'placed the tips of their fingers' upon it, as he called 'Is there peace?' three times and each time got the answer *Heddwch*. At the close of the ceremony the Archdruid admitted seventy men and seven women into membership of the American Gorsedd and, as suitable robes had failed to arrive, each one was given a ribbon of green, blue or white, according to the Order admitted, to tie round the right arm, and each was given a bardic name.

The assembled company, numbering around eight thousand, then adjourned to the Exposition Hall for the ceremony of chairing the bard.

Once more, the Archdruid observed 'the rite of the sword' and read the adjudication, in Welsh. When he announced that the winner bore the pseudonym 'Roger Williams', no one responded, and it later transpired that the successful bard was William Roberts (Gwilym Ceiriog) of Llangollen. Wiliam B. Jones of Pittsburgh acted as a substitute for the chairing ceremony and had the sword held above his head as he was installed in 'a splendid throne on which the winner's name will be inscribed under a Welsh motto upheld by the dragons of Wales carved upon it.'

Forty-one initiates were admitted, by examination, at the International Eisteddfod held at San Francisco in 1915, but by 1919 admission was open to 'all worthy compatriots eligible', which meant any American who was able to prove Welsh descent. On St David's Day that year, a Gorsedd national headquarters was opened at Pittsburgh and some two hundred members were initiated. A similar number gained admission the following June at a Gorsedd ceremony held at Schenky Park, Pittsburgh.

The first Archdruid of the American Gorsedd was Thomas Edwards (Cynonfardd), a native of Landore, Swansea, who emigrated to the United States for the benefit of his health in 1870 and became the minister of Congregational churches at Wilkes Barre and Edwardsville, and was later appointed Professor of Elocution at Wyoming College, Kingstone, Pennsylvania. He was well regarded as an eisteddfod conductor in the USA, as he had been, between 1891 and 1897, at the National Eisteddfod. He was invested Archdruid at the Pittsburgh Eisteddfod in 1913 by the Archdruid Dyfed, and was succeeded in that office by Dr William Surdival of Middlepoint, Ohio. The third and last archdruid was Senator James J. Davies (Cyfunydd) who was the president and generous supporter of the 1913 Eisteddfod. He had left Wales as a child and worked as a puddler at the Pittsburgh steel mills before rising to eminence in the industrial world and serving as Secretary of Labour under Presidents Harding, Coolidge and Hoover. He was the 'regarded Founder' of the Loyal Order of Moose and its first Director General, until his death in 1947. The archdruid wore a white robe with a breastplate of a metallic braid bearing the Gorsedd symbol. The robes for members do not appear to have materialised.

The Gorsedd survived until 1946. By then, its *raison d'etres* had substantially changed, and the descendants of the founding fathers had become more American than Welsh.

INDEX